RAIN ON A STRANGE ROOF

A Southern Literary Memoir

Jan Whitt

Hamilton Books
A member of
The Rowman & Littlefield Publishing Group
Lanham · Boulder · New York · Toronto · Plymouth, UK

Hamilton Books
4501 Forbes Boulevard
Suite 200
Lanham, Maryland 20706
Hamilton Books Acquisitions Department (301) 459-3366

10 Thornbury Road
Plymouth PL6 7PP
United Kingdom

Printed in the United States of America
British Library Cataloging in Publication Information Available

Library of Congress Control Number: 2011945862
ISBN: 978-0-7618-5829-4 (clothbound : alk. paper)
eISBN: 978-0-7618-5830-0

Cover image: Library of Congress LC-USF33-T01-000666-M3.
"School Scene at Cumberland Mountain Farms (Skyline Farms)
near Scottsboro, Alabama," June 1936.

∞™ The paper used in this publication meets the minimum
requirements of American National Standard for Information
Sciences—Permanence of Paper for Printed Library Materials,
ANSI Z39.48-1992

In Memory of

Rutherford Hurst (1913-1971)

and

Nadine Elizabeth Nash Miracle (1919-1996)

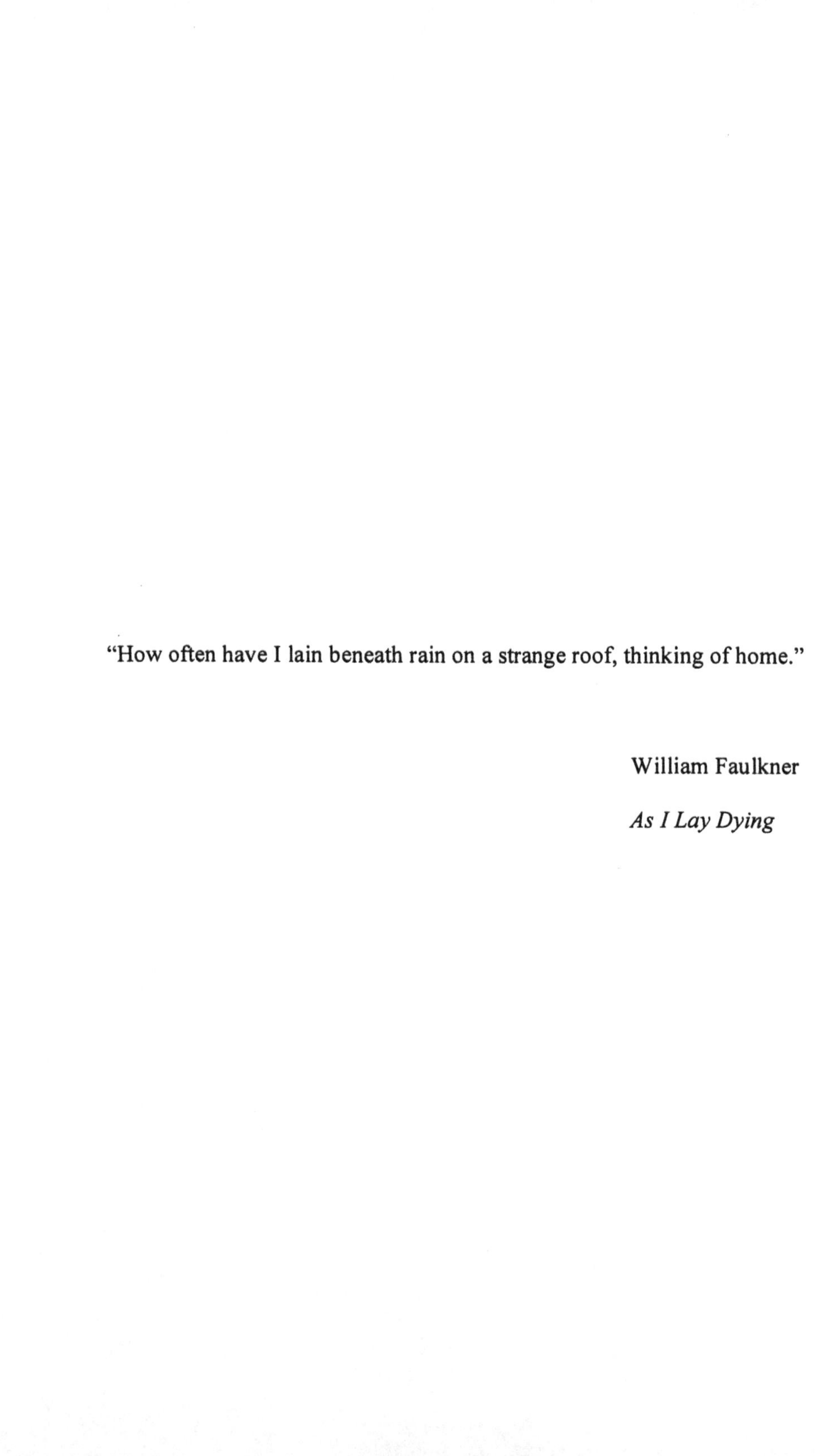

"How often have I lain beneath rain on a strange roof, thinking of home."

William Faulkner

As I Lay Dying

Contents

Acknowledgements

Autobiographies, memoirs, and personal essays allow us to reconstruct our lives and to celebrate those who influence and sustain us. Reminiscences also make it possible to organize our experiences around important events, particular timelines, or, in my case, significant people. *Rain on a Strange Roof: A Southern Literary Memoir* depends upon the stories of families—both traditional and unconventional ones—and upon a belief in the resilience of the human heart.

First, I thank colleagues and friends from Baylor University, the University of Denver, the University of Colorado at Boulder, and other academic institutions. These people collectively comprise one of my most treasured families. Whether I engage with these friends only at annual conferences or see them almost daily in hallways and offices, I rely upon their kindness and their willingness to share their experiences with me. In short, I am grateful for what Professor Jane Tompkins calls a "life in school" and for those who have accompanied me on my academic journey.

Too many to list here, these colleagues and friends have disparate interests and vastly different life stories from my own, but they care about their students and their academic mission. They support the humanities and social sciences, knowing that a devotion to the study of art, literature, media, philosophy, religion, and other fields is as much about the heart as it is about the mind.

I am especially grateful to David Abrahamson, Maurine H. Beasley, Martin Bickman, Diane L. Borden, Christopher Braider, Elizabeth Burt, Andrew Calabrese, Carole Capsalis, Ann Carlos, Tom Connery, Caryl Cooper, Jeffrey Cox, Hazel Dicken-Garcia, Kathleen Endres, Michael Grant, Steve Jones, Mary Klages, Paul Levitt, Therese Lueck, Jeanne Meyer-Brown, Janice Peck, Nancy

Roberts, Elizabeth Robertson, Jeffrey Robinson, Willard D. (Wick) Rowland, Elizabeth Skewes, Rodger Streitmatter, John Stevenson, Patricia Sullivan, Michael Tracey, Robert Trager, and Judy Van Slyke Turk: Whenever I turn a corner and see your smiling faces, I celebrate the joy you bring to me and to our shared profession. I am thankful to have known Barbara Cloud and Sandra Haarsager, scholars and teachers extraordinaire. They died far too soon.

An artist, scholar, and longtime friend, Sarah Hankins once said, "Other people have families. You have institutions." Although she said these words partly in jest, they are hauntingly true. My first family was Baylor University, an institution that struggles to balance teaching and research and represents both the life of the mind and the elevation of the human spirit. As an undergraduate from 1973 to 1977 and a graduate student from 1977 to 1980, I became friends with professors who were more than classroom teachers. I babysat for their children, joined them for lunch between classes, and celebrated their achievements. Perhaps more importantly, I emulated them. I chose a profession in which I could reach out to students in the way those teachers and scholars once reached out to me.

Relationships with Baylor friends did not end when I moved to Colorado in 1980. As recently as December 2010, for example, I joined former professors Rachel Hunter Moore and her husband Andy J. Moore to commemorate their 50th anniversary in Colorado Springs, Colorado. The Moores, now retired from the Department of English at Baylor, continue to light up every room they enter. As a student in an introductory literature course in 1973, I could never have dreamed that I would enjoy a quiet dinner with them decades later or that we would on that occasion reaffirm a shared commitment to our students and to the role of the humanities at our respective institutions.

As the Moores and I talked at the Broadmoor Hotel, I remembered their warmth and enthusiasm in the classroom. I could almost hear them reading poetry by Robert Frost and William Butler Yeats and excerpts from novels by Carson McCullers and William Faulkner those many years ago. It was as though I was still sitting in their sun-drenched classrooms, transported by their passion for words on a page. I thank them for helping me to find my way.

Friends and professors at Baylor—Robert Baird, James Barcus, Wallace Christian, Robert Collmer, Genie Dyer, Preston Dyer, Tom Hanks, Leta Horan, J.R. LeMaster, Mary Massirer, Robert Reid, and others—challenged, entertained, guided, and parented me. The late Frank Leavell is among those who brightened the days his students spent with him, and he introduced many of us to the wonder of Southern literature. "You don't go to college to learn how to make a living," he told us earnestly. "You go to learn how to make a life." Professor Leavell and others at Baylor University inspired their students in ways we could not then express —or perhaps ever fully comprehend.

Second, I thank Sherry Castello, who since I was 15 years old has elevated my spirit and embodied the values that inspire so many of us. Her children—Bill, Kenneth, Laurie, and Charlie—made room for me in their home and treated me as one of their siblings. In gratitude to them, I often open my home to others.

Formerly executive editor of *The Baylor Line* alumni magazine, Sherry now commits her life to serving the hungry and the poor through a ministry in Waco, Texas. Her friends are legion.

Sherry gave me many treasures over the years—a Bible, a bracelet that commemorated my work in a Christian organization for girls, cards and letters expressing her love and encouragement, a job as her editorial assistant, and her time. Sherry and I have talked about children, about friendship, about love, about mortality. We have camped and water skied and tramped through fall leaves. We have always laughed more than we cried.

Third, I acknowledge with love and gratitude the place that Michael Danny Whitt has in my life. During our marriage, he and his children—Charles and Wintry—provided what can only be described as a traditional family, complete with Sunday morning church services; bike rides; trips to Disney World, Hawaii, and Santa Fe; quiet evenings; and chaotic holidays. I treasure the school essays, photos, and poems from those years. I thank Wintry for her beautiful letters; Charley, for the notes of encouragement he taped to my steering wheel; and Michael, for never giving up on the people he loves. Hope springs eternal.

Although we met late in life, I also pay tribute to my new family. I deeply appreciate contact with my cousin and his wife, Jack and Carolyn Bunch; my sister, Geraldine (Gerri) Cheatham; my half-sister, Faustine Miracle Heiser; and my aunt, Helen Petre, who died before I completed this manuscript. I also thank my cousins Ron Vance and his sister Paula Vance Phillips, who sent me photographs of my father and their mother. In a message dated June 26, 2010, Paula wrote, "I couldn't imagine never even seeing a photo of my Father!" All of these people have restored portions of a life I missed. Since I was old enough to speak, I longed to find them.

I dedicate this book to my mother, Nadine Elizabeth Nash Miracle, with whom I spent a day in 1986, and to my father, Rutherford Hurst, whom I never knew but who shadows my journey. I owe them my existence and wish only that we could have known one another well. They deserved easier lives.

Finally, I acknowledge those who make genealogical research possible. The phrase "genealogical research" is clinical and unemotional; however, these experts connect people to one another and help them to define and understand themselves and their geographical and historical contexts. I appreciate the contributions of Denny and Marla Brubaker of the Claiborne County (Tennessee) Pioneer Project and all of those who conduct research and post their discoveries on the web site. Their work saved me hours of time and helped to put me in touch with others interested in particular surnames.

One of these people, the late Harry K. Till (1942-2010), established a web site that contains photographs of my father, grandmother, great-grandparents, and great-great-grandparents. These photographs constitute a treasured link to generations of Bunches, Bundrens, and Hursts—people whom I do not know but whose lives made mine possible. Those who have always had extended families cannot imagine the impact of clicking on a link and seeing for the first time the face of one's grandmother: "I look like her," I thought.

Like Harry K. Till, Nancy Cassada Nelson is one of my cousins with an avid interest in genealogical study. Periodically, she drops into my life to provide additional information about our ancestors. Her interest in the Hopson family intersects with my own, since Georgia Hopson was my father's first wife. Georgia Hopson Hurst and Rutherford Hurst are the parents of Wanda Jo Hopson Hurst (September 29, 1933-December 27, 1939), my "little sister," born 22 years before I was. I wish that I could have protected her from the accident or illness that ended her short life.

After learning that Wanda Jo Hopson Hurst and her mother and grandparents are buried in the Fairfield Baptist Church Cemetery in Morristown, Tennessee, I called the church and talked with Bruce and Cheryl Morgan, who offered to take photographs of the gravestones. Georgia Hopson Hurst Howerton and her parents, George Caleb and Laura Breeding Hopson, are buried next to my sister. All of us are in some way indebted to the kindness of strangers, and I thank the Morgans for the photographs and for the compassion they showed me.

Most importantly, I acknowledge the readers who found this book and who may identify with parts of my pilgrimage. Some of you were adopted or have lived in foster homes, some of you may have lost a parent or both parents when you were young, and some may struggle with your identities. I celebrate your quest and empathize with your disappointments. I hope you find solace and direction in literature, film, and other creations of the mind and heart as I have done. May you endure and prevail.

Introduction.
The Reading Life

In the television series "Damages" that began in 2007, Arthur Frobisher (Ted Danson) is a narcissistic, manipulative corporate raider. At a low point in a career peppered with jubilation and regret, Frobisher sits in front of his laptop in the office of his elegant home. Frowning, he types the title at the top of the page: *My Life*.

Leaning back and pondering the extent of the task at hand, Frobisher looks up to see his son in the doorway, requesting his help. Sighing, he temporarily abandons the daunting project.

Those familiar with the hour-long drama may recognize Frobisher's decision to write his memoir as one of the ironic moments that define the series. Like dramatic monologue, his desire to (re)construct his life on paper tells the television audience more than he intends to tell them. Vain, pretentious, and self-absorbed, Frobisher has found the penultimate way to guarantee his immortality and, in the short term, to justify his unethical business practices.

The moment when viewers first see the title of his autobiography is amusing and terrifying, compelling and off-putting. Who would read his story? Who would believe anything he has to say? Would those who were the victims of his Ponzi schemes read the chronicle of his life in order to understand his motivations to defraud them? Would those who never knew him read the memoir, perhaps for the same reason they might screech to a halt on the interstate to view the aftermath of a collision? Does anyone love him enough to want to know his innermost disappointments and dreams?

Fans of the mysterious, twisting, fast-paced "Damages" know that Frobisher completes his manuscript and in the third season contracts with actors and filmmakers to create a movie based on his autobiography. The title of the published memoir is *My Long and Windy Road,* a source of humor because Frobisher intends for "windy" to be pronounced with a long "i," although no one complies. He plays a significant role in selecting the actor who will play him.

The seriousness of the crimes he once committed against his colleagues and investors puts a damper on any desire to laugh at Frobisher, and arrogance propels his life story and his efforts to turn the book into a film. Season 3 of "Damages" deals with the intertwining of fiction and fact that is now Frobisher's life on paper and on the screen.

Over the years, my students at Baylor University, the University of Denver, and the University of Colorado at Boulder sometimes tell me they are writing their memoirs. I respond respectfully, albeit with some surprise. A memoir suggests that they have lived full lives, have something to offer to readers, and understand the value of reminiscence. In the case of the 20-somethings who share their memoirs with me, I smile, remembering how intensely I, too, once felt their passions about a future career, about love lost, about the world and its mysteries.

To be writing a memoir is disconcerting at any age. After all, I am not Barbra Streisand or Hillary Clinton. The unordinary ordinariness of my life has prompted me to compose a "literary memoir"—a tribute to literature that is held together by the chronology of my life. I have written the book in the most appropriate genre I can, combining memoir with literary, biographical, and historical criticism.

This is a story about adoption, about childhood abuse, about the role of caring people with a commitment to justice, and about the resilience of the human spirit. It is not about someone who has reached the pinnacle of personal or professional success; however, it is the story of someone who has against all odds found joy, an achievement I could not have imagined when I was a child. Trapped and afraid, I did not then know that days of torment spill into days of wonder. I did not yet know that literature is both a diary of the human spirit and a respite from confusion and despair.

Rain on a Strange Roof is a tribute to the role of reading in our lives. Those who love literature and understand both its mesmerizing quality and its ability to provide escape and solace will understand that it is impossible to separate the books we have read from the lives we lead. Just as watching "The Sound of Music" (1965) allows me to remember what it was like to be 10 years old and to long for a world in which Julie Andrews sang to me about her favorite things, books are a connecting thread in our own personal histories. Pages bound in books and volumes carefully shelved in libraries reassure some of us that there is order in the world. The first time I stood outside the home of English department colleagues Jeffrey Robinson and his wife Elizabeth Robertson, I gazed longingly through the front window at the bookshelves that lined every wall. "Insulation," I thought.

The challenge in writing *Rain on a Strange Roof* is telling my story after a lifetime of studied detachment. As a journalist, I understand the impossibility of impartial observation, but I work to relay news and human interest stories in a balanced and fair way. I force myself to step outside of what is familiar and to explore another person's point of view. Even as a teenager working at the Waco Tribune-Herald, I doubted the likelihood of objectivity but understood its theoretical purpose. Much later, as a professor of journalism and literature, I emphasize the value of examining a text without relying entirely upon a personal filter.

However, I am now persuaded that the emotion with which writers approach their own experiences may be of value to others. Empathy and personal identification provide relevant context. In fact, creative nonfiction and literary journalism continue to be popular American genres precisely because of their personal filter, which reassures readers about the intent of an author to tell the truth as she or he best understands it. On April 29, 2010, Patricia Sullivan, former director of the Program for Writing and Rhetoric and now a professor of English at the University of Colorado at Boulder, wrote to me: "Your academic writing always seems to want to get personal, but stops (by necessity) a few inches short."

Studied academic prose has its limits. With Pat's encouragement and with respect for her own contributions to creative nonfiction, I began to think about ways to discuss literary texts without omitting the reasons I first turned to them and invested them with importance. I concluded that others would substitute the titles of books, poems, and short stories in my study with those significant to them and that they might identify with my dependence upon the magic of language.

And so it is that I have sewn the personal into the academic—with one recurring impediment: I have been ever fascinated by people and animals who dig things up. If my life has been devoted to anything, however, it has been to knowing where the bodies are buried—and to keeping them there. To unearth memories and people—even selectively—is a journey from which I may or may not return intact.

The Ancient Mariner tells his tale.

The appeal of autobiography, memoir, the personal essay, and other similar literary forms can be partially explained by our interest in stories that are based on fact. Often at least as compelling as fiction, nonfiction satiates those who prefer to read about people who live in real time and whose lives are at least partially documented by birth certificates, scrapbooks, high school diplomas, marriage certificates, photographs, and other materials.

Roger Rosenblatt, author of the memoir *Making Toast: A Family Story,* has told his share of narratives during his rich journalistic career. In a 1999 essay for a series entitled "Once Upon a Time," Rosenblatt describes the diary entries, poems, letters, and news stories that Jews wrote in the final days of the Warsaw ghetto, even when they knew they would soon die:

> Why did they do it? Why bother to tell a story that no one would hear? And why make the telling of that story their last act on earth? Because it is in us to do so, like a biological fact—because story-telling is what the human animal does, to progress, to live with one another.
>
> Horses run, beavers build dams; people tell stories. Chaucer's pilgrims go back and forth from Canterbury and feel compelled to pass the time by telling tales. The Ancient Mariner, crazy as a loon, grabs the wedding guest and forces him to listen to an incredible yarn. (n.p.)

Samuel Taylor Coleridge's "The Rime of the Ancient Mariner" lies at the heart of this book because—just as Sisyphus must roll his boulder up the mountain—the Ancient Mariner must tell his autobiographical tale over and over until he finds solace and understands the purpose behind the telling. He seeks and finds forgiveness. The cycle of telling and retelling both exhausts and saves him.

There are, of course, more recent examples of those who organize their lives into paragraphs and market their stories. Each one of them has a different motive, reason, or purpose. And readers expect the narratives to ring true, to be authentic, to tell them something the media overlook. These mariners may be actors, authors, journalists, ministers, politicians, or others.

For example, political memoirs proliferate and find an enthusiastic audience. Although Bill Clinton's portrayal of himself in his 2004 memoir *My Life* might be no more "true" than the description of the fictional Miss Havisham, whose bridal gown catches fire in *Great Expectations,* we feel as though we know the former president because we once shook his hand or voted for him or identify in some manner with his relationship with his wife or his daughter (or don't identify with him at all).

Clinton talked directly to us from the television screen; we were connected to him in real time in a relationship that those in media studies understand to be both false and still undeniably compelling. We may read *My Life* and trust his perspectives; few of us wonder what he omitted or why he might exaggerate particular narratives. We tell ourselves that Bill Clinton's story is "true"; Miss Havisham's, invented.

Reality television is one of the most recent incarnations of our fascination with what purports to be factual. At least partially true and presumably occurring in real time, ordinary people are afforded an extraordinary opportunity. They provide at least partial access to themselves, while controlling to some extent what we make of them and of their desires and interrelationships. Celetoids—those who are instant and short-term popular phenomena—seduce us and then vanish, to be replaced by more balloon boys and dancers with the stars.

As Tom Wolfe predicted in the early 1970s, nonfiction has usurped the place of fiction in American popular culture. For example, the bestselling re-creation of the life of Chris McCandless by Jon Krakauer, *Into the Wild,* became a film by the same name and is but one example of a singular life writ large. We are drawn to McCandless's story because it promises adventure, because he might have been anyone's son, because Krakauer was deeply affected by McCandless' fate, and because of a thousand other reasons. Like Truman Capote's *In Cold Blood* and other dramatic chronicles about what we believe to be real life, we are entertained by mystery, we compare our lives to those in nonfiction novels, and we hope to learn something about ourselves and the world that might make our own existence more rewarding, more rich.

But who thinks about writing a memoir in contemporary America? To some extent, the answer is obvious. Celebrity accounts are like grains of sand. Political memoirs by Hillary Clinton, John McCain, Barack Obama, and Sarah Palin served a strategic purpose during the 2008 presidential campaign and since. Roger Rosenblatt's lyrical *Making Toast* is a tribute to the love that family members often have for one another as they deal with loss and new possibilities. Joan Didion's *The Year of Magical Thinking* showcases her sharp, incisive, clipped prose and narrates life after the death of her husband John Gregory Dunne and during the illness of their daughter Quintana Roo. (Didion would suffer the loss of her daughter, too.)

In short, human beings write memoir for multiple reasons, for multiple purposes, and with strikingly different results. Furthermore, we write memoir for drastically different audiences, often without anticipating accurately the target market for a story about our constructed selves. As a journalist, I am always aware of the audience, the nameless, faceless people who watch CNN or read The New York Times and are the targets of marketing surveys. However, Marianne Wesson, a professor of law and author of several riveting mystery novels, said to me in the summer of 2010, "Write the book you want to write." And so I have.

As a scholar of journalism and literature, I could not begin a memoir without acknowledging the arrogance implied in telling one's own story. Why should I tell my story and not that of my next-door neighbor, who completed several years of medical school and opted for life as a full-time mother? Her family adores and relies upon her. Why tell my story and not that of a Jewish friend whose mother was forced to flee Austria for the United States to avoid persecution? A psychotherapist in Denver, this woman guided some of her clients from despair into the light of self-awareness. Why tell my story and not that of a favorite professor at Baylor University, who introduced generations of students to William Wordsworth's poetry and traveled with many of those same students to visit Tintern Abbey? Several of us have dedicated books to her and remain in awe of her influence and her consummate joy in simply being alive.

What kind of person thinks about writing a book about himself or herself? If one is Didion, a genius whose reputation is rooted in writing news through a personal lens, perhaps *The Year of Magical Thinking* is a logical response to grief. If one is Sara Davidson, perhaps it makes sense to follow the nonfiction chronicle of three best friends at the University of California at Berkeley, entitled *Loose Change: Three Women of the Sixties,* with another largely autobiographical story, entitled *Cowboy: A Love Story*. Like *Loose Change, Cowboy* also became a best seller, signifying the manner in which one's personal tale may resonate for others. And when Rosenblatt's daughter Amy died, the journalist and author addressed his pain and provided solace for others by—what else?—writing a personal reflection.

If several decades ago one was a prominent publisher or executive editor of The Washington Post—such as Katharine Graham or Benjamin C. Bradlee, respectively—then books such as *Personal History* and *A Good Life: Newspapering and Other Adventures* inform us about Watergate; the Pentagon Papers; the professional rise of reporters Bob Woodward and Carl Bernstein; the making of the film "All the President's Men" (1976), based on the book by the same title; and their individual and family lives. I celebrate their contributions.

Historical and political memoirs are genres unto themselves, and no one can question their popularity with American readers. Hillary Clinton and Sarah Palin, for example, found it imperative to employ long-form texts to address gender and political issues and to inspire activism. In *Living History* and *Going Rogue: An American Life,* respectively, these prominent women relied upon years in American political life to address contemporary issues. Clinton published *It Takes a Village: And Other Lessons Children Teach Us* and *Living History* as precursors to running for political office; Palin wrote her first book as a reaction to having already run and lost. Clinton wanted to persuade the electorate; Palin wanted to address the role of media and political handlers after her failed but notable vice presidential run. Palin followed *Going Rogue* with *America by Heart: Reflections on Family, Faith, and Flag,* an even more personal look at the way in which she interprets Christianity and patriotism. Barack Obama and John McCain, too, made use of memoir, dealing with their fathers, their ancestries, and their commitments to public service.

In a *Newsweek* column entitled "Good Grief," Mary Pols argues, "The best memoirs of loss and tragedy teach us universal truths. The worst just teach us suffering" (7). In her article, she compares memoirs by Jill Bialosky *(History of a Suicide: My Sister's Unfinished Life)* and Joyce Carol Oates *(A Widow's Story: A Memoir)*. Because *History of a Suicide* "probes larger issues," Pols finds it superior to Oates's story about living as a widow after a 47-year marriage. She writes:

> If only Oates had waited, if not on the writing then at least on the editing. Both memoirs are filled with truths of human suffering, but while Bialosky's offers a source of solace and understanding for the bereaved, Oates piles her grief onto the page and walks away—a reminder that sharing does not always mean giving. (7)

As I write *Rain on a Strange Roof,* there is little doubt about the ongoing popularity of memoir. Actress Ashley Judd penned *All That Is Bitter and Sweet,* and Meredith Baxter, best known for her role as Elyse Keaton on television's "Family Ties," published *Untied: A Memoir of Family, Fame, and Floundering.* Both were published in 2011. William Styron's *Darkness Visible: A Memoir of Madness* in 1990 perhaps inspired his youngest daughter Alexandra Styron to write *Reading My Father: A Memoir,* also published in 2011. Actress Tatum O'Neal followed her 2004 *A Paper Life* with *Found: A Daughter's Journey Home* in 2011. I see no end to the genre.

"Life is not a novel."

Although other chapters explore my relationship with my adoptive father, a few of his comments are writ large more than 40 years later. One is especially important here. In anger, he once said to me, "Life is not a novel." Perhaps his statement was the result of my living on some particular cloud on some particular day; perhaps it was the result of the fact that I lived to read (and read to live).

Wisely, I did not share my theories about the importance and purposes of literature in that moment. However, much of the research I have conducted for more than 30 years deals with the borderland between fact and fiction and with the difficulty we face in reliably distinguishing between them. For example, *Settling the Borderland: Other Voices in Literary Journalism* explores the ways in which truth is sometimes stranger than fiction and fiction sometimes imitates life. Because we find it difficult to remember and relay memories accurately, it is important to ask why anyone would presume to write autobiography or memoir, even during a time when nonfiction continues to gain popularity. And presuming that an author is able to re-create experiences accurately, why do we want to read her or his story? In short, what makes personal stories—especially after debacles such as *A Million Little Pieces* by James Frey—worth reading?

Certainly, my reasons for writing *Rain on a Strange Roof* do not lie in career aspirations or in a desire for political office. I am not a celebrity. My reminiscence is not an attempt to persuade anyone or to account for my past. I will include some anecdotes and exclude others. I will color particular events and protect particular people. Memoir is true primarily in its intention to be true: As a product of memory, it is at least as suspect as other nonfiction forms. However, my motivation, at least, is pure. As a person notoriously private about her life (I don't have links on social networking sites, for example), I have no desire to set my own record straight and no confidence that others would believe me if I did.

The reasons for this particular memoir separate me from those who have already penned their personal stories. My reasons are as different from theirs as people are different from one another. The title of the book is drawn from a line in William Faulkner's *As I Lay Dying:* "How often have I lain beneath rain on a strange roof, thinking of home" (81). Spoken by Darl, the apparent question is not a question at all. Instead, it is a declarative statement about the number of times the fictional character has been alone and unmoored and has longed for safety and peace and a familiar emotional and geographical space. I selected the quotation because Faulkner is for me the greatest author of the 20th Century and because I identify with Darl's wistful stream of consciousness. Often, I have lain awake, imagining home.

Faulkner, Eudora Welty, and other Southern writers celebrate place, a theme that is pervasive, enriching, and tenacious in its appeal. Home may be four walls with a door and windows and a mailbox by the street; just as likely, it may be a state of mind; an island off the coast of Portland, Maine; or an imaginary but evocative period of time. For those of us without a clear sense of family (I often boast that I have been afforded the luxury of choosing—not inheriting—those I love), geography provides its own sanctuary. Quoted in the "Acknowledgements," artist and scholar Sarah Hankins once said of me, "Other people have families. You have institutions." Certainly, I walk the grounds of universities from Boston to San Diego with a reverence others might find strange, but their desire to surround themselves with family members during the holidays similarly mystifies me. I am rooted in place and find solace there.

Ultimately, the reason for this book is not self-revelation but a desire to celebrate the collision of life and literature. For those who already make their home in the shadowy borderland between a real and a remembered past, this explanation is immediately clear. For those who doubt the relevance of fiction except as entertainment for a quiet evening—when others have appropriated the flat-screen TV—*Rain on a Strange Roof* addresses not simply one person's life but social issues, including abortion, abuse, adoption, children's rights, family connections and the lack of those connections, genealogical puzzles, and a desire for meaning in a world in which, as the Bible says, "moth and rust doth corrupt" and in which "thieves break through and steal" (King James Version, Matt. 6.19). The reminder that the people we treasure are mortal and that the things we collect are transient is one of the best explanations for memoir, which is at its heart a suggestion that the stories we tell might outlast us.

Interspersed throughout this narrative are references to popular novels that have defined decades of American life and whose characters are a part of the cultural lexicon. It is no surprise that Americans think of Atticus Finch, played by Gregory Peck in the Academy Award-winning film "To Kill a Mockingbird," whenever they remember famous fathers in American popular culture. Depending upon their age, they may remember fathers portrayed on television shows such as "Bonanza," "Father Knows Best," "Leave It to Beaver," "Little House on the Prairie," "The Waltons" and "The Cosby Show." They may also remember celluloid fathers as different as Charlie Anderson (Jimmy Stewart) in "Shenandoah" (1965) or Benjamin Martin (Mel Gibson) in "The Patriot" (2000).

These iconic images infiltrate American households and individual sensibilities; we measure ourselves, our fathers, and the men in our lives against these fictional giants, even though those who have known Mel Gibson or Michael

Landon, who played Charles Ingalls on "Little House on the Prairie," often describe a far different person from the heroic figures each played on the large or small screen.

The center doesn't hold.

Literary journalists such as Sara Davidson and Joan Didion have appropriated "The Second Coming" by William Butler Yeats to better describe the chaos that characterizes certain eras in America. Of course, Yeats's acknowledgement that things come apart resonates with many of us, making this particular poem one of the best known.

Yeats writes about a falcon that is not able to hear the falconer and about "mere anarchy" and a "blood dimmed tide" that engulf the world. "Things fall apart; the centre cannot hold," Yeats writes. "The best lack all conviction, while the worst/ Are full of passionate intensity" (158). Davidson and Didion employ "The Second Coming" to describe the 1960s in America, a period during which societal revolution reached an unprecedented pitch. Didion even entitles one of her most famous collections *Slouching Towards Bethlehem,* which is drawn from the description of the beast in the last line of "The Second Coming" as he "slouches towards Bethlehem to be born" (158).

During personal periods of chaos and near-despair, I have turned to friends, lovers, and literature for solace. Using books to escape a difficult childhood became a habit, although there certainly are many who simply read for knowledge, pleasure, and a temporary respite. For me, literature is a life-or-death proposition.

Counting those who love literature is like counting the stars. Finding well-known authors who pay tribute to their own personal literary development, however, is less common. One of those who explores a dependence upon literature is Southern novelist Pat Conroy. In *My Reading Life,* he celebrates the work of Charles Dickens, James Dickey, Margaret Mitchell, Thomas Wolfe, and others. The shine on the apple, however, is Conroy's self-effacing description of his development as a writer and the tribute he pays to literature and its role in our lives. He writes:

> I take it as an article of faith that the novels I've loved will live inside me forever. Let me call on the spirit of Anna Karenina as she steps out onto the train tracks of Moscow in the last minute of her glorious and implacable life. Let me beckon Madame Bovary to issue me a cursory note of warning whenever I get suicidal or despairing as I live out a life too sad by half. If I close my eyes I can conjure up a whole country of the dead who will live for all time because writers turned them into living flesh and blood. There is Jay Gatsby floating face downward in his swimming pool or Tom Robinson's bullet-riddled body cut down in his Alabama prison yard in *To Kill a Mockingbird.* (11)

The author of *Beach Music, The Great Santini, The Prince of Tides, The Water is Wide,* and other beloved novels here acknowledges his debt to the writers who came before. Just as importantly, Conroy understands the sanctuary that literature provides for the fragile and sometimes damaged readers who rely upon it.

Rain on a Strange Roof: A Literary Memoir is divided into four chapters, each with themes drawn from my own life but reliant upon specific works of literature. Because the literature of the American South is rich with references to childhood, family, home, place, and religion and because it often relies upon character more than plot or theme, most of the novels to which I refer are set in the Deep South and are written by Southerners. References to families lost and found are especially evocative. Conroy writes in *The Prince of Tides* about having "brought to my adult life a nostalgia for a lost childhood": "I longed to raise my children in a South stolen from me by my mother and father" (484), he writes.

Although I have studied and taught literature from across the English-speaking world, this is a tale about the longing for home, the desire for community, and the place of stories in our quest for identity. Nowhere are these themes more resonant than in modern and contemporary Southern fiction. I share with Conroy a nostalgia for a childhood lost to me.

From Harper Lee's *To Kill a Mockingbird* in 1960 to Conroy's *South of Broad* in 2009, the novels in this study are popular with general readers of all ages as well as with historical, literary, and sociological scholars. The novels span several decades and reflect rural American life, although *The Prince of Tides* is partially set in New York City. This allows Conroy to define the South by juxtaposing it with a fast-paced American metropolitan city, and the Carolinas profit greatly from the comparison.

Some of the novels, including *As I Lay Dying, The Heart Is a Lonely Hunter,* and *To Kill a Mockingbird,* are familiar to high school students, while others are more familiar to older readers. *To Kill a Mockingbird* invites one to read quickly; Pat Conroy's *The Prince of Tides* and William Faulkner's *Light in August* require time and multiple readings. Several of the novels—*To Kill a Mockingbird* and *The Prince of Tides,* for example—are so beloved that they also became major motion pictures and garnered Academy Awards.

In each case, literature provides a temporary stay against chaos, an escape from a world in which the center does not hold. The short stories and novels included in these chapters are almost exclusively written by Southerners and/or set in the South. An exception is Cormac McCarthy's *No Country for Old Men,* although it is a novel so dark and brooding that Faulkner might have written it. A literary memoir celebrates the opportunity we have to read and to transport ourselves into the other worlds that make this one richer and more satisfying.

Chapter 1, "An Imagined Childhood," addresses adoption, identity, and the secrets we choose to keep or to make public. I am among those who argue that *To Kill a Mockingbird* is the quintessential American novel, and I have read and reread the book throughout my academic career. Unlike others, perhaps, I also appropriated the fictional world it provides and lived inside its pages when my immediate environment was too difficult to bear.

The chapter pays tribute to those who protect and love us and addresses the lucky few whose fathers remind them of Atticus Finch. Scout's father is not demonstrative but makes his children and their life lessons his priority. The mother of Jean Louise Finch and her brother Jeremy Atticus Finch is dead; the children grow up with their father and Calpurnia, the family's black housekeeper. Like Carson McCullers in *The Member of the Wedding,* Harper Lee is familiar with the significant role played by employees of white families in the post-Civil War South. Calpurnia provides not only safety and stability for the children, but she also cooks for them and reminds them to obey the rules their father taught them. Calpurnia is a moral center in the household, a caring and compassionate maternal figure.

The importance of figures such as Calpurnia in *To Kill a Mockingbird* and Berenice Sadie Brown in *The Member of the Wedding* cannot be exaggerated. The phenomenal success of Kathryn Stockett's 2009 novel *The Help* is testament to the central role of black childcare workers in the lives of white American families in Mississippi and elsewhere. We can now add the names of Stockett's Aibileen, who raised 17 white children, and Constantine, beloved by a young Mississippi child, to a long list of well-known caregivers in American literature.

When I first read *To Kill a Mockingbird,* I realized that I wanted Calpurnia's encompassing presence and stern but loving guidance in my own life. Although she was not a biological member of the Finch family, she loved the children, and they depended upon her. Throughout *Rain on a Strange Roof,* I pay tribute to those who parented me without receiving anything but love in return. They deserve luxury vacations and mansions on a hill.

Unlike those who nurture only their family members, these people made someone outside their circle feel contained and sane. Over the years, I have written letters to say "thank you" to some of these people, but I remain overwhelmed by my debt to them. Like Harper Lee and Carson McCullers, I was dependent upon people of character, people who were long-suffering and deeply compassionate and who did not include or exclude me based upon socially sanctioned definitions of "family."

In the first chapter, I argue that a child who is adopted must to some extent create herself or himself, and literature provides imaginative constructs to facilitate that process. Adopted children cannot readily ask questions about their ancestry or easily access their medical records. Even when the adoptive parents are mature, kind, and engaged, adopted children must at some point address the unknown. Who are their biological parents? Whom do they resemble? Did their parents grieve their loss? Might they meet siblings or other relatives aboard an airplane or in a convenience store? How would they recognize them?

The realization that I might walk unknowingly past a sister or brother haunted me for many years. Decades later, when I identified my biological family, I learned that my half-sister Faustine Miracle Heiser had, in fact, driven through the University of Colorado campus where I teach. As I read her account of the visit in a 2011 letter, I learned that she and her husband traveled to Colorado "four or five times in the past 17 years" and that they stayed with cousins who lived in Longmont and Berthoud, Colorado, only a few miles from my home.

Of course, I wonder where I was when my sister toured the university. Did we see one another? Might we have passed on the sidewalk? These kinds of questions plague adopted children and others separated from their families. What role does chance play in their being united or reunited with people who look like them or who share their DNA?

The questions that adopted children ask are not incidental, and too many people thoughtlessly underestimate their impact. The exploding popularity of web sites such as ancestry.com suggests that most of us consider our personal history a birthright. How often do we consider the position of adopted children, many of whom long for information about their origins—and who deserve to have it?

Adoption is not inherently positive or negative. Having once dated a Waco, Texas, attorney who said he did not want to raise someone else's "bastard," I am a staunch supporter of those who believe that all children are our responsibility. I advocate for adoption when prospective parents are carefully screened and when follow-up visits occur. However, the Tennessee Department of Human Services in 1955 conducted limited research into my adoptive parents (there is substantially more psychological screening now). Since there are sometimes more tests for admission to college than there are for parents hoping to adopt or conceive children, adoption is fraught with peril.

Admittedly, adoption is not better or worse than being born to a woman who might or might not be in love, might or might not have a supportive extended family, and might or might not have the financial means to provide for a child. However, adoption does suggest a second layer of chance, which I will address through references to literature and film. Suffice it to say that no one chooses those to whom she or he will be born, and those adopted as infants face additional challenges.

In the first chapter, literature, articles in news magazines, and references to television programs and films illustrate the role of fate in our lives. As unsettling as it is to consider how chance might impede our desires, adopted children understand the roll of the dice more clearly than most. The novel and film *No Country for Old Men* prod us into considering how little of our lives we actually control. The 2010 film "Mother and Child" reminds us what occurs when we don't beat the odds and when we run out of time to fulfill our dreams.

Just as some literary and visual texts address adoption and its discontents, they also celebrate its possibilities and raise questions about the nature of belonging and about societal definitions of family. What does it mean to draw boundaries around one's family and exclude others who deserve the same level of care? What does it mean to say, "We plan to have our own children. If we can't, we would consider adoption"? What does it mean to divide the world into "my family" and "everyone else"? How tribal are our needs to fold in on ourselves in order to feel safe and contained? How are family units constituted, and who defines "traditional family values"?

As someone who believes in nontraditional families—and who often depended upon those who readily included me—I would argue that we might find it helpful to embrace broader definitions and to extend our emotional borders. Our children too readily imitate our exclusion of others, thereby reifying the status quo. In my experience, clannishness limits our development as individuals and suggests false parameters. Inclusiveness defines families, too.

In addition to childhood, Chapter 1 deals with adolescence, a time that was particularly evocative for Carson McCullers (and for me). In both *The Heart Is a Lonely Hunter* and *The Member of the Wedding,* McCullers addresses the difficulty of sustaining relationships and the necessity of building a community for oneself.

Themes of isolation and a failure to communicate distinguish her short stories and novels and reflect events from her own life. McCullers was excluded from groups in high school—a reality that surfaces in her portrayal of Mick Kelly in *The Heart Is a Lonely Hunter*—and from relationships with some of those whom she loved—a phenomenon that arises in her portrayal of Frankie Addams in *The Member of the Wedding.* McCullers also believed that it is better to love than to be loved, which makes the merry-go-round of lovers in novels such as *The Ballad of the Sad Café* a strange sight indeed.

McCullers found only temporary respite from loneliness, and she rarely believed she was deeply loved. Although McCullers had a devoted mother and sister, she was largely incapable of understanding that she was the recipient of loyalty and affection. Certainly, this is true for many who long for their own "we of me" *(The Member of the Wedding* 497), their own accepting and safe community. Readers do not have to be alienated to appreciate McCullers' fictional universe, of course, but like Flannery O'Connor, McCullers populates her short stories and novels with memorable misfits.

Chapter 2, "Southern Fictions," introduces classics by Dorothy Allison, William Faulkner, Fannie Flagg, and Flannery O'Connor and suggests how Christian allegory, imagery, and symbolism inform Southern literature. Several times throughout the manuscript, I address the Christ-haunted South of O'Connor's artistic vision and the Christian imagery that permeates both the geography of the American South and its literature. A Catholic growing up in Savannah and Milledgeville, Georgia, O'Connor was surrounded by images of Christ and by Christian icons, and she employed these symbols effectively in her didactic prose.

For example, Hazel Motes, who hailed from Tennessee and whose very name is an allusion to Scripture ("And why beholdest thou the mote that is in thy brother's eye, but considerest not the beam that is in thine own eye?"—King James Version, Matt. 7.3), struggles to save himself. For this ardent protagonist in *Wise Blood,* Jesus becomes a figure who moves from tree to tree in the back of his mind, a haunting and persistent representation of God that has been central to my life as well.

Like Bone in *Bastard Out of Carolina,* I could not count on adults to protect me. Beaten by her stepfather and betrayed by her mother, Bone is a victim of both physical violence and passivity; it is the latter that takes the greater toll on her spirit. Passivity is a theme in O'Connor's "The Displaced Person" and Faulkner's *Light in August,* two texts central to "Southern Fictions." I argue that those who stand and watch as injustice plays out are as culpable as those who commit the actual crime or who perpetrate the actual wrong.

Another character central to the chapter is Idgie Threadgoode of *Fried Green Tomatoes at the Whistle Stop Café.* Confronting injustices with courage and defending those whom she loves, Idgie laughs loudly and often and finds joy in the world. Flagg introduces dark themes, balancing them with humor. Dealing with everything from domestic violence to murder, Flagg creates characters who show us how to love and how to build and sustain an inclusive community.

From "The Minister's Black Veil" to *The Scarlet Letter*, Nathaniel Hawthorne suggests that we are saved through meaningful connection to one another; certainly, this has been true for me. From childhood friends in Alamo, Tennessee; to a compassionate family in Waco, Texas; to professors at Baylor University; to friends in Colorado; and to newly found family members in Tennessee, I am blessed with the memories and presence of those who light my way. I find strength in solitude and joy in community. In this chapter, I pay tribute to those who embrace one another and risk rejection by doing so. I identify some of these people by name, but all are symbols of the people who enrich our finite time on this earth.

Chapters 2 and 3 depend upon a quotation from William Faulkner's *Light in August:* "Memory believes before knowing remembers" (119). I explore the similarities between characters such as Addie Bundren in *As I Lay Dying* and Byron Bunch in *Light in August* and my ancestors, the Bunches, Bundrens, Hursts, Miracles, and Nashes of East Tennessee. "Bunch" and "Bundren" are names drawn from Faulkner's own "little postage stamp of native soil" (Stein interview, *Lion in the Garden* 255), and I taught classes about these characters long before I identified my biological family. Since my home state borders Mississippi, families with these surnames were familiar to Faulkner, and I now identify with and feel compassion toward these fictional representations of my family.

"Southern Fictions" concludes with a tribute to the sustaining role of memory in our lives and an acknowledgement of its discontents. I have only shards of information about my family, and both of my parents and many of my siblings are dead. I am unlikely to learn much more about them without oral histories, since whatever photographs or letters there might have been are lost or missing. Therefore, reconstructing the lives of my family is itself a Southern fiction.

In Chapter 3, I continue the exploration of memory as narrative. "Memory and Knowing" deals with my journey from innocence to experience; with a 1986 visit to Knoxville, Tennessee, to meet my mother; and with the poverty I shared with my relatives from Appalachia. The chapter title alludes both to the novels I introduce throughout the memoir and to the stories I created about myself and about others in order to survive.

Late one night in 2010, I typed the name "Rutherford Hurst" into the computer. A photograph of my father sitting in the front row of the Ridge School of Claiborne County, Tennessee, appeared on the screen. He was 6 years old, a somber child posing for the camera. Clicking on another link, I discovered a 1912 photograph of David Washington Bundren; his wife Mary Barlow Bundren; and their children. In the back row stands Cornelia Bundren, my grandmother.

Realizing that David Washington Bundren and Mary Barlow Bundren are my paternal great-grandparents, I began on that night a search that would yield enough information for a book about adoption but not enough information to satisfy my lifelong desire for connection. When I saw the name "Bundren," I thought immediately about the desperate and poverty-stricken family of Faulkner's *As I Lay Dying* and their pilgrimage to bury their matriarch. Abandoning sleep, I reread the novel that night and stepped into a fictional world that was—as it always has been—a sanctuary.

In "Memory and Knowing," I seek to explain to readers—and to myself—how as an undergraduate I gravitated to the literature of the American South and why I wrote both a thesis and a dissertation about William Faulkner's novels and short stories, never knowing that names such as "Bunch" and "Bundren" would one day lead me home. The thesis, *William Faulkner's Panoramic Vision,* deals with *Go Down, Moses; The Unvanquished;* and *The Hamlet.* The dissertation, published in 1994 by Mercer University Press, is entitled *Allegory and the Modern Southern Novel* and contains a chapter about Faulkner's work.

Little did I know that the characters whom Faulkner describes are drawn from my own extended family. Was my interest in Faulkner's fictional world—a world populated with poor whites from Alabama, Mississippi, and Tennessee—accidental? Or does it signify something more mysterious and compelling? I don't read tea leaves or look up my horoscope. But I believe in the mysteries of the universe, and I believe that the literature of the South provided me with a map to the Bunches, Bundrens, Hursts, Miracles, and Nashes of East Tennessee.

"Memory believes before knowing remembers" *(Light in August* 119) is one of Faulkner's most paradoxical lines, and I now consider it the central truth of my personal life and much of my academic career. The words are magical and prophetic, unfamiliar concepts to those of us who shun Tarot cards and scorn even the suggestion of extra-terrestrial life. But I remembered my biological family long before I knew them, and, without knowing them, I grieved their loss. I still do.

The chapter "Memory and Knowing" addresses the necessary stories we tell ourselves and the strategies we employ to "prepare a face to meet the faces that you meet" (483), as T.S. Eliot writes in "The Love Song of J. Alfred Prufrock." In this chapter, I explore the intersections between fiction and autobiography, biography, and history. For example, Conroy draws from his own experiences when he creates Tom and Savannah Wingo in *The Prince of Tides*. He remembers his own father's rage as he brings character Henry Wingo to life. In short, Conroy's portraits are both fictional and altogether real.

A portion of the chapter is devoted to the seasons of gratitude in our lives and to those who reach out to love and sustain us. "Memory and Knowing" reintroduces Tom Wingo of *The Prince of Tides* and focuses upon the word he repeats as he crosses a bridge off the South Carolina coast at the end of each working day. Alluding to a past relationship, he whispers, "Lowenstein, Lowenstein." The words—which signify both sadness and celebration—refer to Susan Lowenstein, a psychiatrist in Conroy's tale. Lowenstein treated Tom's sister Savannah, a poet tormented by her past, and, although Tom was not Lowenstein's patient, he, too, was transformed by her compassion and her wisdom.

Conroy juxtaposes the raw and relentless abuse perpetrated by Lila and Henry Wingo against their children with the healing that Sallie, Tom's wife; Luke and Savannah, Tom's siblings; and Susan Lowenstein provide. "But it is the secret life that sustains me now, and as I reach the top of that bridge I say it in a whisper, I say it as a prayer, as regret, and as praise. I can't tell you why I do it or what it means, but each night when I drive toward my southern home and my southern life, I whisper these words: 'Lowenstein, Lowenstein'" *(The Prince of Tides* 567). This chapter pays tribute to those who save us, whether they are characters in the pages of books or people whose journeys intersect with ours.

Chapter 4, "Children Not Our Own," explores the responsibility we have to future generations and our commitment to those who are unrelated to us. Here, I recount moments in the classroom with other people's children and, to a lesser extent, address the years I spent with Charles and Wintry Whitt, my stepchildren. A stepparent relationship is problematic for many reasons; perhaps most importantly, it is not protected in the event of one's divorce from a biological parent. Nonetheless, I treasure my years with Charley and Wintry and the cards, school essays, and letters with which they entrusted me.

Although I cannot document it, I suspect that my separation from my stepchildren helps to account for at least some of my commitment to the graduate and undergraduate students I am privileged to know. Parenting and teaching are high callings, and they are more alike than many might acknowledge. Both require that one listen intently, respond respectfully, and value what is said as well as what goes unsaid. Both are focused upon the happiness and success of others.

Literature often pays tribute to the art of teaching. In *The Prince of Tides,* Tom Wingo tells Susan Lowenstein, "I'm an English teacher, Lowenstein, a wonderful English teacher with astonishing, outsized gifts for making slack-jawed southern morons fall in love with the language they were born to damage" (139). Both Wingo's affection for and frustration with his students are apparent in this excerpt.

Poet W.D. Snodgrass, too, analyzes teaching and the role of the university in modern life. In "The Campus on the Hill," he describes the privileged students who populate a prestigious campus as "the vaguely furiously driven" (34). In his 1987 poem, Snodgrass suggests that "tomorrow has broken out today"—with chaos and struggle from Algeria to Alabama. He asks himself that which engaged and caring professors often ask: "What shall I say to the young on such a morning?—/ Mind is the one salvation?—also grammar?" Although Snodgrass is critical of the students and their lack of awareness of their surroundings ("They look at the world—don't they?—the world's way?"—34-35), he cares about them and believes in his role in their lives.

In "The Campus on the Hill," Snodgrass critiques the myopia of the privileged and the young. Guaranteed an education and the opportunities that education makes possible, these "Whites" who "resist/ Their souls with such passivity" (34) may never champion the welfare of those unlike them. I worry about the news quizzes my students fail because it suggests a lack of engagement with political and social issues. For other reasons, I grieve the lack of seriousness with which they take written communication. But I have lived my life in the classroom, and I believe in its possibilities for the students and for me.

Chapter 4 begins with the experiences with which extraordinary teachers provided me and ends with my own classroom challenges and successes. The academy provides an unbroken circle. I honor the memory of two particular students who died—one after a skiing accident and the other after a drug overdose—during semesters when they were taking classes with me. They are my children, too.

I wish for my former students—and for those whom I have yet to meet—joyful lives in which they can unite their vocation and their avocation, as Robert Frost writes ("Two Tramps in Mud Time" 275-77). I am quite certain that my students rarely understand the role they play in the lives of their professors; after all, it is not their responsibility to contribute to our collective sense of purpose. However, I sometimes enter the classroom exhausted and emerge with new enthusiasm, and my students are the only possible explanation. Jane Tompkins describes much of what I have experienced in her philosophy of teaching entitled *A Life in School: What the Teacher Learned*, and I cite her ideas liberally in Chapter 4.

I cannot separate the tenets of my faith from my goals as a teacher. I do not privilege Christianity over other world religions, but I draw from a lifetime of biblical study each time I describe my affection for students and each time I enter what is for me a sacred classroom space. I believe that I am called to teach in the way that others are called to the ministry or to social service. I celebrate the classroom and the magic that can occur in the interchange among students and between students and professors.

As an adopted child of Southern Baptist missionaries, I learned early the practices and principles held sacred by devout Christians; however, the physical and verbal abuse I endured at home was incongruous with the forced "family devotions" to which I and my adopted brother and sister were subjected. Unlike others, I do not reject Christianity because of these early experiences. In fact, I identify myself as a "Christian," attend a United Methodist church, and seek to emulate the teachings of Christ. Because of my childhood, however, I have had to explain to myself how I could espouse the beliefs of people I avoided and feared.

Eventually, I solved the conundrum by identifying with the slaves who provided labor for white people in the Deep South. Beaten and objectified, some of them adopted Christianity, the very religion of those who subjected them to cruelty. In making peace with my faith, I considered the history of gospel music and novels such as Alice Walker's *The Color Purple,* in which Shug Avery sings with conviction in both a juke joint and a church. I understand the desire to adapt and re-appropriate important narratives, such as the story of the life of Christ, because I have done so.

Watching plantation owners as they assembled for Sunday morning church services, slaves must have wondered how their oppressors could sing hymns and read Scripture and then continue to perpetuate the horrors of slavery. How often must they have questioned how Christian slave owners reconciled their beliefs with their daily lives. I do not in any way compare my upbringing to slavery, nor was my abuse comparable to anything field laborers experienced. But what Samuel Taylor Coleridge calls a "willing suspension of disbelief" *(Biographia Literaria* 14:398) helps to explain how I rejected my adoptive parents while appropriating their faith.

From the first moment that I can remember being conscious of my adoptive parents, I wanted to live elsewhere. However, when they introduced me to the church, I was drawn to the stories about Jesus and his kindness to children; to Zacchaeus the tax collector; to Mary Magdelene; and to other biblical figures. Gradually, I simply divorced the Jesus I "knew" from the one my adoptive father worshipped. Jesus was my refuge from him and from his wife, from their limitations, and from their cruelty and detachment. I had fallen under the spell of biblical tales as well as secular ones.

Although as a child I could not explain the paradox between the life my adoptive parents lived and the doctrines they perpetrated, in time I would meet compassionate Christians who provided me with love and a sense of community. I would learn that Christianity is merely a doctrinal system until it is made flesh, until it becomes a force for change. Although I no longer teach at a church-related institution, I often find that those I most admire rely upon their faith in God to sustain and motivate them.

Christian symbolism permeates Southern literature, making it even more compelling for me. In *Wise Blood,* for example, a train porter tells Hazel Motes, "Jesus been a long time gone" (27). He then provides a rye commentary on the state of the world that operates, it appears to him, without moral center. The literal statement that Jesus has been dead for many years is an anathema to Haze, a tormented man who seeks meaning and direction from a living Christ. I, too, rely upon the values embodied in the historical Jesus and understand why O'Connor employs grotesque figures to represent her world view. The porter's observation that Jesus is "gone" refers to O'Connor's belief that life without a spiritual center is devoid of meaning.

In some ways, I am an unreconstructed Southerner, as the conclusion suggests. I am committed to justice for those of all races, ethnicities, and sexual orientations, but I also celebrate the best of the South—including its arts, diversity, food, literature, manners, and music. I seek out Southerners with their soft drawls and their hospitality. I like it when students hold doors open for each other and for me, and I appreciate the occasional "yes, ma'am."

I believe that some of the best and most compelling literature was forged in the fires of discord and inequality in the Deep South by those who used their creative energies to try to make sense of the chaos and despair that surrounded them. I understand the isolationism that developed in a society weary with being invaded and—often—despised. When one of my professors at the University of Denver said he would relocate "anywhere but the South," I felt as though I had been struck. When a lovely young Jewish man in a media history class said he would not take a road trip through the South because he feared he would later be found "lying dead on the side of the road," I dropped my gaze so that he could not see my reaction. I hope he will one day discover the emerging South.

"Reconstructed (But Unregenerate)" acknowledges that we have much to learn from the tortured history of the Deep South (and, for that matter, the genocide of the American West and the challenges faced by the people of other regions as well). For me there is nothing more alluring than swings on front porches and flickering lightning bugs on a Georgia night. William Faulkner, Flannery O'Connor, William Styron, Robert Penn Warren, and Eudora Welty are old friends. I hear their voices, and on dark nights of the soul—when pretensions fall away—I acknowledge the fact that literature may have saved my life. At a minimum, literature makes difficult times endurable; at most, it makes the days shine with promise.

Finally, I should mention that although I identify actors, authors, critics, filmmakers, friends, literary figures, relatives, and others in the memoir, I do not name my adoptive parents. Because it is easy enough for readers to identify them if they choose, I clearly do not omit their names in order to protect them. Instead, I want the discussion of their role in my life to suggest their symbolic rather than their corporeal presence. What they represent is far more important to me than their names or the details of their lives. Also, having left my adoptive parents more than 40 years ago, I can describe them only through the filter of memory. I have no way of knowing how they might have changed or grown.

It is appropriate, too, that I mention the cover photograph by Carl Mydans (1907-2004). Used with permission from the Library of Congress, the photograph originated at Cumberland Mountain Farms near Scottsboro, Alabama, in June of 1936. While working for the Farm Security Administration and *Life* magazine, Mydans chronicled the lives of the rural poor and later covered World War II and the assassination of President John F. Kennedy. Other notable photographers who worked for the FSA include Walker Evans and Dorothea Lange.

Although Mydans took the photograph in the South during a time that is important to my own genealogical work, I intend for it to represent the enjoyment involved in the act of reading. I wish the child in the photograph were identified because she, too, had a story worth telling—and I would have liked to hear it. I appreciate her quiet contemplation. I hope she had a happy life.

My goals in writing *Rain on a Strange Roof* are to celebrate the magic of reading and to describe a personal journey. Some might identify with the story and draw pleasure, strength, and understanding from it. I dedicate the narrative to those with troubled childhoods, to those who have been separated from their families, and to those who live courageously. For me as well as for them, what matters is this day—with all its joys, sorrows, and promise of things to come.

Chapter 1.
An Imagined Childhood

When my adoptive parents decided to seek their first child, Nadine Elizabeth Nash Miracle was in no position to argue. Exhausted, poor, and desperately alone, she already had given birth to nine children, seven of whom survived. With the tenth, her will splintered, and she gave the baby, whom she named "Betty Ann Miracle," to well-meaning people from a faceless institution.

Perhaps she believed that they were in a better place than she to know what would be best for the child. Perhaps she was too tired to care much one way or the other. Perhaps she was devastated by her decision; perhaps, relieved.

Whatever the case, officials from the Tennessee Department of Public Welfare came to the dilapidated white frame house at 2212 Western Avenue in Knoxville, Tennessee, where the child was born. Presumably, they arrived with the best of intentions and the determination of those who serve the disenfranchised.

Although most of those charged with placing children in new homes no doubt do so carefully and thoughtfully, adopted children experience a level of uncertainty other children do not face. Not only do adopted children have biological families who relinquish them, but they also become part of a mysterious institutional placement process that might or might not serve their best interests. In short, although there are no guarantees for anyone born into any family, adoption puts lives into the hands of the state.

I am Betty Ann Miracle. I was born February 25, 1955, and only my mother and the oldest children in the family knew about me. One of my sisters, Geraldine (Gerri) Cheatham, was fathered by the same man I was, and we share a tenuous and precious connection; however, she doesn't remember having seen me or knowing anything about my birth or the adoption until years later. I met Gerri in 1986, but that is a story for another chapter. For now, suffice it to say that, according to Gerri and my half-sister Faustine Miracle Heiser, I am the only one of Nadine Elizabeth Nash Miracle's children to be relinquished.

Author of *Bastard Out of Carolina,* Dorothy Allison wrote a memoir to explain her landmark semi-autobiographical novel about families and violence. In the memoir, she states: "Two or three things I know for sure, and one of them is just this—if we cannot name our own we are cut off at the root, our hold on our lives as fragile as seed in a wind" (12). Although I searched for my family for many years, it was not until 1986 that I found my mother. In 2010, I finally talked with someone who could describe my father and his family. In short, I have spent most of my life "cut off at the root," feeling as "fragile as seed in a wind."

The vagaries of chance are especially significant for adopted children. In addition to their birth, which no child controls, adopted children confront orphanages, adoption agencies, and/or foster homes. Like other children, they are innocent and helpless, but they also must rely upon adults to whom they are not related.

In "Design," Robert Frost creates a word picture about the vulnerability of people caught in an unpredictable world. He describes a spider web into which a hapless moth has flown. Frost asks the reader, "What brought the kindred spider to that height,/ Then steered the white moth thither in the night?/ What but design of darkness to appall?—/ If design govern in a thing so small" (302). In this poem, Frost explores the concept of a divinely instituted process, or "design," that contributes to the death of an insect. Is there a divine plan, or does chance determine universal processes? Using the predicament of the moth to argue that human beings, too, are at the mercy of natural law, Frost addresses the manner in which chance—or what we define as chance—is set into motion.

Of course, all infants are helpless and dependent upon their birth parents for nurturing and sustenance, and none of them can choose parents or a preferred set of financial or emotional circumstances. Their existence depends upon the maturity and the stability of those who brought them into the world.

However, adopted children are especially vulnerable. If adoptions go well—if children are reared with patience and attention to their needs and if those children then pass on the love they came to depend upon—then surely the adoption was successful (one might even say "meant to be"). If a child's early years are spent in a house of horrors, however, then perhaps it was ill fortune that "steered the white moth thither in the night." Either way, both the birth and the placement of adopted children are to some extent dependent upon fate and upon an additional layer of decisions.

I was adopted five months after I was born. My adoptive parents provided health care and the opportunity for a public school education, significant benefits for which I am thankful every day. Many of those in my biological family died young because of medical problems that resulted from poor or nonexistent medical care and/or from personal choices. When I took my concerns about my genetic history to physician Laurence Granston in Boulder, Colorado, he reminded me that health care during the 1950s in rural areas of Tennessee was poor. In addition, tobacco was as important as cotton to Southern farmers, and smoking was a leading cause of illness and death. In fact, several of the photos I have inherited show my mother and her sisters smoking. My mother died of lung cancer that migrated to her liver; according to Gerri, she also suffered from chronic obstructive pulmonary disease (COPD).

I am not safe from the cancer and other serious medical conditions that afflicted my biological family, but I am grateful for the regular doctor visits, nutritious food, and attentive dental care that my adoptive parents provided. With the exception of being diagnosed with melanoma, I have enjoyed good heath, and I possess seemingly endless energy. I do not take these advantages lightly.

As important to me as health care is the chance I had to attend school. I am a university professor, committed to research and teaching and deeply grateful for the opportunity to make the halls of academia my home. I was not destined to teach; in fact, my adoptive father once recommended that I get a teaching certificate to "fall back on," and I rejected the idea. Perhaps he thought journalism would not be a wise career choice. I do remember thinking, "Are there really people who choose teaching because they need a safety net?" Even then, I believed that teachers are special and that only those who love communicating and inspiring others should teach. I said nothing in response to his advice—nor did I ever pursue a teaching certificate.

In spite of my gratitude for medical care and educational opportunities, I acknowledge that the adoption was otherwise disastrous. My adoptive parents are not the reason I succeeded in school or in any other venue; in fact, what successes I had were the result of their inability to express affection or to encourage their adopted children. Craving external validation, I sought it elsewhere.

Not surprisingly, it was teachers who reached out to me—beginning at Edgar D. Park Elementary School in El Paso, Texas, and continuing until I completed my Ph.D. at the University of Denver. The classroom provided both a system of rewards and a safe haven. It reassured me that there is order in the world and that hard work often leads to success. Teachers responded to my curiosity and my desire to do well. I have never been the most intelligent student in the room, but few ever tried harder. Learning was and is a powerful drug, and so was gaining the affection and notice of my instructors.

During elementary and junior high school, I was more attached to my teachers than many children are, anxious to please them and anxious to be validated. I lived for their praise, and their positive responses suggest that they appreciated my desire to learn. They encouraged me to participate in spelling bees, girls basketball and volleyball, and cheerleading.

One teacher at Magoffin Junior High School drove my boyfriend Richard Monroe Armes and me to a spelling competition sponsored by the El Paso Times. She tried without success to suppress a smile as Richard and I walked to her car, opened our respective doors, and sat together in the back seat holding hands, as though it was the most natural thing in the world for her to chauffeur us. I wish I could remember her name; more importantly, I wish I had found a way to thank her. Quiet and attentive, Richard and I sat in her classroom and participated enthusiastically for the rest of the term, reinforcing behaviors that would serve me well with teachers and professors during the 12 years of college that lay ahead.

My teachers parented me when I did not understand enough about my own needs to ask them to do so. As a child, I lived only a few doors from the elementary school, and I did not want to leave my homeroom class with its colorful bulletin boards and expansive windows at the end of the day. The classroom was a sanctuary with reliable rules and rewards. Walking back to the house, I knew that nothing that awaited me there was predictable.

After more than three decades in academia, I cannot deny the impact of those early days in the classroom or my debt to the caring and invested teachers whom I met. Daily, I seek to emulate their commitment by reaching out to my own students, and unlike some of my colleagues who prefer to work at home, I treasure my time on campus.

When I travel, I seek out libraries and college campuses and gain reassurance from walking through university bookstores and handling legal pads and pens adorned with school colors. Only after I have walked across the campus and interacted with students on their way to class do I remember that others are waiting for me at a conference or at the beach or at a restaurant. In the way that athletes are at home in the stadium and judges rely upon familiar codes of conduct in the courtroom, I understand the geography of a college campus and celebrate its distinctive culture.

Although friends describe my adoption as going from a frying pan into a fire, I am grateful for the opportunity to attend school and for the teachers and other loving adults who reached out to me during a difficult childhood. Had I grown up in East Tennessee, it is unlikely that I would have earned a Ph.D. As a teenager, I might have been pregnant. Like my sisters and brothers, I might not have had enough to eat. It is tempting to imagine that I would have enjoyed school and made my way out of poverty on my own—it is tempting but unlikely.

My biological mother graduated from high school and spent her working life as a machine operator and factory supervisor. She sometimes depended upon welfare. In addition to rearing seven children in poverty before I was born (two other children died at birth or in infancy), my mother suffered an emotional breakdown prior to my being born.

My father, Rutherford Hurst, completed only the eighth grade and worked as a machine operator for much of his career. Before he died of a heart attack at age 57, he had been fired from a job at which he made $3.15 an hour. He died penniless and alone, slumped over the steering wheel of his car at the end of a road in Claiborne County, Tennessee.

Memory allows us to treasure what was special and to recreate—or relinquish—what was not. In *The Prince of Tides,* Pat Conroy writes, "There are no verdicts to childhood, only consequences, and the bright freight of memory"

(64). No one has a perfect childhood. The consequences of my upbringing were fear and self-doubt, but—perhaps sensing my vulnerability—classmates and teachers compensated. The classroom became a magical and sustaining place, one that I enjoy more every year.

I've been putting it up my whole life.

Ideally, childhood experiences make us more responsive to the needs of others, more confident about our place in the world, and more capable of making good decisions. As a young child, I understood that I had been born to someone who had relinquished me. I did not know where I had lived in the interim five months before I was adopted. I did not know who decided to allow my adoptive parents to take me. I felt powerless and unable to control my fate.

I knew I was too young to leave El Paso, and I was trapped and fearful. Having had so little control over my life, I realized how important it is to be in charge of as much as I can be. Even now, I prefer to be independent, a positive enough quality, but because I rarely choose to live with others, I am not skilled at negotiating decisions in a primary relationship. A desire to control my environment limits the amount of companionship I can enjoy, and it also affects my career choices. I chose a life in the academy, partly because it is fulfilling and partly because it allows me to have autonomy in the classroom and in my research.

Adopted children may decide to find their biological parents, or they may make peace with what they know about their early lives. Those of us who seek our families may be glad we took the first step, or we may regret forever the truths we uncover. As early as I can remember, I decided to find my mother. An unhappy home life played into my desire to take this particular leap of faith, but it is not necessarily a catalyst for other people. For example, some adopted children are simply curious; some adoptive parents encourage their children to fill in the blanks of their past; some adopted children face a crisis and subsequently want more information about their roots; and others who were adopted want detailed medical records. There are as many reasons to seek information about our past as there are people who opt to do so.

The impetus to seek my biological family was twofold: First, I wanted to address the anxiety that accompanied my times alone. Every abandonment—even a friend who went home when her parents summoned her or a boyfriend who dropped me off at the house—was a reenactment of my mother's disappearance. I wanted to feel enclosed, contained. Second, my friends and teachers had convinced me that I was lovable—a person worthy of being happy. I wanted to find my birth family because I believed that they might be magically—or at least biologically—predisposed to love me.

I was certain of only one thing: I could not continue to live with my adoptive parents, whose public personas as Southern Baptist missionaries established them as caring people engaged in a sacrificial life. My experience with them suggested otherwise, but I was afraid to talk to adults and ask them to confirm my impressions. I suspected that my adoptive parents would portray me as angry (I was) and rebellious (I was) and that I would have to pay for having reported them. I knew only that I wanted to flee.

Those who are raised without affection—by people whose lives are supposed to exemplify love—must be some of the most confused of creatures. I certainly was. As an adult, I marvel at the way my adoptive parents so convincingly maintained their image as humble followers of a righteous God. Having been a journalist, I now understand, of course, that actors, ministers, politicians, presidents, priests, and others are often not what they appear to be. Because I grew up understanding that everything is not as it seems, I later became particularly adept at reading people and at paying attention to the nuances of self-expression. I also became a person largely incapable of trusting others.

As a child, I feared that no one would believe me if I talked about the abuse I experienced and the terror I felt; in fact, with the exception of a family therapist who was a member of the First Baptist Church, I remember confiding in only four people, Richard Monroe Armes; Martha Eugenia Angulo, my Sunday School teacher; and Nancy and Earl McCuin, who worked at a local children's home. Although they believed me, none was in a position to intercede for me. It didn't matter: I learned from these few that I could speak about my experiences and that others were willing to validate me. It was a lesson that would stand me in good stead. In 2010, I located Nancy McCuin, now in her 80s, and we enjoy sporadic e-mail exchanges and share memories of her husband and their time in El Paso. Nancy McCuin is not intrusive, but she remembers my childhood anxiety and never misses an opportunity to tell me that she is proud of the person I have become.

Since becoming an adult, however, I have talked to others about my early memories. Several of those who knew the family that adopted me describe the rigid discipline to which I was subjected and cite a lack of tolerance for normal childhood behavior, including crying. It is impossible to exaggerate my gratitude to these people; first, I know that they shared information with me at some risk to themselves and to relationships that were important to them; and 2) I know that without their confirmation, I would doubt myself and my perceptions.

Trusting our instincts is essential to making good decisions and capably navigating both professional and personal relationships. Children are in an especially vulnerable position when those around them appear oblivious to their silent torment, or, worse, when those who should intercede for them do not believe them. As a result of early self-doubt, I often do not trust my instincts, consulting with colleagues, counselors, friends, family members, and ministers before I make important decisions.

During junior high and high school, I appeared to be a good student but was otherwise an unexceptional person. I did not take drugs or drink alcohol or have sex. I wanted to be loved, and I knew that if I made poor decisions, I would confirm the opinions my adoptive parents had—and no doubt shared with others—about me.

However, our parents are the first line of defense against the world, and in my case, the world was more welcoming than they. Even now, I remain in awe of those who seem comfortable divulging their failures and who have perfected the art of uttering sincere and seemingly effortless apologies. These people are emotionally healthy and approachable and appear to be happy with themselves and others. I never heard my adoptive parents apologize for anything, and I grew up believing that admitting guilt or making mistakes would be used against me. I still struggle valiantly but often unsuccessfully against this early training. It is impossible to have a trusting adult relationship without at least occasionally and inadvertently wounding the other person and without learning to apologize for commissions and omissions. I often fall short.

My interest in the role of fate in the lives of adopted children led me to particular texts. One of the best examples is the 2007 film "No Country for Old Men," the bleak, dark, and dreadfully wonderful cinematic experience that introduces us to the antihero Anton Chigurh and the quarters he flips in order to determine who lives and who dies. Two scenes in the novel and film are particularly evocative for me. The first involves a hapless gas station owner; the second, a woman returning from her mother's funeral. In both cases, Chigurh—like God—determines without passion who will see another day.

Chigurh is an antihero obsessed with the role of fate in the lives of those with whom he comes in contact and with the mechanistic nature of the universe. Carson Wells, a bounty hunter who pursues Chigurh, survives until a final showdown in an old hotel. After someone suggests he has led "something of a charmed life," Wells responds, "In all honesty I cant say that charm has had a whole lot to do with it" (141). He facetiously suggests that luck is more important than charm. Later, immediately before Chigurh shoots Wells, Chigurh asks him cryptically, "If the rule you followed led you to this of what use was the rule?" "I don't know what you're talking about," Wells replies. "I'm talking about your life," Chigurh says. "In which now everything can be seen at once" (175).

"No Country for Old Men" suggests that we make decisions that lead to unknown destinations; furthermore, much of what occurs to us is outside of our control. Nature is relentless and impersonal. We are at the mercy of natural disasters. We are at the mercy of genetics, of plane crashes, of the strengths and weaknesses of those to whom we are born, of the economy, and of the natural cycles that determine our very health.

In the novel and the film by the same name, Llewellyn Moss stumbles onto a drug deal gone bad. He tracks a briefcase filled with $100 bills and begins a perilous cat-and-mouse game that ultimately will cost him his life. Sheriff Ed Tom Bell, who futilely attempts to save Moss's life, pursues Chigurh but wants to intercept Moss and return him to his wife.

Because of the violence Bell has observed during his many years as a law enforcement officer, he thinks often and passionately about the nature of evil:

> I read the papers ever mornin. Mostly I suppose just to try and figure out what might be headed this way. Not that I've done all that good a job at headin it off. It keeps gettin harder. Here a while back they was two boys run into one another and one of em was from California and one from Florida. And they met somewheres or other in between. And then they set out together travelin around the country killin people. I forget how many they did kill. Now what are the chances of a thing like that? Them two had never laid eyes on one another. There cant be that many of em. I dont think. Well, we don't know. Here the other day they was a woman put her baby in a trash compactor. Who would think of such a thing? (40)

Similarly, Bell later ruminates about newspapers and the nature of humanity:

> What I was sayin the other day about the papers. Here last week they found this couple out in California they would rent out rooms to old people and then kill em and bury em in the yard and cash their social security checks. They'd torture em first, I don't know why. Maybe their television was broke. Now here's what the papers had to say about that. I quote from the papers. Said: Neighbors were alerted when a man run from the premises wearin only a dogcollar. You can't make up such a thing as that. I dare you to even try.
>
> But that's what it took, you'll notice. All that hollerin and diggin in the yard didn't bring it. (124)

When his deputy laughs and seems embarrassed for finding the violence funny, Bell says: "That's all right. I laughed myself when I read it. There aint a whole lot else you can do" (124).

When Chigurh confronts the gas station proprietor, neither of them understands the other. In a compelling example of allegory, Chigurh, a serial killer, speaks with wisdom and awareness about the futility of life. Confronted with what he increasingly recognizes as the embodiment of evil, the station owner understands little that Chigurh says to him. The dialogue follows:

> Will there be somethin else? the man said.
> I dont know. Will there?
> Is there somethin wrong?
> With what?
> With anything.
> Is that what you're asking me? Is there something wrong with anything? (53)

Chigurh then challenges the proprieter to flip a coin:

> Just call it.
> I didnt put nothin up.
> Yes you did. You've been putting it up your whole life. You just didnt know it. You know what the date is on this coin?
> No.

> It's nineteen fifty-eight. It's been traveling twenty-two years to get here. And now it's here. And I'm here. And I've got my hand over it. And it's either heads or tails. And you have to say it. Call it.
>
> I dont know what it is I stand to win.
>
> In the blue light the man's face was beaded thinly with sweat. He licked his upper lip.
>
> You stand to win everything, Chigurh said. Everything.
>
> You aint makin any sense, mister. (56)

On a literal level, Chigurh does not make sense. But in his treatise on chance and its role in human destiny, he speaks as though he were a prophet. Although Chigurh will kill the proprietor if he calls tails instead of heads, he reminds him that his existence is fragile and that going home that night or returning to his place of business the following day is uncertain. Fortunately, the proprietor correctly identifies "heads then," and Chigurh responds, "Well done" (56). The coin has traveled many years to arrive at the gas station, and so, presumably, have the two men engaged in a conversation that determines who lives and who dies.

Throughout the novel and the film are other explorations of the role of fate in human life. We are oblivious to the catastrophes about to occur. We can predict very little and cannot shield ourselves from disaster. For example, finding a dead man on the highway, Bell engages in a conversation with his deputy. Someone has killed the man and set fire to his car, and the two officers acknowledge that the man never dreamed he would meet this fate. The conversation follows:

> It wasn't his day, was it Sheriff.
>
> It surely wasn't.
>
> Why do you reckon they set fire to it?
>
> I dont know.
>
> Wendell turned and spat. Wasnt what the old boy had in mind when he left Dallas I dont reckon, was it?
>
> Bell shook his head. No, he said. I'd guess it was about the farthest thing from his mind. (68-69)

Moss, who appears to be the central protagonist, instead becomes one of Chigurh's pawns. Determined to save Moss from himself, Bell discusses the site of an aborted drug deal, where corpses and dogs lie rotting in the Texas sun. Asked if Moss understands the extent of the evil he has loosed on the world ("You think this boy has got any notion of the sorts of sons of bitches that are huntin him?"), Bell replies, "I don't know. He ought to. He seen the same things I seen and it made an impression on me" (94).

Like a laser, Chigurh's relentless pursuit leads to Moss's momentary self-awareness, similar to the moment of epiphany that occurs between the Misfit and the grandmother in Flannery O'Connor's "A Good Man Is Hard to Find." In her final moments, the grandmother understands that the Misfit is an agent of evil, but she also recognizes his humanity. After he shoots her, the Misfit says,

"She would of been a good woman if it had been somebody there to shoot her every minute of her life" (22). Although he is the embodiment of evil, the Misfit operates in the text as a kind of antihero, bringing both wisdom and violence to those whom he confronts.

Chigurh, too, is a misfit who forces other characters in the novel and the film to confront their own natures and their mortality. Before Moss dies, McCarthy describes him "thinking about his life, what was past and what was to come" (210). At one point in his dangerous journey, Moss shares with a young woman a portion of what he's learning about himself and about humanity: "It's not about knowin where you are. It's about thinkin you got there without takin anything with you. Your notions about startin over. Or anybody's. You dont start over. That's what it's about. Ever step you take is forever. You can't make it go away. None of it. You understand what I'm sayin?" (227).

Bell never calls Chigurh the devil—he doesn't need to. Before Chigurh kills Moss's wife, he talks to her about fate and human choice. Initially, she refuses to call heads or tails. Then she calls "heads," but the correct answer is "tails." "You make it like it was the coin," she tells him. "But you're the one. . . The coin didnt have no say. It was just you." "Perhaps," he says. "But look at it my way. I got here the same way the coin did" (258-59). With the tone of a preacher instructing her or his congregation, Chigurh tells her:

> Every moment in your life is a turning and every one a choosing. Somewhere you made a choice. All followed to this. The accounting is scrupulous. The shape is drawn. No line can be erased. I had no belief in your ability to move a coin to your bidding. How could you? A person's path through the world seldom changes and even more seldom will it change abruptly. And the shape of your path was visible from the beginning. (259)

Loss often accompanies chance as a central theme in the novel and the film. On one occasion, Bell visits an elderly friend who tells him that there's "no point" to what occurs during one's life. He confesses his exhaustion:

> You wear out, Ed Tom. All the time you spend tryin to get back what's been took from you there's more goin out the door. After a while you just try and get a tourniquet on it...Anyway, you never know what worse luck your bad luck has saved you from. (267)

Much of the novel deals indirectly with issues of faith and the existence of God. Thinking about whether or not he believes in evil, Bell concludes that he does and acknowledges the role of Satan in the world: "He explains a lot of things that otherwise dont have no explanation. Or not to me they dont" (218). Having decided to retire, Bell tells his friend that he had hoped God would become more real to him during his life: "I always thought when I got older that God would sort of come into my life in some way. He didnt. I dont blame him. If I was him I'd have the same opinion about me that he does" (267). Pensively, Bell later discusses how difficult it is to evaluate one's own worth: "It's a life's work to see yourself for what you really are and even then you might be wrong" (295), he says.

When I turned my back on my childhood and found a new family, I might have said, "God brought me to where I am now." Today, I would have to say, "It was a coin toss." The adoption, too, might never have occurred. I cannot find it in my heart to believe that my biological siblings were less deserving of good health and of the opportunity to gain a good education than I. I also do not believe that my placement with an adoptive couple ill prepared to be parents was the will of God. I had the good judgment to work hard and to emulate the lives of those around me who cared about relationships and professional success, but none of us entirely controls our destiny.

Much of my good fortune depended upon—and continues to depend upon—chance. Like the owner of the convenience store in McCarthy's dark novel, I have been putting it up my whole life. Unlike him, however, I am entirely conscious of what is at stake.

"Did you hear the rain one night?"

Stories about adopted children finding their biological parents regularly appear in news and popular magazines, and even a reality show devoted to reuniting adoptees with their birth families enjoyed a short run on prime-time television in 2009. ABC's "Find My Family" failed to find its niche, but it raised issues of great importance to those who are adopted and to the parent or parents who relinquished them. At the time the pilot episode aired, the network web site described the short-lived television program by highlighting the human cost of separation:

> We all know people who feel incomplete, searching for something to make them feel whole. The heartache of separation is difficult on all of us, but it's hard to imagine the struggle for those wondering about family they haven't seen since birth, or who don't know if a loved one is even alive after decades of silence.
>
> The producer of *Extreme Makeover: Home Edition* created this show with one simple mission—to bring families back together. With the help of a dedicated team of researchers, hosts Tim Green and Lisa Joyner guide people searching for lost loved ones through the emotional journeys that will change their lives forever.

Testimonials in print and on the small screen often reflect the gratitude that family members express for their good fortune in finding one another. The Aug. 16, 2010, issue of *Time* magazine features Dana Lowrey, a young woman who sought and found what she calls her "first family." Having looked for her birth mother for 30 years, she used social networking sites and found her in one day:

> She combed through county records, searched the online adoption registries and enlisted the help of reunion experts. On Jan. 10, she set up a Facebook page and asked the friends she had made in the adoption community to help her search. Within 24 hours, she was in touch with her birth mother, Mary Stark. And by Jan. 15, she had made contact with her biological dad, Kenny Morse. (Luscombe 45)

But Lowrey's story takes another turn. Mother of two children, Lowrey used her site on MySpace in 2008 to find her own son, whom she had given up for adoption two decades earlier.

The access that social networks provide raises issues for adoption agencies. "We have not yet begun to wrap our mind around what the implications are," said Adam Pertman, executive director of the Evan B. Donaldson Adoption Institute in New York City. "Even in the best of cases, you want a little knowledge first. You want to do this thoughtfully and methodically. With Facebook, you don't have any of that" (Luscombe 46). However, in "Finding Mom on Facebook," Belinda Luscombe concludes her article about Lowrey, Lowrey's birth parents, and Lowrey's son with optimism: "And thanks to Facebook, now they all know exactly where to find each other" (46).

In the 1970s, Karen and Richard Carpenter recorded a plaintive song entitled "Bless the Beasts and the Children" that reached the top of the music charts. One of the lines—"For in this world, they have no voice"—reminds us that children were and are at the mercy of those who are stronger and bigger than they are and those who are convinced of their own wisdom.

If the children survive, those who are victims of abuse, molestation, rape, and violence develop multiple coping mechanisms. Often either fearful or defiant, they stand somewhere along the continuum of mental and emotional health. Although this is no different than it is for biological children reared by their "natural" parents, an adopted child faces a second line of uncertainty and fear. Adopted children understand—perhaps better than others do—the role of chance in their birth and, subsequently, in their placement and upbringing. Often, they are deprived of their health history and other information that others take for granted.

A landmark film dealing with adoption is "Mother and Child" (2010), written and directed by Rodrigo García and featuring a noteworthy cast. García spent 10 years writing the screenplay. Like the novel *The Hours* by Michael Cunningham (and the film by the same name), "Mother and Child" features storylines about three women and demonstrates an unusually nuanced understanding of women.

Viewers meet Karen (Annette Bening), who was 14 when she gave birth, and share her life from the ages of 49 to 51; discover the personal and professional career of Elizabeth Joyce (Naomi Watts) during nine months; and become acquainted with Lucy (Kerry Washington) over the course of six months. Karen, Elizabeth's mother, gave her up for adoption; having lived without one another, both Karen and Elizabeth are anxious and angry, unable to share freely with those around them. The first lines in the film are Karen's, when she wakes from an unsettling dream. At breakfast, she tells her mother, "Her birthday's coming up. She'll be 37."

Although promotion materials suggest the film is about the "unbreakable bond between mother and child," it is also about the arbitrariness of adoption and the errors that the system—in this case a Catholic adoption agency—can make. If letters that Karen and Elizabeth are invited to write to one another had been treated with care, the two would have met and would have enjoyed a relationship with one another. Although it is obfuscated in the film, errors of commission and omission suggest that those who work in the institutional adoption process might not be diligent and might not understand the gravity of procedures that separate parents from their children.

One of the most complex characters in the film is Elizabeth Joyce, who named herself in junior high school. During an interview for a position in a law office, Elizabeth tells Paul (Samuel L. Jackson), her prospective employer, that she often intimidates women and prefers to report to men: "I'm not in the sisterhood," she tells him. "I'm my own person." When Paul asks her to share general information about her personal life, she tells him:

> I was born here in Los Angeles. And I was given up for adoption on the day of my birth. My mother was 14 when she had me. And that's all I know about her. My adoptive father died when I was 10. My adoptive mother and I are not close.
>
> My name—Elizabeth Joyce—is one I picked out for myself in junior high. It's my legal name now. I don't go by any other.
>
> I live alone. I have since I turned 17. I've never been married. And I have no plans to marry. I value my independence above all things. That way I don't have any expectations to fulfill...other than my own...which are great enough.

The viewer and Paul learn about Elizabeth gradually. Asked about why she returns to Los Angeles, she replies, "This part of the world is as good as any." The statement runs much deeper than Paul originally understands; in fact, one job is as good as any other, one law firm is as good as any other, and one man is as good as any other. When she and Paul become intimate, she refers to their "affair." Paul asks how it can be an "affair" when neither of them is married. She tells him an affair is anything "informal" and "temporary," two words that define all her relationships.

Later, when her new boss invites her to a welcome dinner, she arrives and is surprised that only he is attending. Clearly, Elizabeth doesn't like surprises: "I just like to know what everything means," she tells him. "That's all."

Keeping a record of her dreams and thoughts about the daughter she relinquished, Karen talks to an absent Elizabeth after her own mother dies. "She's gone now," Karen says to an empty room. "She will never see your face. And you will never see hers...I know in my heart that we will meet one day, and you will forgive me."

The beautifully subtle film features realistic dialogue, including a conversation between Paul and Elizabeth before he breaks off their sexual relationship to protect himself from his own growing feeling for her:

> Paul: Have you ever looked for your biological parents?
> Elizabeth: No.
> Paul: They might be looking for you.
> Elizabeth: There is no "they." My father's not part of my imagination. I live in her hometown. How hard can it be for her fucking majesty to find me? It's better this way. We're all better off like this. Why do you ask?
> Paul: I thought she'd be very pleased with who you are.

Paul tells her he must "bow out" before he gets hurt. "You want what you want," he tells her. "I like that. In fact, your willfulness is a great part of your charm."

Karen, too, struggles to connect with men, and moments of anger punctuate a colleague's attempts to reach out to her. Paco (Jimmy Smits) perseveres, and as the two of them sit in his car on their way to dinner, she explains her inability to express affection for him. "Everything I do, every thought in my head, takes me back to her," Karen says of her lost daughter. "Everywhere I go, I look for her face in the crowd. I write her letters…buy her birthday gifts…I have nothing else. That's who I am. I have nothing to give."

Paco and his daughter encourage Karen to seek Elizabeth before time runs out. Asked about her greatest fear, Karen replies: "That she'll spit in my face." Karen writes a letter that will be held in her file in case Elizabeth seeks information about her. Under California state law, if both are willing to meet, the agency is free to identify them to each other.

After Elizabeth learns that she is pregnant, she rethinks her response to Paul and also writes a letter for the file. The text follows:

> I don't want to impose myself on you. I don't want to be a nuisance. I am pregnant, and I'd like my baby to know where she comes from. I live in Los Angeles. I'm successful in my work and financially independent. I am open to sharing more about myself, and if you were open to that as well, it would be welcome. If you don't want to communicate with me, I will also understand and accept it. If we were to meet, I think we should look forward, not back, and build something new. I was born November 7, 1973. My name is Elizabeth. I think of you often.

When Elizabeth delivers the missive to the agency, a distracted employee misplaces it. By the time the administration discovers the mistake, Elizabeth has died while giving birth, and her baby has been adopted.

Horrified by their error, the agency puts Karen in touch with her grandchild Ella (Juliette Amara), who—as chance would have it—lives with her single mother only a few blocks away. The two play joyfully in the front yard with the child's adoptive mother Lucy, and that night, before Karen falls asleep, she writes a diary entry for the daughter she will never meet: "I never saw you," she writes. "Did you hear the rain one night when I heard it? What gave you comfort? I've missed it all, and I've accepted it. But today I met Ella...Ella is peace."

What some might call fate plays a role in the film that provides few happy endings. Lucy, whose husband leaves the marriage because she cannot give him biological children, describes the function of chance in her life and in the lives of others. Talking to the birth mother of the first child she tries to adopt, she says: "I believe that when we're born, we come from nothing and that when we die, we go back to nothing—that what we make of our lives is the result of our will and our luck—the strength of our character and the roll of the dice."

García's sensitive and powerful screenplay makes it clear that adoption is something not to be taken lightly and something barely understood by those who have not experienced it. The film, he says, is about a pregnancy and the relinquishment of a child that occurred 35 years before and from which Karen and Elizabeth "took a whole life to recover from."

I identify with the "willfulness" and independence Elizabeth exhibits. I grieve about what those characteristics cost those who fall in love with her; simultaneously, I celebrate what they mean for her career and her sense of stability. I understand, too, her inability to trust and her desire to enter temporary relationships. She does not want to fail. And because she does not want to be abandoned again, she leaves men before they can leave her.

The film chronicles the most primitive kind of loss, the relinquishment of one's flesh and blood and the impact of that decision on a child. I share Elizabeth's fears and recognize the ways in which she compensates for having lost her mother. I understand all too keenly Elizabeth's desire for independence, her disinterest in primary relationships, and her relentless desire to succeed.

I also identify with Karen when she writes to an absent daughter, "Did you hear the rain one night when I heard it?" I understand her longing to believe that—although she has "missed it all"—there still might be forgiveness and a restorative connection with her lost child. At least, Karen suggests, we were bound together in the most intimate of ways, we were alive during the same time, and perhaps we even heard the same rain.

I wonder if my mother and father were conscious of events and experiences—even weather—that may have bound them to one another. I wonder if they shared memories of the soft Tennessee rain. I wonder how much time my mother and I had together before staff from the Tennessee Department of Human Services arrived. I wonder, too, if Nadine Elizabeth Nash Miracle ever commemorated my birthday.

Standing on the Radley porch is enough.

Since childhood, I have been drawn to pseudo-autobiographical narratives by authors who both lived and imagined their childhoods. This interest does not make me special or even unusual. Children who spend their lives in an arid place devoid of emotion and hope flail about for something that will save them. Some people watch television, play video games, or discover adventure and romance in a darkened theater. I read books.

Those who enjoy school have a predisposition to love literature. I don't remember when I first understood that a book could transport me out of myself and into a better world, but the inclination to lose myself in a book—and later a television series or film—is one of my earliest memories.

Although I often purchased paperback novels based on how many pages they contained—a desperate desire to prolong the experience of learning about a particular fictional universe—these books are not necessarily the ones that defined or encouraged me. Instead, like many children, I read *To Kill a Mockingbird,* an archetypal tale of childhood innocence into experience, and it was and is a touchstone.

I was no different from other children who discover Harper Lee's imaginative reminiscence, but I did not long to be Scout as much as I wanted to belong to Atticus Finch. I did not picture Gregory Peck when I read Finch's conversations with his independent and intelligent daughter, but when the film was released in 1962, I thought: "Of course. That's Atticus Finch!" *To Kill a Mockingbird* made me long for an older brother like Jem, too. Rather than believing that the fiction is impossible to attain, I simply used the novel as a template for what could be. As a child who longed to wake up in a sunlit room in Maycomb, Alabama, I had no idea that I would one day teach *To Kill a Mockingbird* in classrooms from Texas to Colorado and watch it work its magic on hundreds of 20-somethings.

To Kill a Mockingbird is indeed a long-form reminiscence, told chronologically in the voice of an omniscient narrator looking back on childhood. It encompasses only three years, although a reader imagines that she or he has followed Scout through more vignettes than can be contained in this deceptively short period of time. Bob Ewell's attempted murder of the Finch children serves as a second climax to the novel, the first being the death of Tom Robinson, played in the film by Brock Peters.

Scout's memory of her long journey home to Atticus is necessarily understated; she must protect herself from reliving the murder in the woods. "When enough years had gone by to enable us to look back on them," Scout tells the reader, "we sometimes discussed the events leading to his accident" (3). The choice of the word "accident" is as interesting as it is misleading. It reflects an adult Jean Louise Finch and her desire to protect herself from the full horror of the night that almost cost her a brother and her own life.

The setting of *To Kill a Mockingbird* reflects quintessential small-town Southern life, slow as molasses and masking the gothic, the grotesque, and the mysterious. Maycomb is civilized, but beneath the red earth lies much that is dark and sinister. The reader steps into the frame of the story, hearing the words of an older narrator but understanding the events through the eyes of a child.

The description of Maycomb introduces both the novel and the film and reinforces the superficial innocence of the time:

> Maycomb was an old town, but it was a tired old town when I first knew it. In rainy weather the streets turned to red slop; grass grew on the sidewalks, the courthouse sagged in the square. Somehow, it was hotter then: a black dog suffered on a summer's day; bony mules hitched to Hoover carts flicked flies in the sweltering shade of the live oaks on the square. Men's stiff collars wilted by nine in the morning. Ladies bathed before noon, after their three-o'clock naps, and by nightfall were like soft teacakes with frostings of sweat and sweet talcum.
>
> People moved slowly then. They ambled across the square, shuffled in and out of the stores around it, took their time about everything. A day was twenty-four hours long but seemed longer. There was no hurry, for there was nowhere to go, nothing to buy and no money to buy it with, nothing to see outside the boundaries of Maycomb County. But it was a time of vague optimism for some of the people: Maycomb County had recently been told that it had nothing to fear but fear itself. (5-6)

Later in the novel, another descriptive section helps to locate the reader in the Deep South, a region with which he or she might not be familiar: "There are no clearly defined seasons in South Alabama; summer drifts into autumn, and autumn is sometimes never followed by winter, but turns to a days-old spring that melts into summer again" (59).

Clearly, the residents of Maycomb have more to fear than fear, in spite of President Franklin Delano Roosevelt's reassurance to the contrary. In the film, Scout asks Atticus Finch if they are poor. He replies that yes, they are, but not as poor as the farmers who were hit hardest by the Depression. With this introductory statement, the reader is reminded that Scout and Jem are safe and protected—at least from financial disaster—and that Atticus is teaching them to be grateful for what they have.

Emotionally, the children are on shakier ground than they are financially, their mother having died when Scout was 2. As the narrator observes, Jem missed her more because he had known her better and had grown to love and depend upon her. In the novel, Calpurnia, Aunt Alexandra, Miss Maudie, and others provide Scout with female roles models and with varying degrees of affection and tenderness. In the film, Aunt Alexandria is omitted, leaving Calpurnia to exemplify motherly care and discipline. Scout is used to her presence and takes her so for granted (as she might her own mother) that she occasionally treats her dismissively.

Other women in the town, such as Mrs. Henry Lafayette Dubose, serve as both foils and metaphors. Although she snaps at the children (she appears only once in the film), Mrs. Dubose exemplifies the kind of courage that Atticus Finch wants for his children, and in the novel he requires that Jem read to her and come to understand the physical suffering that dominates her life:

> I wanted you to see something about her—I wanted you to see what real courage is, instead of getting the idea that courage is a man with a gun in his hand. It's when you know you're licked before you begin but you begin anyway and you see it through no matter what. . . She was the bravest person I ever knew. (112)

The Pulitzer Prize-winning *To Kill a Mockingbird* is a barely disguised autobiography of Harper Lee and is dedicated to "Mr. Lee and Alice in consideration of Love & Affection." The reference to "Mr. Lee" is to Harper Lee's father, Amasa Lee, and the reference to Alice is to Alice Lee, her sister. Scout's childhood friend Charles Baker Harris (Dill) represents Truman Capote, with whom Lee would conduct research for *In Cold Blood* when they were both established writers. Both "Capote" (2005) and "Infamous" (2006), which were in production at the same time, depict the relationship between Capote and Lee. In the novel, Lee writes about Capote lyrically and devotedly:

> Dill was off again. Beautiful things floated around in his dreamy head. He could read two books to my one, but he preferred the magic of his own inventions. He could add and subtract faster than lightning, but he preferred his own twilight world...a world where babies slept, waiting to be gathered like morning lilies. He was slowly talking himself to sleep and taking me with him, but in the quietness of his foggy island there rose the faded image of a gray house with sad brown doors. (144)

In the film, Dill often stands outside while Atticus Finch embraces his children and walks with them into their home. The camera does not linger on Dill, but his sadness and his awareness that he is not part of the insular family unit are reasons I was drawn to the film when I was a child. Aware of his loneliness although unsure of the catalyst, Scout once asks Dill why he thinks Boo Radley never runs away. "Maybe he doesn't have anywhere to run off to" (144), replies Dill, with wisdom born of empathy.

Scout's (and presumably Harper Lee's) life is defined by a series of lessons that include schoolyard fights, arguments with teachers, and social blunders involving "entailments" and other adult issues. Some of the concerns are more important for a young girl growing up in the South than others. When Scout asks Atticus Finch if he defends "niggers," her father tells her to call black people "Negroes." She responds by reminding him that everyone in her community calls African Americans "niggers." "From now on," Finch tells her sternly but with love, "it'll be everybody less one" (75).

Some of the most memorable lines appear in both the novel and the film, including a statement by a mature Scout, who is looking back on her life and remembering the night that she attended a Halloween party with Jem: "Thus began our longest journey together" (254), she says. Depicted with rustling leaves and echoes, the assault on the Finch children in the 1962 film highlights the violence of a segregated South. The events devastate the children and terrify the small community in which they have always felt safe. Jem escorts Scout, dressed as a ham for a play, to and from their school. As the trees tower above the children on their way home, someone stalks them. In the dark and ominous woods, Jem tries to protect his sister from the assailant, but he is attacked. His arm is broken, and he is knocked unconscious.

After the incident, law enforcement officials find Bob Ewell's body in the woods. Atticus Finch wordlessly agrees to let the sheriff claim that Ewell fell on his own knife and killed himself. We learn that Boo Radley (Robert Duvall), a mysterious figure who lives in a ramshackle cabin down the street from the Finch children, has saved Scout and Jem. His voice trembling, Atticus Finch says to his reclusive neighbor, "Thank you for my children, Arthur" (276).

Recovering from his injuries, Jem sleeps. Scout walks Boo Radley down the street to his dark and decrepit house, and the mature narrator tells the reader in a pure and understated manner: "I never saw him again. Neighbors bring food with death and flowers with sickness and little things in between. Boo was our neighbor. He gave us two soap dolls, a broken watch and chain, a pair of good-luck pennies, and our lives" (278).

Didacticism intrudes throughout the novel and film. After Atticus Finch tells Scout about the way in which a mockingbird sings for people and does not hurt their crops, she thinks about his admonition not to hurt or kill any innocent creature. At the end of the novel, an older Scout explains the statement to herself and to us: "Atticus was right. One time he said you never really know a man until you stand in his shoes and walk around in them. Just standing on the Radley porch was enough" (279).

The novel advocates for compassion and a respect for people who are different from ourselves. Boo Radley is a mockingbird, but so are 19-year-old Mayella Ewell, the kind but doomed Tom Robinson, Jem Finch—and Scout. The reader knows that Scout will prevail because her father is intelligent, kind, and invested in his children and their welfare. In a kind of postlude to the novel, Lee writes about her own father and her fictional creation: "He would be there all night, and he would be there when Jem waked up in the morning" (281).

I loved the mockingbirds in my own life. As alienated as I was during my youth, I knew there were others who endured greater discrimination than I. Drawn to Roger Bell, a charismatic African-American high school drum major, and in love with Richard Monroe Armes, a brilliant student and devout Catholic, I learned that not everyone in a white, middle-class, Protestant suburb celebrates difference.

In short, my adoptive parents did not want me to date blacks or Catholics. When I asked why a Catholic is not a Christian, they could not provide a reasonable explanation. As an adult, I wonder if even they believed what they were saying (and not saying). I have no doubt that they were entirely unaware of the devastating consequences their pronouncements had on me. Telling me that the boy I loved might suffer damnation because he had not "accepted Jesus Christ as his personal savior" devastated me, and there was no room in their house or their belief system for rebuttal.

My adoptive parents went to church on Sunday mornings and evenings and returned for evening prayer meeting on Wednesdays. They conducted daily Bible studies in their house. They replaced dice with spinners in table games because they believed that dice were associated with gambling. They prayed before every meal, and I never saw them drink even a glass of wine. I could not play music by the Beach Boys (my adoptive father objected to the reference to "French bikinis" in the song "California Girls"). They did not allow me to see the 1970 film "Love Story" because it featured extramarital sex. Frankly, I might have accepted their conservative world view if they had been able to express compassion, but they lived in an Old Testament world dominated by sin and punishment—and I wanted out.

No logic of mine could prevail in this rigid and sterile world, and I longed for Atticus Finch and a town in Alabama, where the streets turned to "red slop" after a rain and where the courthouse "sagged" in the town square. I wanted to chat with Miss Maudie and run with Jem through the moonlight. I wanted to peer into the window of the Radley house. I wanted to sleep soundly and safely. And I waited for my real life to begin.

In those early days, I could never have predicted that I would become a full professor at one of the nation's most prominent public research institutions. Pat Conroy, too, acknowledges that his own early life did not necessarily suggest that he would succeed: "Yet an intellectual life often forms in the strangest, most infertile of conditions" *(My Reading Life* 3), he writes. So it does.

Remarkably, I escaped into the pages of literature as early as I can remember knowing how to read. I thought I was alone in my fantasy life. I know now that I was not. Conroy, for example, frequents a favorite local bookstore and remarks upon the customers: "For many of them, books were the lifelines to unbearable lives" *(My Reading Life* 124). In *My Reading Life,* published late in his remarkable career, Conroy confesses, "I reach for a story to save my own life" (154).

Like the author of *The Prince of Tides* and *The Great Santini,* I remember finding respite during my childhood and adolescence—not in drugs or alcohol—but in books. More effective and less dangerous to one's health, books became a cherished access to life in the academy. "Though I failed to notice it at the time, my childhood was a long, patient apprenticeship of finding my comfort zone in the ocean of words that rushed through me each day," Conroy writes. "I was drifting toward novels that would one day capture me with the unanswerable power of their rawness, and the sheer need to be told" *(My Reading Life* 88).

Books enticed me into a mystical world and protected me from reality. Commenting on his own difficult childhood, Conroy describes a time when his father beat his mother and he—like Luke, Tom, and Savannah Wingo in *The Prince of Tides*—was told to forget what he saw. "Later my mother would recover and tell us that we had not seen what we had just seen," Conroy writes. "She turned us into unwitnesses of our own history" *(My Reading Life* 189). Through writing, Conroy recovers his memory and learns to trust himself and his own perceptions.

I, too, know what it is like to be an "unwitness" to the events in my own life, and *Rain on a Strange Roof* also describes the times when I was penniless and alone. Gradually, I let go of the anger and the disappointment. I worked hard in school and found a job at a local newspaper that helped to pay my way through college. Each person who liked and encouraged me surprised me more than the previous one, and little by precious little, I learned to believe in myself.

Scout Finch's childhood was a happy and secure one, and her future is full of promise. However, the Radleys remind her that all does not end well; they remind us that chance determines a great deal about who we are. Those of us who suffered pain and shame at the hands of those who were charged with protecting us will never trust others entirely. "If your parents disapprove of you and are cunning with their disapproval, there will never come a new dawn when you can become convinced of your own value," writes Conroy in *The Prince of Tides*. "There is no fixing a damaged childhood. The best you can hope for is to make the sucker float" (134).

As a mature Scout understands years after the perilous night in the woods, Boo Radley saved her life, but she could not save his. Standing on his front porch, she empathizes with his loneliness and poverty and imagines what it would be like to call the Radley house her home. Awaiting her are her compassionate father and her protective brother; Calpurnia and Miss Maudie; and all those whom she has yet to meet.

To Kill a Mockingbird portrays young children and a father's love. Given my own deprivation, it is hardly surprising that Atticus Finch became my fantasy father; in fact, it is not surprising that even today I have on my office wall a photograph of Gregory Peck with his arms around child actors Phillip Alford (Jeremy Atticus Finch) and Mary Badham (Jean Louise Finch). Atticus Finch's tender strength never diminishes in its impact on me.

I share what I have experienced in the hopes that it will sustain others who were adopted, who had difficult childhoods, who were told to forget the past, or who understand the transformative power of literature. I will be as honest as someone unaccustomed to self-disclosure can be. And I will rely upon the comfort of stories told well.

Frankie Addams and Mick Kelly are the "we of me."

Imagined childhoods are topics for the intimate lamp-lit offices of psychotherapists, ministers, priests, and rabbis; for conversations over candles and wine during romantic encounters; for reminiscences during family reunions and birthday gatherings. Some childhoods may resemble those portrayed in Harper Lee's *To Kill a Mockingbird* or Carson McCullers' *The Heart Is a Lonely Hunter*. Both of these novels are fictional accounts of life in the Deep South. Or are they?

Lee and McCullers transformed their own childhood and adolescent yearnings into tales both remembered and created. Like the toys Boo Radley leaves for Jem and Scout Finch, Lee and McCullers left behind treasures of consciousness—reminiscences of a time they imagine they remember.

To Kill a Mockingbird and *The Heart Is a Lonely Hunter* are masterpieces of the retold life, and both novels help to explain my initial attraction to literature. *The Heart Is a Lonely Hunter* is akin to *The Member of the Wedding* in its focus on an adolescent girl trying to make her way in a small Southern town.

Although I did not read novels by McCullers until I was in college, I have always been struck by the author's ability to describe adolescence with such empathy and intensity. Adolescence earns its reputation as one of the most challenging passages in American life, and I vividly remember its pitfalls and discontents. In both *The Heart Is a Lonely Hunter* and *The Member of the Wedding,* McCullers creates female protagonists who long for connection to others. Tomboyish and self-conscious, Mick Kelly and Frankie Addams deserve their place in the memories of the girls who identify with them.

Published when McCullers was 21, *The Heart Is a Lonely Hunter* is a staple in high school and introductory college literature courses. Teaching the novel to undergraduates, I remind them repeatedly how old the author was when she began what some consider to be her best work. I want my students to understand that novels, poetry, and photographs of merit are contributed by those in their 20s. I tell them about McCullers, but I do not stop there.

Other 20-somethings also left their mark on history: I tell students the story of Nick Ut, who took the Pulitzer Prize-winning photograph of children running from a napalm attack in Trang Bang, Vietnam. I tell them about John Filo, too poor to own a camera, and the Pulitzer Prize he won for his photo of the 1971 shootings at Kent State University. I tell them about Dan Eldon, reporter and photographer, who died while covering his first war and who is now remembered in a CNN documentary entitled "Dying To Tell the Story." I remind my undergraduates that they are talented and enthusiastic, a powerful and enviable combination.

In McCullers' first novel, we learn about the deep friendship between two deaf mutes, Spiros Antonapoulos and John Singer. We learn that Singer, whose name evokes both his ethnicity and his ironic role in the novel, is adored by Jake Blount, Biff Brannon, Benedict Mady Copeland, and the 12-year-old Mick Kelly. McCullers describes Singer as being other-worldly, as being invested with the qualities demanded by those around him: "In his face there came to be a brooding peace that is seen most often in the faces of the very sorrowful or the very wise" *(The Heart Is a Lonely Hunter* 11).

McCullers created Singer as the center of the wheel and made the other characters the spokes. Even Mick Kelly—who is trapped in a family that does not express affection for her and who is terrified that she will spend her life working at Woolworth's—looks to Singer for support. Similar to McCullers herself, Mick writes music to express her innermost longing. "I want—I want—I want—was all that she could think about—but just what this real want was she did not know" *(The Heart Is a Lonely Hunter* 46), writes McCullers. Appropriately enough, one of Mick's musical compositions is entitled "This Thing I Want, I Know Not What" *(The Heart Is a Lonely Hunter* 205). McCullers creates a child who embodies the fears and isolation of characters much older than she.

Mick is not alone in her desire to spend time with Singer. As a child, she can be forgiven for not reaching out to address his loneliness. However, none of the adults tries to understand Singer either, and his sorrows multiply as he remains silent and in despair. Because he listens and responds compassionately to those who visit his room, he becomes an unwilling Messiah, a purveyor of grace and love. "He listened, and in his face there was something gentle and Jewish, the knowledge of one who belongs to a race that is oppressed" *(The Heart Is a Lonely Hunter* 115), writes McCullers.

Relying upon biblical narratives, McCullers compares Singer to Christ, whose disciples need much from him. Citing a reference to the disciples, McCullers writes: "And when they had found Him, they said unto Him, 'All men seek for Thee'" *(The Heart Is a Lonely Hunter* 27). The characters who are unable to make sense of their lives find meaning in John Singer and spend hours basking in his presence. He listens thoughtfully, reading their lips and interpreting their body language.

Unaccustomed to having others interested in them, the central characters in *The Heart Is a Lonely Hunter* live for their time with Singer: "For two days now I been talking to you in my mind because I know you understand the things I want to mean" *(The Heart Is a Lonely Hunter* 21), says Jake Blount. Angry and uncontrolled, Jake finds solace in his conversations with Singer, never noticing that he is the only one speaking. "Jake Blount leaned across the table and the words came out as though a dam inside him had broken" *(The Heart Is a Lonely Hunter* 22), writes McCullers. Alone and incapable of hiding his desperation, Jake Blount depends upon Singer to assuage his fears. Jake believes Singer understands him and is unaware that Singer, too, needs comfort. "He had got a lot of things off his chest and the man had listened," Jake thinks. "He had talked himself hoarse, but he could remember the expressions on the man's face better than anything that was said" *(The Heart Is a Lonely Hunter* 48).

Like *To Kill a Mockingbird, The Heart Is a Lonely Hunter* begins with a description that makes geography as important as character development. Of course, the centrality of place distinguishes much regional fiction, whether the novel is *Bless Me, Ultima* by Rudolfo Anaya, *Fried Green Tomatoes at the Whistle Stop Café* by Fannie Flagg, or *Pride and Prejudice* by Jane Austen. Whether the action occurs in the American West, the Deep South, or England, location often drives the plot. In *The Heart Is a Lonely Hunter,* McCullers writes: "The town was in the middle of the deep South. The summers were long and the months of winter cold were very few" (5). The loneliness evoked in the description of the physical place is the central theme of *The Heart Is a Lonely Hunter*, as it is for much of McCullers' fiction. "It was funny, too," Mick thinks, "how lonesome a person could be in a crowded house" *(The Heart Is a Lonely Hunter* 46-47).

Even minor characters in the novel reinforce McCullers' central themes. For example, Portia, the daughter of a detached and uncaring father, tells him, "You think out everthing [sic] in your brain. While us rather talk from something in our hearts that has been there for a long time" *(The Heart Is a Lonely Hunter* 68). Like the other characters, however, her father, Benedict Copeland, is fatally flawed. He cannot hear his daughter's expressions of desire when she tells him how much she longs to connect with him. For Copeland, too, Singer is the only one who provides solace and peace.

Although Singer kills himself and his followers disband in pain and loneliness, McCullers provides some hope at the end of the novel. Biff Brannon probes the meaning of his life without Singer and begins to acknowledge the importance and purity of love, however it is expressed and whoever expresses it: "For in a swift radiance of illumination he saw a glimpse of human struggle and of valor," McCullers writes. "Of the endless fluid passage of humanity through endless time. And of those who labor and of those who—one word—love" *(The Heart Is a Lonely Hunter* 306).

Known for creating believable and passionate adolescents, McCullers constructs near-autobiographical tales about longing and the netherworld between childhood and adulthood. With Mick Kelly and Frankie Addams, McCullers reinforces an image of tough and vulnerable tomboys who struggle to make their way in an often hostile world.

In *The Member of the Wedding,* Frankie Addams is 12 years old when she "belonged to no club and was a member of nothing in the world": "Frankie had become an unjoined person who hung around in doorways, and she was afraid" *(The Member of the Wedding* 461). Frankie is connected emotionally to Berenice Sadie Brown, an African American who balances love and discipline when dealing with her charges, and John Henry West, who is a ready playmate and dotes on her. But she struggles with how she fits into the world and with what she should become. She wants to go to Winter Hill with Jarvis and Janice, her brother and his soon-to-be bride, so that the three of them can travel around the world and provide a safety net for one another.

At the heart of her sadness is a desire to belong, to be a "member of the wedding." "I wish I was somebody else except me" *(The Member of the Wedding* 465), she says. She calls herself "F. Jasmine Addams" so that her name is more similar to the names of her brother Jarvis and his new wife Janice. Instead of feeling safe in a community or family, Frankie is alone and fears she'll grow up to be a freak, like those who perform in a nearby circus: "She was afraid of all the Freaks, for it seemed to her that they had looked at her in a secret way and tried to connect their eyes with hers, as though to say: we know you" *(The Member of the Wedding* 477), McCullers writes.

Frankie's fears intensify one summer when she moves into adolescence and begins to question her own identity. "This was the summer when Frankie was sick and tired of being Frankie," McCullers writes. "She hated herself, and had become a loafer and a big no-good who hung around the summer kitchen: dirty and greedy and mean and sad" *(The Member of the Wedding* 478). Especially observant and vulnerable, Frankie feels deeply and has only Berenice and John Henry with whom to share her fears:

> Things she had never noticed much before began to hurt her: home lights watched from the evening sidewalks, an unknown voice from an alley. She would stare at the lights and listen to the voice, and something inside her stiffened and waited. But the lights would darken, the voice fall silent, and though she waited, that was all. She was afraid of these things that made her suddenly wonder who she was, and what she was going to be in the world, and why she was standing at that minute, seeing a light, or listening, or staring up into the sky: alone. She was afraid, and there was a queer tightness in her chest. *(The Member of the Wedding* 480-81)

In February 2011, I presented academic papers at the Carson McCullers Interdisciplinary Conference at Columbus State University in Columbus, Georgia. On the streets where the imaginary Mick Kelly and Frankie Addams once walked, it was easy to imagine a young McCullers writing her way out of Georgia and into New York City. Her loosely autobiographical novels enchant students and scholars even today, and her simple prose conveys complex and disturbing themes.

Certainly, I am not alone in having gravitated to McCullers' work. I identified with the desire of her characters to become important people and to escape homes in which parents were absent and unaware. I escaped when I was 15 and never looked back. I also am not alone in understanding Frankie Addams' adolescent desire to find a community of supportive people. Longing to be part of her brother's family, she realizes how alone she is. *"They are the we of me,"* she thinks. "All other people had a *we* to claim, all others except her" *(The Member of the Wedding* 497).

Today, the halls of the academy provide sanctuary and purpose. They also provide me with an opportunity to make Mick and Frankie come alive for students who are far more sophisticated than I was at their age. Even now, my students are drawn to the stifling small Southern towns that are home to Frankie Addams, Scout Finch, and Mick Kelly, and female students often identify readily with their experiences.

In women's literature or American literature survey courses, I introduce the enigmatical John Singer and his wayward followers. We discuss the historic roles of the fictional Calpurnia and Berenice Sadie Brown. We note the significance of gender stereotypes in the Deep South and debate the meaning of the titles *The Heart Is a Lonely Hunter* and *The Member of the Wedding.* We address why Nelle Harper Lee and Lula Carson McCullers and Mary Flannery O'Connor published under their middle and last names.

I no longer need to escape into the novels I read. When I step into a classroom and engage with students eager to talk about literature and memory, I'm home. I teach *To Kill a Mockingbird, The Heart Is a Lonely Hunter,* and *The*

Member of the Wedding, stories about childhoods and adolescences both real and imagined, and I will continue to do so throughout the remainder of my career.

Chapter 2, "Southern Fictions," deals both with literature of the American South and the stories we tell ourselves and others about who we are and what we remember. We are storytelling animals, and by necessity we construct and reconstruct ourselves throughout our lives. We tell stories selectively. We omit portions that are too painful to relate. Depending upon whether we are talking to children or adults, we adjust even practiced stories. We remember things differently from our partners and closest friends, and arguments sometimes ensue.

Youth is a particularly evocative time. For all of us, childhood and adolescence unfold in a series of events that defy retelling. What do I remember? What was I told? What did I read in a letter or see in a jewelry box? Who was the child who rode on the toboggan and was thrown when she hit the tree? What was the name of my third-grade teacher in the school with too many echoes?

In Katherine Anne Porter's *Old Mortality,* Miranda experiences the stories that her family members tell as legends: "They loved to tell stories, romantic and poetic, or comic with a romantic humor; they did not gild the outward circumstance, it was the feeling that mattered" (109-10). At the end of the short novel, Miranda says to herself, "Let them tell their stories to each other. Let them go on explaining how things happened. I don't care. At least I can know the truth about what happens to me, she assured herself silently, making a promise to herself, in her hopefulness, her ignorance" (182).

Porter's inimitable ability to portray the innocence and ignorance of youth makes it clear that Miranda will grow up and tell the same kinds of "romantic and poetic" stories that her family tells. She, too, will pretend to know "how things happened." "I don't care," Miranda says, although as readers we understand that she cares a great deal. In the same way that children believe they are immortal, we believe that we will always look squarely at the truth; in fact, as Miranda learns, we will know some truth about ourselves and others and invent or remain oblivious to the rest.

Like Miranda, I like drama and the bright enchantment of romance. Unlike her, I am convinced that I rarely understand "the truth about what happens to me." I am impeded by more than the simple failure of memory, a failure that afflicts us all.

From birth, some of us are aware that all is not what it seems. Unable to bond with our biological mothers, adopted children are taken somewhere against our will and without our knowledge. A sense of powerlessness begins here. Filling in the gaps of a past that others take for granted becomes a lifetime exercise in creative writing.

Conroy's *The Prince of Tides* is a semi-autobiographical account of his own childhood. In one of the most memorable scenes in the novel and the film, Conroy depends upon memory and upon the refracted light of imagination. When Tom Wingo and his brother and sister leap off the edge of a pier, they hold onto one another's hands and remain submerged until they must rise for air:

> I could feel the dazzling connection between us, a triangle of wordless, uplifted love as we rose, our pulses touching, toward the light and terror of our lives. Diving down, we knew the safety and silence of that motherless, fatherless world; only when our lungs betrayed us did we rise up toward the wreckage. The safe places could only be visited; they could only grant a momentary intuition or sanctuary. The moment always came when we had to return to our real life to face the wounds and grief indigenous to our home by the river. (380)

Friends, literature, music, and school defined my childhood and adolescence. I longed to know more about myself and about the people who might look like me. I thought often about a parallel universe in which my imaginary mother lived. Like the Wingo children, I located momentary sanctuaries. Like Elizabeth Joyce, I began to develop coping mechanisms, began to construct an identity, began to desire success—and began to dream.

Life is a slide show, flashes of light and color.

I am no different from anyone else in selectively remembering events from childhood. My biological sister Geraldine (Gerri) Cheatham, with whom I was reunited in 1986 when I was 31 years old and she was 36, admits that entire portions of her childhood have disappeared from memory. I think she would like to remember and share the events of her life when I ask her to do so, but her desire is compromised by her own psychic damage.

When I ask questions about our family, Gerri somewhat dismissively says that she was never much for family reunions and refers me to an older half-sister who attended those reunions and who keeps in touch with her extended family. Faustine Miracle Heiser has indeed been a reservoir of memories, and I treasure her letters and the information within them.

Although we did not grow up together, Gerri and I are failed repositories of our family histories. Although she has never said it, I believe that her inability to share certain memories results from her desire to forget them. Because I hide from memories of abuse and know how difficult it is to talk about them, I do not pressure her to say more than she wants to say about her own sadness.

However, because I long for information, I grieve about her unwillingness or inability to unearth her past. So many of Gerri's memories intersect with those of others, family members I will never know. We have little in common, and I alienate Gerri even more by asking too much about our family. On the other hand, she cannot imagine a life spent wondering who might be her mother and her father—nor would I want her to.

The desire to bury remembrances of childhood is a common theme in Pat Conroy's work. In *The Prince of Tides,* for example, protagonist Tom Wingo says:

> But there is no magic to nightmares. It has always been difficult for me to face the truth about my childhood because it requires a commitment to explore the lineaments and features of a history I would prefer to forget...It's an act of will to have a memory or not, and I chose not to have one. (6).

Of his own sister Savannah, Wingo says, "Whenever she turned to her childhood, she could recall only disconnected fragments, all of them attached to a vague and debilitating sense of terror" (386).

In my case, the loss of memory is calculated, deliberate, systematic—an act of will—although I have been unable to erase all of the abuse and sadness from my childhood. Fortunately, after all these years, only the most traumatic times retain the heat to disrupt me in mid-sentence or to wake me in moments of half-sleep. Conroy describes such times with brooding intensity: "I was trembling all over now and a great sadness had bivouacked in my heart again," Wingo says. "I burned with the despair that slips up on the powerless and the disinherited" *(The Prince of Tides* 141).

When I'm "powerless" and "disinherited," certain submerged stories do indeed surface: I remember hating to return to the house where my adoptive parents lived. I remember long silences during meals in a sterile kitchen. I remember the tedious and regimented "family Bible studies" to which the children were subjected. I remember my adoptive mother's unpredictable anger. I remember anti-Catholic rhetoric and their fear that electing John F. Kennedy as president would mean that the Vatican would govern the United States. I remember references to a drug we could take if we were in danger of dying in a nuclear war.

Again, it is Tom Wingo with whom I identify: "What I know of human love I took first from my parents," he writes. "With them, love was a deprivation and a withering. My childhood was one of disorder, peril, and small craft warnings" *(The Prince of Tides* 243). Fortunately, there were compassionate people to offset my own deprivation, and they taught me about human love and its restorative promise. Without those outside of the bleak and terrifying house in which I lived, I am certain that my ability to love and to develop a healthy sense of self would have atrophied.

In spite of myself, some memories are tenacious. I have always been devoted to the welfare of animals, volunteering for golden retriever and herding dog rescue organizations and supporting the American Society for the Prevention of Cruelty to Animals and Greenwood Wildlife Rehabilitation Center of Colorado. Currently, I live with two golden retrievers and three cats. Although I eat fish, I stopped eating other meat years ago. While I do not advocate for vegetarianism in my conversations with others, I have no desire to eat animals that live short lives and are destined for slaughter.

Given this compassion for and identification with both domesticated and wild animals, I find one memory from my childhood especially painful. I share it here because it is representative and because it suggests that we are the products of difficult as well as positive experiences. Who we become is a complex, chaotic mixture of positive and negative responses to pain. In the case of animal rights, I rejected entirely my adoptive father's lack of interest in animals and devoted myself to their welfare.

Against my ineffective but passionate protests, my adoptive parents decided to leave Tuffy, my Cocker Spaniel mix, in the back yard while we moved to another city for several months. They paid someone to feed Tuffy and check on him. Even as a teenager, I knew there is no greater loss for a dog than to be separated from those upon whom he depends. He spent the hot West Texas summer in the back yard (he had never been allowed indoors), and after ticks infested the yard, he died a slow and no doubt excruciating death, surviving until the afternoon of our return.

I lifted Tuffy onto my lap as I sat on a lawn chair and immediately felt the welts and swollen bites that covered his body. Crying for help and demanding that we take him immediately to the veterinarian, I failed to persuade either of my adoptive parents to act on his behalf. I couldn't yet drive myself, nor could I think of any neighbors or adult friends who would help me try to save his life.

I cannot remember Tuffy without dissolving into grief and anger. The incident represents more than animal cruelty, of course: it represents the powerlessness and rage that characterized my childhood, and it reminds me of the inability of my adoptive parents to empathize with my suffering or with the plight of a small black-and-white dog. Tuffy died during the night, and I awoke to my adoptive father lifting his body and carrying it away. The image is indelible, searing, and recurring. As irrational as it might be, I cannot forgive myself for not advocating more effectively for a helpless animal.

Even now, when confronted with cruelty against animals, I have difficulty separating those perpetrating the violence from my adoptive parents. When NFL great Michael Vick was arrested for dog fighting, for example, I retreated emotionally for weeks before I could talk about his actions, his rehabilitation, or his time in prison. It is difficult for me to watch former vice presidential candidate Sarah Palin and others shoot wild game. As a journalist, I am not accustomed to hiding from such events, and understanding the origin of my anger about the suffering of animals does not protect me from my response to these stories. I identify with the animals that are subjected to the will of human beings, and I have had to learn to address my own overwhelming grief by advocating on behalf of the creatures we are charged to protect.

Life is a slide show, flashes of light and color that interrupt us during even the most ordinary of days. I do not miss having a clear chronology of my early years. Failing to remember what we long to forget is one of God's gifts.

Even though I was a newspaper reporter during and after college and relied upon facts and specifics, I remember events viscerally and can rarely attach what occurred to a particular date. It is logical then that in my research, I am drawn to the borderland between fiction and nonfiction. For a journalist, time and place are essential to the story. For a victim of emotional and physical abuse, those details are less important than the residual effects of the events themselves.

Those who write memoirs are well served by having kept diaries or journals during their childhood or adolescence. My students often keep records of their lives on their laptops. Although professionally I am tied to the who, what, when, why, and how of an event, I remember my childhood in the way that a blind person might vaguely and imperfectly remember a hallway leading to a spiral staircase. I kept no notes.

Like the poet Savannah Wingo in *The Prince of Tides,* I rely upon fellow travelers to help me remember details—although unlike Savannah I have no twin brother to explain what happened to me. I remember with Emily Dickinson in what she describes as a "certain Slant of light" (118). I do not chronicle the events of my life with the meticulous notations of an attorney or historian.

But as we all know, there are multiple ways to tell the truth to ourselves and to others, and memory can be precise or diffuse, locked in time or eternal. For me, writing memoir requires dismantling an imagined childhood and confronting what has been. Walking through cobwebs into rooms where the memories reside is not for the weak of heart.

Chapter 2.
Southern Fictions

Rain hammered the tin roofs on the ring of cabins in Fredericksburg, Texas. Falling into sleep, I felt safe and loved, unable to imagine dawn and the journey back to Waco, Texas. I knew I would pay for the joy of swimming with other children, of swinging into the warm water from a rope high above the pond, and of spending the weekend with the couple I had chosen to be my parents. Aware of what awaited me, I prepared as best I could for the inevitable reaction to my most recent betrayal.

Even as a young child, I knew there was something wrong with the house in which I lived. I didn't look like the couple that raised me, and they did not express affection toward me. I sometimes saw the kind of family I wanted when I visited my friends or when I watched families interact on television. ("Father Knows Best" and "Leave It to Beaver" portrayed happier families in those days than did "The Simpsons" or "Married With Children" decades later.) I read books such as *To Kill a Mockingbird* and sank into the redolent town inhabited by Atticus Finch and the children he adored. It would be years before I understood that I was not at fault—that I was not unlovable—years before I would reach out to others and make the word "family" an active verb.

Being the adopted child of a fundamentalist Southern Baptist minister and a housewife who had suffered abuse when she was young would not be my choice for anyone. My adoptive father was absent from the house and from my life. Vaguely, I remember his being at the Formica dinner table and his reading *Time* magazine in a white recliner. I don't remember having a conversation with him, nor do I remember that he accompanied me to any school event. Once, he walked me to the swimming pool where I spent summer days. Dressed in knee-high socks, plaid shorts, black dress shoes, and a white t-shirt, he was no different from any other parent who horrified his children with his choice of attire. But it was not his manner of dress that alienated me.

I don't remember hating my adoptive father or feeling much of anything at all. His wife seemed frustrated and tired, the victim of endometriosis, a painful and sometimes debilitating disease, and other less discernible demons. Depending upon the severity of her health problems, she either completed household tasks or stayed in her bedroom.

My adoptive mother knew of my affection for other families and my desire to spend time with them. She opened mail that I wrote to other people and used the words and feelings in those letters against me. She appeared to be jealous of their involvement in my life, and since I was so happy to be separated from her, I could not understand why she didn't simply let me spend as much time away as possible.

In *The Prince of Tides,* Pat Conroy writes of Tom Wingo's father, "If Henry Wingo had not been a violent man, I think he would have made a splendid father" (4). This ironic statement is true for my adoptive mother as well. I suspect that she never told her husband about her rages or the slapping and other physical abuse that punctuated my days. Even if she did, I believe he was emotionally unable to deal with her and most certainly incapable of privileging the needs of his children over hers. My adoptive father's betrayal of his children had a profound impact on my understanding of relationships.

For example, I do not celebrate the number of years people spend with one another. Friendship, inclusiveness, laughter, and passion are at least as important to me as a relationship that appears to weather well. Anniversaries mean less to me than even one authentic moment of sharing between people. My adoptive parents have been married for more than 50 years, and I know first hand the cost of their complicity. When couples are together for many years, I can't stop myself from wondering what secret price they may have paid, what impossible compromises they may have negotiated. I am ashamed of my cynicism, although it is well earned.

Psychiatrists, psychologists, and sociologists often compare the damage from emotional abuse to the effects of physical abuse. I will not venture into this labyrinth. I will say that both can snuff out the light in a child's eyes, and I will align myself with those who find corporal punishment of any kind unconscionable. To hit a child or an animal or to frighten or threaten a creature smaller than ourselves should be unthinkable.

In a chapter entitled "Challenging Violent Discipline," Aaronette M. White writes:

> The American Academy of Pediatrics, the American Psychological Association, and the American Medical Association oppose the use of corporal punishment as a disciplinary strategy because empirical findings associate its use

> with negative outcomes: violence permits and encourages behaviors inconsistent with nurturance. (166)

White's summary of the conclusions drawn by the mental health and medical communities is compelling. Being slapped and hit with wooden spoons, flyswatters, and other objects taught me to fear but not to obey. Gradually, I grew to despise the woman who sought to bring me to my knees. Rather than immobilizing me, anger became an ally and a motivator, but it came at a terrible cost.

Even now, I am mystified by the detachment my adoptive parents exhibited. They had not been able to have biological children. I often wonder what motivated them to adopt three of us, when it was clear that they did not enjoy talking to or interacting with us. I accepted their disinterest the way children accept other aspects of their surroundings, although not a day passed in which I did not dream of another place to live. Until I found a family that represented hope and compassion, I imagined what a supportive and sustaining family might be. I simply willed one into existence.

On the morning I returned from Fredericksburg with Sherry and Don Castello, whose family would define my teenage years, I opened the door to the apartment where my adoptive parents lived that year and encountered silent rage. The warmth of the Castellos and their children evaporated into cold, stoic despair. I heard the Castellos drive away, and as I closed the screen door behind me, I escaped into an imaginary world. As devastated as I was to be separated from them, I now knew there were people who did not live like we did, people who gathered around tables laden with food, people who welcomed others into their circle, and people who celebrated the day.

As a missionary couple, my adoptive parents did not seek help for our dysfunction, perhaps because doing so risked their being embarrassed publicly. More destructive than the physical abuse were the unspoken lies, the subterfuge, the daily rituals of silence and denial. It is perhaps impossible for those raised outside of organized religion to understand fully how much pretense is required to maintain one's place in the church hierarchy. There was never an open acknowledgement that our relationship was violent and destructive or that days often passed in silence. They kept the secret because reality was not consistent with their opinions of themselves; I kept the secret because I feared no one would believe me.

In *The Prince of Tides,* Tom Wingo ultimately tells his father that the physical abuse he experienced was less toxic than the denial. I, too, find denial more dangerous than violence. I know how to respond to the latter but am immobilized by the former. Wingo says:

> This is what makes me crazy in this family, Dad. I don't care that you hit us. I really don't. That's over and there's nothing any of us can do about it. But I can't stand it when I state a simple fact about this family's history and I'm told by you or Mom that it didn't happen...We learned how to be afraid without making a sound. And Mom was a loyal wife to you, Dad. She would never let

> us tell a soul that you were hitting us. Most of the time, she was like you and would simply tell us it didn't happen the way we remembered it. (486-87)

The relationship that developed between the Castellos and me during those early years was authentic. I did not need to lie to them or to myself. Like the books I read, the Castellos didn't seem quite real, but I wanted to share in the family life that they enjoyed. They were not the first people who embraced me, nor would they be the last. Their impact on my life is direct (I became a journalist in part because Sherry worked for many years as the editor of the Baylor University alumni magazine) and indirect (for years, I bought Joy detergent because it reminded me of helping Sherry wash dishes in a bright and noisy kitchen where her family and friends gathered).

During the years that followed, an already difficult home situation intensified. Old enough to stand my ground, I began to retaliate more directly against my adoptive mother's flash-point temper and her husband's passivity. In fact, while I was a teenager, anger, denial, and passivity began to emerge as themes that I would explore later in literary and film studies.

My interest in works by Pat Conroy, William Faulkner, Flannery O'Connor and others evolved in part because of their choice of particular themes. Often, I quote from "The Displaced Person," a story by O'Connor in which an immigrant worker is killed while those who should protect him do nothing. I write about William Faulkner's *Light in August* and the predetermined death of Joe Christmas, who as a child was abused and provoked until he eventually commits murder. I write about *The Prince of Tides* and other novels in which Conroy addresses the danger of looking the other way.

I identify with Tom Wingo, who admires his brother Luke because Luke is courageous and proactive. In one scene, Luke tells Tom, "But somewhere along the line you turned from something into not much. And you've got a good chance of turning into nothing, nothing at all. A man's only got so many yeses inside him before he uses them all up" *(The Prince of Tides* 515).

By the time I was 15, I had used up all my "yeses" and had set a course for a life that did not include being hit or ridiculed. When I left El Paso, Texas, and all it represented, I was too young to understand what might happen to me. I was poor and unsure of how I would go to college, but I never doubted that I would find a way. Little did I know then that I would support myself financially through 12 years of college—applying for scholarships and paid internships and working too many jobs to list here—and that my financial independence would continue until I married at the age of 28. I could not know then that I would worry for most of my life about whether or not I could afford food and shelter. Worry became a state of being.

During college, I listened carefully to the parents of my friends who taught me about balancing a checkbook and handling insurance, and I struggled to pay tuition and living expenses. I adjusted gradually to the reality of being poor, although the fear of being homeless never dissipated. Even now, I compensate for the fear—alternately spending lavishly or regressing into the miserly habits of my teenage years. I am paying off my house. Even though claiming mortgage interest into my retirement years might be the wiser course, I will not feel safe until I own my home. A fear of homelessness is the silent demon that haunts me, one I rarely confess to others.

As a professor at the University of Colorado, I am surprised by the affluence of many of my students and by the involvement of their parents in their lives and successes. I cannot imagine attending classes without also working full time. At the first of each semester, I wonder if my students have food and affordable places to live. I will never adjust to a world in which some parents save toward their children's college educations or check in with them to be certain they're safe and happy. Often, I tell my students how lucky they are. I think a few of them understand.

Mrs. McIntyre watched while the tractor rolled.

Much of my research deals with the theme of passivity in fiction and nonfiction. I emulate people who advocate for one another. I trust those who readily express their feelings and opinions without an obvious filter. It is no surprise that I was for several decades either a newspaper reporter or a professor of journalism —a profession defined by its charge to find and disseminate the truth. I am uncomfortable with secrets, fearful of those whose eyes mask their souls, scornful of those who try to hide shameful behavior with lies. I am not happy inhabiting a subterranean world, often startling those around me by identifying the elephant in the room and by asking friends to share more than they are comfortable discussing in a public venue.

In *The Prince of Tides,* Pat Conroy writes about Tom Wingo, a Southern man who loved his beautiful mother: "I learned from my mother that loyalty was the pretty face one wore when you based your whole life on a series of egregious lies" (133). I am not Tom Wingo, nor did I learn the lesson of loyalty at all costs. Instead, my childhood taught me a hatred for passivity and a distrust of those who ignore the hurricane as it slams into the shore. I would not have lasted long in Lila Wingo's home.

The advantage of the lessons I learned is that I am not one who hesitates. When another is in pain or when an emergency occurs, I don't watch as the smoke fills the room or rely on someone else to step in. The disadvantage is that I spend life on high alert and often act too quickly and before I have all the facts. Those who love me forgive my impulsive nature; however, I often cannot forgive myself for words spoken too hastily or for the conflicts that inevitably occur when I intervene. I'm the person I'd most like to have in the room if danger threatens. I'm the last person who should be there if the situation calls for careful, thoughtful, and deliberate action.

The theme of passivity appears often in literature, and it surfaces in my own research as well. In *Burning Crosses and Activist Journalism: Hazel Brannon*

Smith and the Mississippi Civil Rights Movement, I retell the story of a Dixiecrat who lost her livelihood during the 1960s because she believed African Americans deserve the same legal protections that whites enjoy. An ardent segregationist, Smith was anything but liberal in her views about racial issues, believing, for example, that blood collected for transfusions should be separated so that no white person risked receiving blood from a black person. However, Smith's comparatively moderate stance in her community alienated her from even her friends and neighbors in the cauldron of unrest and violence that was once Mississippi.

Passivity is central to the story of Hazel Brannon Smith and to the biographies of the white male editors who supported her personally and financially (Hodding Carter Jr., Mark Ethridge, Ira B. Harkey Jr., John Netherland Heiskell, and Ralph Emerson McGill are among them). Although fear of personal injury and bankruptcy affected them all, it was not white supremacists who posed the greatest threat. The real threat lay with the masses—the citizens who stood passively by while the editors and their families were targeted, ridiculed, threatened—and in some cases—bankrupted and driven out of their respective counties.

Vengeance, cruelty, and passivity lie at the heart of the story of Hazel Brannon Smith. Those wearing white sheets and venting their hatred were not the ones who destroyed her. Instead, those who remained silent are the ones responsible for destroying her livelihood. Although she is the first woman to win a Pulitzer Prize for editorial writing, Smith lost her Tara-like home to foreclosure and after her husband's death moved to Tennessee to live with her sister. Afflicted with dementia, Smith died in a nursing home in 1994.

My interest in passive behavior and its origins dominates *Burning Crosses and Activist Journalism* and other studies. As a child, I often wondered why so few people interceded to protect me, especially when so many of them were Christians who espoused kindness and advocated for others. Some people internalize the effects of criticism and corporal punishment; others externalize their anger to maintain their own self-worth and to deflect the pain. It is difficult to know which response is healthier, but there is no doubt that I opted for the latter.

During adolescence, I grew to hate my adoptive mother for her compulsion to punish others for her own emptiness and despair, but my adoptive father simply confused me. I believed he was capable of interceding, of saving us from his wife's barely disguised loathing. As I grew, I came to believe that those who choose not to know are at least as dangerous as those who know and do nothing.

At the heart of my research about the effects of passivity is "The Displaced Person." In it, O'Connor describes a fictional world in which an immigrant becomes the target of discrimination. When he is murdered, those responsible stand nearby and watch. No one shouts a warning. No one intercedes on his behalf.

In O'Connor's story, Guizac, a Polish immigrant, works longer and harder than the other hired help on Mrs. McIntyre's farm. Recommended to Mrs. McIntyre by a local priest, Guizac and members of his family are tormented. Those on the farm ridicule even the children in Guizac's family by distorting their Polish names into "Gobblehook" and "Sledgewig." As is often true in O'Connor's tales, a central character's pride and lack of compassion drive the plot, and the title of the story alludes both to the immigrant Guizac and to Christ. Jesus and the Polish immigrant, according to the Catholic writer, were displaced, mistreated, and murdered by those who should have respected and cared for them.

Ignorance and fear motivate the characters in "The Displaced Person." Unfamiliar with life anywhere but the Deep South, one of the characters, Mrs. Shortley, expresses the racism prevalent throughout the short story:

> She began to imagine a war of words, to see the Polish words and the English words coming at each other, stalking forward, not sentences, just words, gabble gabble gabble, flung out high and shrill and stalking forward and then grappling with each other. She saw the Polish words, dirty and all-knowing and unreformed, flinging mud on the clean English words until everything was equally dirty. ("The Displaced Person" 216-17)

A perpetrator of the same racism that drives Mrs. Shortley, Mrs. McIntyre begins to plot to rid herself of Guizac. Because she is aware of the hatred of others on the farm toward Guizac and because she lacks the courage and integrity to protect him, she begins to fabricate problems with her employee. Telling the priest that she is not responsible for Guizac and did not "create his situation" ("The Displaced Person" 239), Mrs. McIntyre blames the immigrant for what she perceives to be his lack of gratitude. Although he is by far her most industrious worker, Mrs. McIntyre says: "Mr. Guizac...is very efficient. I'll admit that. But he doesn't understand how to get on with my niggers and they don't like him. I can't have my niggers run off. And I don't like his attitude. He's not the least grateful for being here" ("The Displaced Person" 238).

Christian imagery and symbolism dominate the story. When Mrs. McIntyre tells Father Flynn that Guizac is "extra" and "didn't have to come here in the first place," he tells her that Guizac came to "redeem us" ("The Displaced Person" 239-40). This reference to Christ is lost on Mrs. McIntyre, whose anger fuels the plot and makes it ultimately possible for Mr. Shortley to kill Guizac. Caring for someone who is lost in a new land would be an act of redemption, but Mrs. McIntyre cannot see the ways in which her prejudice facilitates murder.

Guizac, lying under a tractor while repairing it, never suspects that he will be killed. The following lengthy excerpt is one of the most effective examples of calculated understatement in all of O'Connor's work. Time moves in slow motion. Like a warning that is lost in the screaming of a train whistle, we want to tell Guizac to move—move *now*—but the story proceeds to an inevitable end. O'Connor writes:

> Mr. Shortley had got on the large tractor and was backing it out from under the shed. He seemed to be warmed by it as if its heat and strength sent impulses up through him that he obeyed instantly. He had headed it toward the small tractor but he braked it on a slight incline and

> jumped off and turned back toward the shed. Mrs. McIntyre was looking fixedly at Mr. Guizac's legs lying flat on the ground now. She heard the brake on the large tractor slip and, looking up, she saw it move forward, calculating its own path. Later she remembered that she had seen the Negro jump silently out of the way as if a spring in the earth had released him and that she had seen Mr. Shortly turn his head with incredible slowness and stare silently over his shoulder and that she had started to shout to the Displaced Person but that she had not. She had felt her eyes and Mr. Shortley's eyes and the Negro's eyes come together in one look that froze them in collusion forever, and she had heard the little noise the Pole made as the tractor wheel broke his backbone. ("The Displaced Person" 250)

As a child, I learned to deal with physical cruelty; however, even now, I have not come to terms with the collusion among those who watched while I was beaten and did not intercede. As a result, I fear people who ignore the cruelty around them more than I fear those who perpetrate it. Ignorance, it seems to me, requires effort. Passivity is an act of will, not merely the absence of action. Too many watch quietly while the tractor rolls.

O'Connor is not the only Southern writer who addresses the role of passivity in the lives of the disenfranchised and victimized. In William Faulkner's *Light in August,* Mr. McEachern hits his adopted son, Joe Christmas, for failing to learn his catechism. Afterwards, Joe returns to the house and lies in the pungent and heavy darkness. Mrs. McEachern comes in—stealthily—and tries to placate him. But Joe hates her—as he is destined to hate anyone who sidles in, pitifully and without courage, throughout his life. His adoptive father's brutality is easier to take—predictable, like the reassuring ticking of a clock—than his adoptive mother's kindness. It is tenderness that he can never anticipate in others, and when it surfaces, there is no way for him to understand it. Simpering kindness becomes intolerable, unbearable, humiliating.

When I first read *Light in August,* the parallels to my own experience were not lost on me, although there are obvious differences between the fictional tale and life in the household where I grew up. Like my adoptive parents, McEachern is determined that his adopted son will study the Bible and learn obedience. Faulkner describes the 8-year-old boy sitting "in a straight chair beside the table on which was a nickel lamp and an enormous Bible with brass clasps and hinges and a brass lock" (146). Repeatedly, McEachern orders Joe Christmas to learn the Scripture, and in increments of one hour, returns to check on his progress.

Relentlessly and viciously, Joe Christmas is punished for his failure to learn his catechism, just as he was punished the day before for failing to polish his adoptive father's shoes correctly. Faulkner writes:

> McEachern took from the wall a harness strap. It was neither new nor old, like his shoes. It was clean, like the shoes, and it smelled like the man smelled: an odor of clean hard virile living leather. He looked down at the boy. . .
>
> Then the boy stood, his trousers collapsed about his feet, his legs revealed beneath his brief shirt. He stood, slight and erect. When the strap fell he did not flinch, no quiver passed over his face. He was looking straight ahead, with a rapt, calm expression like a monk in a picture. McEachern began to strike methodically, with slow and deliberate force, still without heat or anger. It would have been hard to say which face was the more rapt, more calm, more convinced. *(Light in August* 148-50)

Continuing to refuse to study the catechism, Joe Christmas eventually collapses from the repeated beatings. He loses consciousness. Later, roused from his tormented sleep, the boy is ordered to accompany McEachern once again. This time, McEachern forces him to kneel and pray. He asks that "the child's stubborn heart be softened" *(Light in August* 152), and then he once again demands that the boy study the Bible. Again, time passes, and the boy refuses.

Mrs. McEachern is absent during the beatings, but it is clear that she understands what has occurred and is complicit in it. Faulkner describes Mrs. McEachern as "dressed, in black, with a bonnet—a small woman, entering timidly, a little hunched, with a beaten face. She looked fifteen years older than the rugged and vigorous husband" *(Light in August* 147). After McEachern finally leaves the house, Joe Christmas lies on his bed. McEachern's terrified wife comes into the room and offers the boy food:

> He sat up then. While she watched him he rose from the bed and took the tray and carried it to the corner and turned it upside down, dumping the dishes and food and all onto the floor...He could see her motionless shadow, shapeless, a little hunched. Then it went away. He did not look, but he could hear her kneel in the corner, gathering the broken dishes back into the tray. Then she left the room. *(Light in August* 154-55)

Being beaten by someone bigger and stronger—by someone over whom you have no control—is an experience familiar to far too many children. Pain and humiliation are only a portion of the experience; in fact, it is the awareness that they cannot protect themselves or alter the event that is the most destructive. Beatings teach children to despise the perpetrator of the violence, to react to pain and humiliation with rage or self-loathing, and to believe that they have little ability to control their own destinies. "He was just eight then," Faulkner writes about Joe Christmas. "It was years later that memory knew what he was remembering; years after that night when, an hour later, he rose from the bed and went and knelt in the corner as he had not knelt on the rug, and above the outraged food kneeling, with his hands ate, like a savage, like a dog" *(Light in August* 155). To save himself, Joe eats, but the act of kneeling and picking up the scraps reinforces both his humiliation and his fury.

During my own childhood, the genders were reversed. My adoptive father was a minister and an editor for a Christian publishing company. He was rarely present and rarely harsh—I remember only twice when he physically restrained me, once when I lost a key in a trashcan and another when I was argumentative. After the second incident, he gripped my wrists and forced me onto the kitchen floor until I knelt, demanding that I ask God to forgive me for what he perceived to be my insolence. In a loud voice, he prayed over me.

I was never afraid of him; instead, I was numb and uninterested. Like Joe Christmas, I considered passivity barely worth notice. Had he come to me after one of the beatings I received at the hands of his wife (he did not), I imagine that I would have seen him in the same way that Joe Christmas perceives his adoptive mother, as "shapeless" and a "shadow" *(Light in August* 155). At other times, I'm not as certain. I might have welcomed his intervention if I could have relied upon it.

My adoptive mother, on the other hand, merited my full attention. Small of stature and shy in public, she had grown up with violence perpetrated by her older brother and, perhaps, by others whose identities she never disclosed. Once, she said, her brother threw scalding water on her, and her older sister intervened to protect her. At some point—between enduring her brother's abuse and adopting children—she forgot what it is like to be small and to be emotionally and financially dependent. She worked out her rage—not in therapy (admittedly, therapeutic sessions with licensed practitioners were not as common in the 1950s and 1960s)—but in episodes of barely contained fury toward her three adopted children. Her tight, angry visage and what I believe to be her lifelong depression are evidence of how little the shouting and the beatings she inflicted relieved her own pain.

As a child, I was terrified when my adoptive mother approached me; later, I felt sorry for her. Eventually, though, I ceased to feel anything at all. I began to focus on the times I could spend with my teachers, with my friends, and with the Castellos, the couple who shared a cabin with me and their children in Fredericksburg, Texas; who taught me to water ski and to love camping; who walked with me in the woods near their home in the fall; and who introduced me to the music of Carol King, The Carpenters, John Denver, Simon and Garfunkel, and James Taylor.

I would eventually spend a great deal of time at the Castellos' home in Waco, Texas, even staying there full time during one semester of college. Because it was my favorite color, the Castellos painted a desk and chair yellow and bought a flowered yellow quilt to adorn a bedroom in their house. Although large enough for all of us—Sherry and Don, their four children, me, and others whom they rescued during the years I knew them—their house reminded me of a cottage in the woods, and, until I moved to an apartment on the Baylor campus, it was a sacred place.

To this day, I believe that the joy of which we are capable is directly proportionate to the pain we have endured, although I am predisposed to identify with something Katherine Anne Porter says in a July 18, 1951, letter to her nephew: "I think joy is just as instructive as pain, and I like it better. I never meant to suffer any more than I could help; my nature was meant for happiness, a daylight art and living" *(Letters of Katherine Anne Porter* 402). Because of the serendipity of love, those who have had less-than-ideal childhoods may one day experience the joy that Porter describes. I count myself among them.

I turned to dust and stone.

Like Faulkner, O'Connor, and Smith, Dorothy Allison also addresses the impact of passivity. Her partially autobiographical novel *Bastard Out of Carolina* can reduce a class of optimistic undergraduates to despair. I, too, take days to recover after living in its pages. Allison employs themes central to this study, including abuse, biological connections, courage, determinism, and parental betrayal. The young protagonist Ruth Anne, whose nickname is "Bone," takes the reader into a world of grief and despair, one she barely survives.

The chapter title "Southern Fictions" refers both to literature by writers in the Deep South and to the fictions that some families create to protect themselves from accountability. Central to *Bastard Out of Carolina* is the line between fiction and fact, a line that families often cross when they have something to hide. The price we pay to maintain the image of a perfect family often is nothing less than truth itself. In *Bastard Out of Carolina,* Bone remembers her own family's mythology:

> Granny wouldn't talk much about my real daddy except to curse his name, but she told me just about everything else. She would lean back in her chair and start reeling out story and memory, making no distinction between what she knew to be true and what she had only heard told. The tales she told me in her rough drawling whisper were lilting songs, ballads of family, love, and disappointment. Everything seemed to come back to grief and blood, and everybody seemed legendary. (26)

Those of us who love literature appreciate its beauty as well as its cathartic potential. We escape into its imaginary worlds. Bone discovers that the way to survive her mother's lack of courage and her stepfather's rage is to transport herself imaginatively. Allison writes:

> The stories I made up for myself changed. In the half-sleep that preceded full sleep I began to imagine the highway that went north. No real road, this highway was shadowed by tall grass and ancient trees. Moss hung low and tiny birds with gray-blue wings darted from the road's edge to the trees. Cars passed at a roar but did not stop, and the north star shone above their headlights like a beacon. I walked that road alone, my legs swinging easily as I covered the miles. No one stopped. No one called to me. Only the star guided me, and I was not sure where I would end. *(Bastard Out of Carolina* 259)

Allison weaves a lyrical story told from a child's unmediated perspective. What results is poetry—"I stood in the garden and spun myself around and around, pouring out heat and rage and the sweet stink of broken flowers" (103)—and raw, haunting prose—"Somewhere far away a child was screaming, but right then, it was not me" *(Bastard Out of Carolina* 193).

The complicity and desperate need that bind Anney and Glen, Bone's mother and stepfather, would destroy most children, but Bone couples courage with determination and saves herself. "I had always been afraid to scream, afraid to fight," she said. "I had always felt like it was my fault, but now it didn't matter. I didn't care anymore what might happen. I wouldn't hold still anymore" *(Bastard Out of Carolina* 282). Her stepfather's cruelty and violence are less likely to be her undoing than her mother's passive betrayal: "Rage burned in my belly and came up my throat. I'd said I could never hate her, but I hated her now for the way she held him, the way she stood there crying over him. Could she love me and still hold him like that? I let my head fall back. I did not want to see this" *(Bastard Out of Carolina* 291), Bone said.

Bone's Aunt Raylene believes and supports Bone in her quest for a new life, but the loss of her mother is more than Bone believes she can bear. "How do you forgive somebody when you cannot even speak her name, when you cannot stand to close your eyes and see her face?" (302-303), Bone asks. When her mother says, "I just loved him so I couldn't see him that way. I couldn't believe. I couldn't imagine" (306), the statement is worse than the physical pain Bone experiences at Glen's hands. "She was a stranger," Bone says of her mother, "and I was so old my insides had turned to dust and stone" *(Bastard Out of Carolina* 306).

Eventually leaving town with Glen, Anney is both a victim and victimizer. It is unthinkable that she needs a relationship with the man who nearly killed her own child. I am among those who cannot understand the choice to preserve a marriage at the cost of a child. Like Bone, I understand the relentless despair that follows such a betrayal: "The grief. The anger. The guilt and the shame. It would come back later. It would come back forever. We had all wanted the simplest thing, to love and be loved and be safe together, but we had lost it and I didn't know how to get it back" *(Bastard Out of Carolina* 307). For a child who is betrayed, there is no getting it back, no recovering the love or the time that is lost.

Dedicated to her own mother ("For Mama/ Ruth Gibson Allison/ 1935-1990"), *Bastard Out of Carolina* is a stark, semi-autobiographical chronicle of a family gone wrong. Allison suggests that we have a responsibility to save ourselves and to become the people God intended us to be: "It wasn't God who made us like this, I thought. We'd gotten ourselves messed up on our own" (306), says Bone. *Bastard Out of Carolina* is an epic novel about a child's courage in the face of terror and loss. There is no Atticus Finch, no hopeful conclusion to a nightmare that never ends.

Fiction is at the heart of my personal and scholarly career, although I have no tolerance for the fictions we spin in order to hide from responsibility or to demonize others. The fictions we read can be reassuring and sustaining; in fact, *Rain on a Strange Roof* is a testament to bibliotherapy and a love of narrative.

However, the fictions we tell in order to protect our public selves are nothing if not destructive. "Things come apart so easily when they have been held together with lies" *(Bastard Out of Carolina* 248), writes Allison.

I know something about lies. As the child of Southern Baptist missionaries, I learned that people who bear false witness against their neighbors—or their children—can survive their crimes if they protect themselves with the trappings of their religion. Few came to my rescue when I was a child, and those who did dealt with the same rage and defensiveness that had grown so familiar to me. My adoptive parents could not forgive my deep affection for those outside their family, nor could they tolerate the people who violated their dark inner circle. They were not inclusive and had few friends. Although they did not want to deal with my obvious unhappiness, they did not want me to talk to others about it either.

I spent most of my adolescence and adulthood telling those who inquired that I had no family. Even now, I have no connection to family that resonates with others. My lack of understanding about family dynamics provides me with an important detachment in evaluating the role that family members play in each other's lives; specifically, I am never startled by their betrayals of one another, nor, conversely, am I surprised by their sometimes unqualified allegiances.

However, my childhood makes me a difficult partner and spouse: I don't understand the complicated dance steps that come readily to others, and I never fall back on family or believe with the characters in Robert Frost's "The Death of the Hired Man" that "home is the place where, when you have to go there,/ They have to take you in" (38). My friends might take me in. (I most assuredly would take them in.) But I have little confidence in the arbitrary bonds so often touted by people who share a similar genetic makeup.

Having spent a lifetime seeking and finding my biological family, I now have a personal narrative with a beginning and middle (I'm in no hurry for the end). I no longer mark "no family history" on medical forms. I have a few photographs from times I never knew, and I have come to treasure these images and to rely upon them. But my experiences set me apart, and I do not presume to speak for anyone else. I am simply someone with a story to tell, and, like the Ancient Mariner, I have a desire to share it.

The abuse I endured does not compare to that experienced by Joe Christmas, Bone, or other literary figures. Certainly, I have friends who suffered emotional damage I can only begin to imagine. I do, however, identify with those who describe the impact of emotional and physical abuse on their self-esteem and with those whose parents ignore and deny their pain. I identify with the silence that makes it possible for a family to enact (and reenact) its violence. And I identify with a child who cannot fathom how one parent stands by and allows the other to mistreat him or her. Torn asunder by her love for and hatred of her mother, Bone finds some solace in the home of her aunt but never regains her innocence or her sense of security.

Dorothy Allison's account of her own life in *Two or Three Things I Know for Sure* reveals again the collision between fiction and fact, between a novel and a memoir. Raped by her mother's new husband when she was 5 years old, Allison describes how she protected herself by relying upon her own imagination. "If I know anything, I know how to survive, how to remake the world in story," she said. But survival comes at a cost, and Allison spent much of her life simultaneously confronting and avoiding her past: "I ran because if I had not, I would have died," Allison writes. "No one told me that you take your world with you, that running becomes a habit, that the secret to running is to know why you run and where you are going—and to leave behind the reason you run" (4).

Instead of losing herself in other people's stories, Allison escapes into her own narratives: "Behind the story I tell is the one I don't," Allison writes. "Behind the story you hear is the one I wish I could make you hear" *(Two or Three Things I Know for Sure* 39). I identify with Allison's fear that others will not believe her, and, in fact, only her mother actually believes her story about rape:

> I need to say that my mama didn't know what was going on, that I didn't tell her, that when I finally did tell someone it was not her. I need to say that when I told, only my mama believed me, only my mama did anything at all, that thirty years later one of my aunts could still say to me that she didn't really believe it, that he had been such a hardworking, good-looking man. Something else must have happened. Maybe it had been different. *(Two or Three Things I Know for Sure* 42)

Rather than arguing with her aunt, Allison said that she "just looked at her, feeling finally strong enough to know she had chosen to believe what she needed more than what she knew" *(Two or Three Things I Know for Sure* 43).

Passivity is an act of will, an act as powerful and destructive as any violence. "Evil is the act of pretending that some things do not happen or leave no mark if they do" *(Two or Three Things I Know for Sure* 44), Allison writes. I remain skeptical of families and primary relationships when they survive because of what people refuse to see. Protecting myself comes at the price of intimacy and a sense of security, and, unlike Allison, I have found it impossible to leave behind the reason I run.

It is no surprise to those who knew me when I was a child that I would choose to write about longing and about nostalgia for a time that never existed. I am not alone in imagining a better life or in willing that fantasy might become real. Throughout my life, I have met others who understand the role of the imagination in keeping us moored and sane. Cathartic and reassuring, fictional narratives provide important escapes and may even suggest blueprints for a more rewarding life.

Because I am not alone in my memories of a painful childhood, I often wonder what fictional constructs others employ in order to protect themselves from their own realities. Perhaps some turn to other people for comfort; perhaps some, to religion. I chose literature as a way out: Not only did I read at the table and in the car and late into the night to avoid contact with my adoptive parents, but I rapidly learned to replace the silence and unspoken rage with stories that featured David Copperfield or the Hardy boys or Elnora from *A Girl of the Limberlost* or Lorna Doone.

Fictional characters protected me from daily sadness and fear and promised adventures if I could endure. I checked books out of school and neighborhood libraries. I bought paperbacks based upon the number of pages they contained. If the book was short, I dreaded how quickly the magical world would dissipate. I learned, of course, that narratives could not ameliorate the anger in the house to which I returned each day. Hostile silences, sudden slaps across my face, and what my adoptive mother called "spankings" punctuated the years. She was the perpetrator of the violence against me; her husband, an absent but complicit figure. I wish I had been courageous enough to flee years before I did. At least I was wise enough to find solace in books.

Attending school and reading became my escapes. Reading helped me to avoid contact with my adoptive parents, although even that strategy sometimes failed. On one occasion, my adoptive mother snatched me by the arm and took me into my brother's bedroom. She hit me repeatedly with a wooden spoon as I ran in circles around her, crying and begging for her to stop. Her mother-in-law stood outside of the room, knocking on the door and asking her to come out. Instead of being grateful for my grandmother's failed intervention, I wondered why she did not intercede with more force. Mercifully, I cannot remember all the violent episodes.

Although I avoided provoking their anger, I grew increasingly defiant when it erupted. One day when I was 15 years old and taller than my adoptive mother, I challenged her authority. As she stepped forward to hit me, I realized with a rush of adrenaline that I was taller than she. As she raised her hand, I said, "If you hit me, I will knock you to the floor." It was the last time she touched me, and it was one of the last times I remember our confronting one another directly. No one surrendered, but until I moved out of the house soon after, there was détente.

I was not a perfect child—especially after I learned how to retaliate— but I was not malicious and I was anxious to please. I didn't lie. I did well in school. Dutifully, I practiced the piano and other musical instruments. Meticulously, I cleaned my room. However, although I had been adopted as an infant, I did not belong to them. I knew it. And more ominously, they knew it.

As I grew older, I'm certain that my increasing rage showed in my face and defined my interaction with them. Helping my adoptive father carry a piece of heavy furniture, I slammed my hand into a wall. "Damn!" I yelled, as he responded with loud disapproval. I remember throwing a Bible at a sliding glass door, a violent and spontaneous response to the relentless and hypocritical "family Bible studies" to which my siblings and I were subjected.

From the outside, my adolescence appeared to be like anyone else's. In junior high and high school, several boys, including Richard Armes, Claude Barron, Michael Bradley, David Burroughs, Tom Courson, John Kirby, and Danny Morris, were good friends to me. I relied upon their attention, often trusting them more than I did the girls in my classes. It would be many years before I thought about how safe I felt with men and how threatened I was by women. Experience helped me shed some of my guardedness around female friends in college and in the years that followed, but I'm quite certain that my adoptive mother's unpredictable nature clouded my relationships with girls in junior high and high school.

In other ways, I was very much like the adolescent girls I knew. I dreaded the rites of passage and being judged by my peers. I was certain that I would forget the combination to my locker. I feared I would be the last person chosen for the volleyball team. I wasn't sure I was cute enough to be a cheerleader. I did not want to trip while I carried my tray through the lunchroom. I did not want to believe that I was a good student only to have a teacher discover that I was all pretense and posturing.

Adolescence was a time of heightened anxiety—and joy. Like Wyatt Earp's true love, Josephine Marcus (Dana Delany), in the film "Tombstone" (1993), I thought, "I don't have time to be proper. I want to live." However, to avoid conflict and to be loved, I adhered to most rules and bided my time. I learned to laugh and to appreciate the absurdities of the human condition—absurdities nowhere more apparent than in the interaction of teenagers who are discovering who they are and exploring boundaries.

An appreciation for the fusion of tragedy and farce is one byproduct of a difficult childhood. I am drawn to everything from novels by Franz Kafka, to television series such as "Roseanne," to films such as "Little Miss Sunshine" (2006) because they encourage us to laugh in the face of absurdity—thereby rendering it powerless. Humor holds a powerful sway, and it characterizes some of the literature I find most compelling. The subversive laughter of women, especially, reminds me that courage lies in using humor as a tool—both to protect oneself and to mount a counterattack.

Laughter reverberates in Dixie.

Farce, humor, parody, and satire are alive and well in Southern fiction. Because Southerners appreciate social hierarchy, because Southern belles and gentlemen dominate popular culture, and because a system of manners prevails in the region, I am particularly drawn to Southern films and works of literature that challenge the status quo and undercut preconceptions about appropriate behavior. Films such as "Steel Magnolias" (1989) and "Something To Talk About" (1995) take on entrenched definitions of femininity and introduce bawdy and courageous women who march to different drummers.

Two of my literary heroines are Idgie Threadgoode and Ruth Jamison of *Fried Green Tomatoes at the Whistle Stop Café*. Like Scout Finch of *To Kill a Mockingbird* and Mick Kelly of *The Heart Is a Lonely Hunter,* Idgie Threadgoode is a tomboy, and her rejection of feminine apparel and behavior underscores her independence. "Seems like Idgie was always in overalls and barefooted. . . you'd swear she was a little boy" (34), writes Flagg.

In an article entitled "What Happened to Celie and Idgie?: The 'Apparitional Lesbians' of American Film," I focus on Idgie's love for Ruth in the novel and film *Fried Green Tomatoes at the Whistle Stop Café* and Celie's love for Shug in the novel and film *The Color Purple.* The sexual orientation of both Celie and Idgie is muted (some would say deleted) in the films that were derived from the novels by Alice Walker and Fannie Flagg, respectively. As many critics acknowledge, Idgie's evolving relationship with Ruth and Ruth's son suggests far more than the devotion of one friend to another. As adults, these women love one another deeply, and they make a home together in a community that has more on its mind than same-sex relationships. Humor defines and saves the two of them as they turn local customs upside down. They have no time to be proper. They want to live.

Family members and residents of the town understand that the two care deeply about one another. "Now, children, your sister has a crush," says Idgie's mother, "and I don't want one person to laugh at her. Is that understood?" (81). The crush grows into the devotion of adults who sustain and support one another, although the childlike humor they share remains:

> Momma said Idgie would have jumped off a mountain backwards if Ruth had asked her to. And I believe that!...Everywhere Ruth was, that's where Idgie would be. It was a mutual thing. They just took to each other, and you could hear them, sittin' on the swing on the porch, gigglin' all night. Even Sipsey razzed her. She'd see Idgie by her self and say, "That ol' love bug done bit Idgie." *(Fried Green Tomatoes* 82)

When Ruth tells Idgie not to put herself in danger because "I don't know what I'd do if anything ever happened to you," Flagg writes that "Idgie's heart started pounding so hard it almost knocked her over" (86). Idgie tells Ruth she would kill for her, and, as the reader later learns, she is, in fact, an accomplice in a murder and protects those who save Ruth: "Anybody that would ever hurt you, I'd kill them in a minute and never think twice about it" (86), Idgie says. With humor and deep seriousness, Flagg captures the joy that the women experience with one another. Understanding that Ruth loves her, too, Idgie "smiled back at her and looked up into the clear blue sky that reflected in her eyes, and she was as happy as anybody who is in love in the summertime can be" *(Fried Green Tomatoes* 87), Flagg writes.

When reading *Fried Green Tomatoes at the Whistle Stop Café* for the first time, students often are startled that they're laughing while reading a narrative about cannibalism, domestic violence, gender stereotyping, racism, terminal illness, and murder. Subversive humor sustains and empowers many of us—especially women—who are accustomed to living on the edges—the fringes—of society. Often not taken seriously, women learn to employ humor as both a refuge and a sword. Flagg masterfully distracts readers from the horror of the novel by celebrating the joy and love that characterize the lives of those who frequent the Whistle Stop Café.

Unlike *Bastard Out of Carolina; The Beans of Egypt, Maine; The Color Purple;* and other novels that deal with similarly bleak topics, *Fried Green Tomatoes at the Whistle Stop Café* relies upon black humor. Flagg does not ignore topics such as loneliness and mortality, but humor is the antidote to despair. Idgie retells a story about ducks that transport a lake to another location in order to help her deal with Ruth's death. Idgie tells the tall tale for the same reason Ruth names her one-armed son "Stump." The women use humor to help them cope with the catastrophic accidents of our lives. Idgie and Ruth face the world as they find it, making no excuses and never asking for quarter.

Some of the most comedic moments in *Fried Green Tomatoes at the Whistle Stop Café* involve Evelyn Couch, a woman afraid of assertiveness, conflict, middle age—and her vagina. The questions that torment her—"She wondered why she had to live in a body that would get old and break down and feel pain" (59)—are universal and unsettling, but Evelyn responds to them with courage and humor.

In the midst of the humor that characterizes the novel lie issues as sobering as death and loss. Much of the action takes place in a residential home for the elderly as Evelyn devotes herself to Ninny Threadgoode. Crying as much for herself as for her friend, "Evelyn stopped the car and sat there, sobbing like her heart would break, wondering why people had to get old and die" (384), Flagg writes. At the end of the novel and the film, we face the grief that follows death. On Ruth's grave is a note from Idgie, which reads: "I'll always remember. Your friend, The Bee Charmer" *(Fried Green Tomatoes* 390).

Fried Green Tomatoes at the Whistle Stop Café is a novel that springs naturally from the character-driven fiction of the Deep South, and it is not alone in its celebration of the subversive humor that saves us. "I may live in California, but I have never, as they say, left the South, nor has it left me" ("A Conversation with Fannie Flagg" n.p.), Flagg said in an interview. The humor she employs is part of a rich heritage of farce, parody, and satire that define a region of contradictions.

Like *Fried Green Tomatoes at the Whistle Stop Café, Confessions of a Failed Southern Lady,* emphasizes the saving power of humor. An autobiography that reads like fiction, *Confessions of a Failed Southern Lady* is the account of a lesbian in the land of Southern belles. In it, Florence King writes about her grandmother and highlights the predicament of tough, rebellious women born into a world that expects them to be ladies:

> She was a frustrated ladysmith and I was her last chance. Mama had defeated her but she kept the anvil hot for me and began hammering and firing with a strength born of desperation from the day I entered the world until the day she left it.
>
> This is the story of my years on her anvil. Whether she succeeded in making a lady out of me is for you to decide, but I will say one thing in my own favor before we begin.

No matter which sex I went to bed with, I never smoked on the street. (2)

As a bisexual woman, I celebrate those who challenge heteronormativity and its constraints. The platonic and romantic love women feel for one another is reflected in the literature and film of the American South and is a source of humor in the land of Southern belles.

There are numerous examples of Southern writers who balance despair with comedy. Even William Faulkner had to escape *Absalom, Absalom!* and *The Sound and the Fury* with a rollicking tale of misfits in *The Reivers*. And as painful as the portrayal of family life in the *The Prince of Tides* might be, Tom Wingo and Susan Lowenstein banter wickedly in the novel. Humor in the face of tragedy is the heart of Pat Conroy's later novel, *South of Broad,* as well. For example, in the novel Conroy lists the 10 most common reasons some Americans hate the South. Number 10 reads: "All Americans who are not Southern hate the South because they know Southerners don't give a rat's fanny what the rest of the country thinks about them" (247).

Acknowledging the forces over which we have no control, Conroy creates a universe of friends in *South of Broad*—some of them orphans, some of them gay, some of them deeply wounded—who persevere. The leading protagonist, Leopold Bloom King, survives the deaths of his parents, the betrayal of a teacher, the murder of his friend Sheba, and his friend Trevor's diagnosis with AIDS and in spite of it all maintains his sense of humor. Leo lives with his fist raised toward the sky, laughing at fate and celebrating life.

In Southern literature, racial and ethnic conflict is as serious a topic as are death and loss, but Conroy creates humor even in his descriptions of the differences that divide us. In *South of Broad,* a black football coach tells Leo that if the coach's son "makes [Leo] mad enough that you want to rip his head off and call him the worst name you can think of, then call him Dr. George Washington Carver, after a great black scientist from Tuskegee University." The coach then tells Leo that he will offer his son similar advice: "He's got to call you Strom Thurmond. That's about as big an insult as a black man can yell at a white man" *(South of Broad* 59).

From the Whistle Stop Café to Charleston, Southern writers respond to the vagaries of life with full-throated laughter. Rude and ever inappropriate, laughter reverberates in Dixie, where the veneer of civilization periodically gives way to children named Stump and to women who sleep with both women and men but would never smoke on the street.

"Southern Fictions" deals with the lies we tell ourselves in order to survive, with customs that dictate particular attitudes or behavior, and with a region in which centuries of dissent and turmoil seem to make storytelling inevitable. The American South is my home, although I do not reside there. Its food, geography, history, music, system of manners, and weather are familiar to me. In particular, I am drawn to Mississippi and to a parcel of land near Ole Miss. Shaded by the trees that line the drive, I come home whenever I travel to Faulkner's home, a place he named Rowan Oak.

Some go to Lourdes, while others go to Rowan Oak.

Much of Southern literature celebrates the centrality of place and the intrusive power of the past. Pat Conroy's canon is an exploration of the ways in which the past determines the present. William Faulkner, too, tells of those who live life in the shadow of a former time, sometimes more glorious, sometimes vapid and perverse.

In one of his many tributes to the role of the past in our present circumstances, Faulker writes, "Memory believes before knowing remembers" *(Light in August* 119). Both suggestive and explicit, this statement summarizes the life I have spent searching, understanding some things without knowing them and knowing some things without understanding them. I knew my family before I met them, forgave them without being aware of the specific wrongs they had committed, loved them without knowing their names.

I am drawn to Faulkner's short stories and novels, reading "Barn Burning," "A Rose for Emily," *Absalom, Absalom!, As I Lay Dying, The Sound and the Fury,* and *Light in August* often and with an equal mixture of celebration and despair. Like the Bible and the histories and tragedies of William Shakespeare, Faulkner's canon both sustains and destablizes me. Whether I am primarily a student of Faulkner or a professor charged with the responsibility of making his work relevant to the young, I am humbled by his genius.

Two of Faulkner's novels—*As I Lay Dying* and *Light in August*—are particularly appropriate for this memoir because of their themes; their rich regional description; their references to the names "Bunch" and "Bundren," which are central to my family history; and their allusions to the past. Faulkner creates characters who reckon with time and who understand that the past permeates the present. Conroy, too, describes the past as it "rose up like a pillaged city" *(The Prince of Tides* 135), but it is Faulkner whose most famous statement is that the past is never really past *(Requiem for a Nun* 535).

As I Lay Dying revolves around the Bundren family, who journey across daunting terrain to bury a family member. *Light in August* tells the story of Joe Christmas, a lost and victimized man who does not know his racial or ethnic origin and pays for his lack of self-knowledge with his life. The surnames in *As I Lay Dying* and *Light in August* are common to Kentucky, Mississippi, North Carolina, South Carolina, Tennessee, and Virginia. When I first taught the novels during graduate school, little did I know that two of the names in these novels—"Bundren" and "Bunch"—are common in my family. I could not know then that I would one day have grandparents, aunts, uncles, and cousins with these surnames.

One of the central characters in *Light in August* is Byron Bunch, a generous and kindly soul who—with Lena Grove—provides at least some hope in a world peopled by the doomed Joanna Burden and the anguished Joe Christmas. *As I Lay Dying* describes a pilgrimage by the Bundren family. I will discuss at greater length the importance of the names "Bunch" and "Bundren" in Chapter

3; for now, I simply acknowledge how often these families intermarried and how familiar the names would have been to Faulkner. For example, my grandmother Cornelia Bundren Hurst Bunch is the daughter of David Washington Bundren and Mary Barlow Bundren. She first married Harrison Hurst, a descendant of Eliza Jane Bunch, and then married Simon Peter Bunch, the son of John Wesley Bunch and Sarah Hurst Bunch. Jack Bunch, the son of my father's half-brother Lawrence Bunch, is a caring and attentive cousin; in fact, I associate Jack with Byron Bunch, who reaches out to those around him in *Light in August.*

Inexplicably drawn many years ago to Faulkner's *Light in August,* I now realize that Faulkner could be describing my own father when he writes about a man whom Byron Bunch observes at a distance:

> Byron Bunch knows this: It was one Friday morning three years ago. And the group of men at work in the planer shed looked up, and saw the stranger standing there, watching them. They did not know how long he had been there. He looked like a tramp, yet not like a tramp either. His shoes were dusty and his trousers were soiled too. But they were of decent serge, sharply creased, and his shirt was soiled but it was a white shirt, and he wore a tie and stiffbrim straw hat that was quite new, cocked at an angle arrogant and baleful above his still face. He did not look like a professional hobo in his professional rags, but there was something definitely rootless about him, as though no town nor city was his, no street, no walls, no square of earth his home. (31)

I am tempted to romanticize my father or to think of him only as the victim of addiction, ignorance, and poverty. When I read *Light in August,* I think of Rutherford Hurst, his shoes dusty and his heart heavy. I can imagine that he often felt as though there was "no square of earth his home." A childhood photograph of a 6-year-old Rutherford Hurst—sitting with other children in the front row outside of a mountain schoolhouse—suggests that even then he bore the weight of an unremitting sorrow.

When I teach the novel, I often discuss Flannery O'Connor and allude to *The Faerie Queen, The Handmaid's Tale, Lord of the Flies, Lord of the Rings,* and "A Modest Proposal." Unlike the critics who find allegory simplistic and outdated, I do not underestimate its power. As someone schooled in Scripture and Christian parables, I appreciate Faulkner's novels *A Fable* and *Light in August,* although I consider the latter to be far better articulated.

In it are characters with suggestive names such as Lena Grove, Gail Hightower, and Joanna Burden. Lena Grove, who is pregnant when the novel begins, represents in equal parts light, hope, and procreation. "Lena" means light, and "Grove" suggests that she might one day be the mother of many. Guileless and kind, Lena marvels at simple things. For example, late in the novel, she says quietly, "My, my. A body does get around. Here we aint been coming from Alabama but two months, and now it's already Tennessee" *(Light in August* 507).

The Rev. Gail Hightower is a minister tormented by the past and a slave to nightmares. Prone to detaching himself from the tragedies and quandaries of others, the Rev. Hightower understands and grieves his limitations. His heroic moment in *Light in August* is brief and without the import it might have had if he had been able to mobilize his energies earlier and with the force of those whose heroism he admires. The minister represents several themes in *Light in August,* in particular the impotence of the church and the inability of Christians to advocate for others and promote the values they espouse on Sundays. Of Hightower, Faulkner writes:

> It seems to him that he has seen it all the while: that that which is destroying the church is not the outward groping of those within it nor the inward groping of those without, but the professionals who control it and who have removed the bells from its steeples. *(Light in August* 487)

Finally, Joanna Burden carries the weight of slavery and of her family's dark history. Trapped in sorrow and guilt, she is unable to save those for whom she feels responsibility. Like others in the novel, she dies before she can come to terms with the torments of her personal history and the sorrow of growing up in the slave-holding South.

The abandonment of a child lies at the heart of *Light in August.* In the novel, an infant named Joe Christmas is left at the door of an orphanage on Christmas Eve. Later, one of his relatives describes him by saying mysteriously, "'I reckon you ought to know what God is, because dont nobody but God know what you is.' But God wasn't there to say…" (384). By the end of the novel, we learn that Joe Christmas is the grandson of Doc Eupheus Hines and that Hines took him from Milly, his mother, and delivered him to the orphanage. Although the quotation refers to the character's race and ethnicity, those of us who are adopted understand all the ways in which only God knows who we are.

When he was a child, one of the rare few to whom Christmas is drawn is a 12-year-old named Alice. He had liked her, the reader is told, "enough to let her mother him a little" *(Light in August* 136). When she, too, must leave him, she tries to wake him to tell him goodbye, but he is deep in sleep and unable to understand why she wants to rouse him: "He went back into sleep while still suffering her, and the next morning she was gone. Vanished, no trace of her left, not even a garment, the very bed in which she had slept already occupied by a new boy" *(Light in August* 136). And so goes his life, with people coming in and out of it without explanation and without warning.

One of those who comes into his life is Mr. McEachern, a stern and devout man who adopts him when Joe is 5 years old. Immediately and without consulting Joe, he changes his name, partly as a sign of ownership, partly as the result of the adoption, and partly because he considers the name "Christian" to be pagan. "He will eat my bread and he will observe my religion," McEachern says. "Why should he not bear my name?" *(Light in August* 145).

Joe Christmas listens to McEachern without feeling and without visible response, not realizing that both his neutrality and his lack of expression will unsettle his adoptive father and elicit punishment. "The child was not listening," writes Faulkner. "He was not bothered. He did not especially care, anymore than if the man had said the day was hot when it was not hot. He didn't even bother to say to himself *My name aint McEachern. My name is Christmas* There was no need to bother about that yet. There was plenty of time" *(Light in August* 145).

McEachern is unable to feel or convey love. Even as a child, Joe Christmas sizes him up and understands him better than he understands himself:

> He could feel the man looking at him though, with a stare cold and intent and yet not deliberately harsh. It was the same stare with which he might have examined a horse or a second hand plow, convinced before hand that he would buy. His voice was deliberate, infrequent, ponderous; the voice of a man who demanded that he be listened to not so much with attention but in silence. *(Light in August* 142)

As noted earlier, McEachern beats the child for failing to learn his catechism and for other missteps, and his adoptive mother pitifully intercedes—but only when McEachern has left the room.

Faulkner's initial description of Mrs. McEachern foreshadows her cowardice and detachment from her adopted son: "She was dressed in black, with a bonnet—a small woman, entering timidly, a little hunched, with a beaten face" (147). Christmas identifies with the oppressor and not with the woman who helplessly reaches out to him. He learns to admire violence as a reflection of power and masculinity. In fact, Faulkner tells the reader that Christmas feels an odd kinship with the man who abuses him: "Perhaps he was thinking then how he and the man could always count upon one another, depend upon one another; that it was the woman alone who was unpredictable" *(Light in August* 159).

Through stream of consciousness, Faulkner tells the reader what Joe is thinking and feeling. In one particularly evocative description, he writes:

> It was not the hard work which he hated, nor the punishment and injustice. He was used to that before he ever saw either of them. He expected no less, and so he was neither outraged nor surprised. It was the woman: that soft kindness which he believed himself doomed to be forever victim of and which he hated worse than he did the hard and ruthless justice of men. "She is trying to make me cry," he thought, lying cold and rigid in his bed, his hands beneath his head and the moonlight falling across his body, hearing the steady murmur of the man's voice as it mounted the stairway on its first heavenward stage; "She was trying to make me cry. Then she thinks that they would have had me." *(Light in August* 168-69)

As Joe Christmas becomes independent, he leaves the McEacherns behind, but many of his relationships with others mirror their ill treatment of him. Faulkner describes Christmas as he seeks to find his place and to understand who he is, but he travels down nameless and terrifying roads: "Knowing not grieving remembers a thousand savage and lonely streets" *(Light in August* 220), writes Faulkner.

After living on his own for three decades, Christmas enjoys only one day when he feels as though he has broken free from his past and from the cruel universe he is destined to inhabit. Fleeing from a crime he has committed, Christmas wakes:

> It is just dawn, daylight: that gray and lonely suspension filled with the peaceful and tentative waking of birds. The air, inbreathed, is like spring water. He breathes deep and slow, feeling with each breath himself diffuse in the neutral grayness, becoming one with loneliness and quiet that has never known fury or despair. "That was all I wanted," he thinks, in a quiet and slow amazement. "That was all, for thirty years. That didn't seem to be a whole lot to ask in thirty years"...When he thinks about time, it seems to him now that for thirty years he has lived inside an orderly parade of named and numbered days like fence pickets, and that one night he went to sleep and when he waked up he was outside of them. *(Light in August* 331-32)

Like the kindhearted Byron Bunch in *Light in August,* characters in *As I Lay Dying* also share my family's names. The novel chronicles the travels of the Bundren family and their pilgrimage to bury matriarch Addie Bundren. The shiftless father and siblings embody the stereotypes of poor white trash. "A Bundren through and through, loving nobody, caring for nothing except how to get something with the least amount of work" (22), writes Faulkner of one family member.

But the Bundrens are more than a stereotype of uneducated and poverty-stricken Southerners. They represent the land on which they live, land that fails to reward even those who work hard for a living: "That's the one trouble with this country: everything, weather, all, hangs on too long. Like our rivers, our land: opaque, slow, violent; shaping and creating the life of man in its implacable and brooding image" *(As I Lay Dying* 45).

Ignorance and corruption take their toll, but Faulkner occasionally employs humor in describing people of the rural South. Deeply aware of the flaws in those whom he creates, Faulkner suggests that some characters are incapable of thought and others willfully avoid it. Faulkner describes one of the latter, Vernon Tull, when he writes:

> Now and then a fellow gets to thinking about it. Not often, though. Which is a good thing. For the Lord aimed for him to do and not to spend too much time thinking, because his brain it's like a piece of machinery: it wont stand a whole lot of racking. It's best when it all runs along the same, doing the day's work and not no one part used no more than needful. *(As I Lay Dying* 71)

Other characters struggle in an incomprehensible universe, destined to be sorrowful and alone. Tormented by the death of his mother and trying futilely to deal with mortality, Darl thinks:

> I don't know what I am. I don't know if I am or not. Jewel knows he is, because he does not know that he does not know whether he is or not...Beyond

> the unlamped wall I can hear the rain shaping the wagon that is ours...Yet the wagon *is*, because when the wagon is *was*, Addie Bundren will not be. And Jewel *is*, so Addie Bundren must be. And then I must be, or I could not empty myself for sleep in a strange room. And so if I am not emptied yet, I am *is*. *(As I Lay Dying* 80-81)

As he wrestles with his own existence, identity, and purpose, Darl thinks, "How often have I lain beneath rain on a strange roof, thinking of home" *(As I Lay Dying* 81). The answer, of course, is that he has always lain quiet and afraid under many strange roofs, seeking answers for questions he cannot articulate.

Although Addie Bundren dies—and most of *As I Lay Dying* deals with her family's response to her unexpected absence—the novel is central to the themes that Faulkner develops, including mortality and the impossibility of human communication. "I could just remember how my father used to say that the reason for living was to get ready to stay dead a long time" (169), Addie says, foreshadowing with both humor and despair her own long sleep. Realizing that language is deeply flawed, she recounts a time when she realizes that "words are no good" and that "words dont ever fit even what they are trying to say at" *(As I Lay Dying* 171).

Addie Bundren is uneducated, but she is not willfully cruel and ignorant like her husband Anse. She understands that Anse, like others she has known, employs words to describe abstract ideas that he cannot begin to comprehend, including love. "He had a word, too. Love, he called it. But I had been used to words for a long time," Addie Bundren thinks. "I knew that that word was like the others: just a shape to fill a lack; that when the right time came, you wouldn't need a word for that anymore than for pride or fear" *(As I Lay Dying* 172).

In spite of her realization that Anse is incapable of feeling what he tries to describe, she does not hate him. Another character in the novel, Peabody, is not as generous. He understands how flawed Anse is and suggests that killing him might have saved Addie and her children: "Then you all could have stuck his head into the saw and cured a whole family" *(As I Lay Dying* 240), he says.

As I Lay Dying is a bleak tale about death and loss and the vicissitudes of family life, a tale told by those who often speak more like Faulkner than like themselves. With language that is more poetry than prose, Faulkner allows Darl to describe the meaning of human life in one glorious moment: "How do our lives ravel out into the no-wind, no-sound, the weary gestures wearily recapitulant: echoes of old compulsions with no-hand on no-strings: in sunset we fall into furious attitudes, dead gestures of dolls" (207).

When I read a short story or novel by William Faulkner, I tumble into another world. I chase fireflies down a lane covered by an arbor of trees. It's muggy and oppressively hot, a Southern summer night that will not cool down before morning. I immerse myself in mysteries told by Quentin Compson and Gavin Stevens, narrative strings that I may never untangle. Lost in Yoknapatawpha County, I forget to read closely, to follow carefully the sprawling dialogue without quotation marks and apostrophes. I'm swept along by a river of words and sink into the atmosphere of each dark tale, knowing that I will have to read and reread in order to make sense of the fragmented timeline.

I know these characters and these places. Faulkner describes my father—tightlipped and clutching a rifle in a photo from his youth—and again before his death—slouching and old before his time. In photographs with his family late in his life, my father wears an expression that mirrors the one on his face when he was 6 years old. Sitting quietly in the front row with his classmates, my father does not smile. He looks like all the other children—many of them related to him—as they pose outside the dilapidated and historic Ridge School of Claiborne County, Tennessee.

My mother, too, is a character in Faulkner's stories, often pregnant, inexpressive, trapped, doggedly weary. When she was a child, I wonder what she dreamed she might become. I wonder why she had 11 children, many of them with different men, and why she never married. How did she meet my father? Were they kind to one another? Was she happy in a 17-year relationship with a married man from Indiana who fathered most of my half-brothers and half-sisters? I want to ask her about so many things, but buried in Bell's Campground in Powell, Tennessee, my mother keeps her secrets.

Nadine Elizabeth Nash was born Sept. 19, 1919, in Grainger County, Tennessee. Her father, Victor Nelson Nash, 27, was a schoolteacher, and Laura Hulda (also spelled "Holdah" and "Huldah" in genealogical records) Welch Nash was a 22-year-old housekeeper. "They were both great people," according to Faustine Miracle Heiser, my half-sister. "They kept us from going hungry until mom got mad and moved to Knoxville where we went hungry a lot of the time."

Life was not easy for my mother and my siblings. It certainly was no easier for my maternal grandparents. Hulda Welch Nash gave birth to one of her children, Jennie May Nash, on June 5, 1925, and buried her the next day. Nadine Elizabeth Nash Miracle had four sisters—Mildred Monday, Valerie Hickam, Lonette Welch, and Julia Ann Lucas—and one brother, James (Jimmy) Nash. To my sorrow, my mother and all of her siblings are deceased.

Living in Liberty Hill, Tennessee, my maternal grandparents, scowling, pose for a photo. Victor Nelson Nash's hands are folded, and he stands next to Hulda Welch Nash, a heavyset woman who does not yet know that she will soon be diagnosed with terminal cancer or that she will bury her husband just a few weeks before she herself dies.

In January of 1972, a mysterious fire broke out in the house with the wooden porch, a house pictured in a ragged black-and-white print that my sister sent to me. My grandmother escaped the fire, but Victor Nelson Nash perished. Members of a local fire department raced to the rural community, but they were too late.

Although information about the Nash family is sparse, my sister Geraldine (Gerri) Cheatham provided two newspaper clippings that refer to our grandparents. One is Victor Nelson Nash's obituary, which discloses that our grandfather died in the Jan. 3, 1972, fire. Entitled "Ex-Teacher Dies/in Grainger Fire," one newspaper article provides some details about how Victor Nelson Nash lost his life:

> RUTLEDGE, Jan. 4 (Special)—N.V. (Vick) Nash, 80, a retired school teacher died in a fire which destroyed his Liberty Hill home yesterday.
>
> Grainger County Rescue Squad found the body in the kitchen of the two-story home, Coroner Sammy Sam said. The body was brought to Smith Funeral Home.
>
> Nash's wife, Hulda, was able to get out of the burning home, the coroner said.

In my single photograph of them, Victor Nelson and Hulda Welch Nash look as though they stepped out of *The Grapes of Wrath.* Although the John Steinbeck novel brings me closer to an understanding of their struggle, I know very little about them. Gerri has only a few memories of her time with them. She said our mother occasionally sent her and the other children to live with their grandparents in the summer and said she remembers that her grandfather was kind to her.

I say out loud that I am the granddaughter of Victor Nelson Nash and Hulda Welch Nash, hoping that the sound of my voice will convince me. I stare hard and long at the photograph of the two of them dated April 1972. The film must have remained in someone's camera after the fire that struck at the first of the year. By the time the photograph was developed, my grandparents had been buried for several months. Their burial ground, Welch Cemetery, is located only a few minutes from where Hulda Welch Nash and Victor Nelson Nash spent their lives.

According to Gerri, "Daddy Vick" and his wife tried to keep Nadine Elizabeth Nash Miracle away from Rutherford Hurst, perhaps because he was married, perhaps because he drank too much, perhaps because she already had several children, or perhaps because he could not (or did not) support the first child they had together. Whatever their reasons, they failed, and I was born.

My father died in 1971, a year before the fire that gutted my maternal grandparents' home and before my grandmother's cancer. Rutherford Hurst's mother and my grandmother, Cornelia Bundren Hurst Bunch—who lived only a few miles from Hulda Welch Nash and Victor Nelson Nash—also died in 1971. I can only imagine their interrelationships, and I wish I could talk to them about my birth in 1955. Did either set of grandparents know about me? Were they angry with my mother for her failures? Were they estranged from her? Did they come to Knoxville to see me, or did I pass out of their lives without a whisper?

Ultimately, my father and my grandparents are strangers to me. Hulda Welch Nash and Victor Nelson Nash live within the borders of unfamiliar photographs and in pages of novels and short stories written by a man known in his community as "Count No Count," a man who lost his job at the local post office and dropped out of the University of Mississippi after three semesters. William Faulkner spent his life writing fiction, and, so, it turns out, must I. Peering into the faces of the people who made my life possible, I imagine their stories in order to make peace with a time and a place I will never know.

I long for days and times I only imagine I know.

My Tennessee roots matter to me in part because I care about history and about Southern literature and culture. However, even if these people were not related to me, I would be enchanted by their grand Southern names: Rutherford Hurst. Harrison Hurst. Cornelia Bundren Hurst Bunch. Nadine Elizabeth Nash Miracle. The name my mother used, "Miracle," also is spelled "Markel," "Merkel," "Merckel," and "Myracle" in genealogical records and can be traced to Germany. And "Bundren," which is an important part of my lineage on my father's side, derives from the aristocratic French name "Bondurant."

The etymology of immigrant names is a topic that interests many of us. "Bunch" is a Scottish name, which originated in Perthshire among the Pictish clans. "Bondurant" came from the Dauphine region of the French Alps, and "durant" means both "enduring" and "stubborn" or "unyielding." "Hurst" is an Anglo-Saxon word considered by linguistic experts to be a topographic surname, meaning that it describes people who lived on a particular type of terrain. "Hursts" were those who resided in woods or thickets, and evidence of the name appears primarily in Yorkshire.

Reading about my family is like reading literature, since, sadly enough, I will never know most of the flesh-and-blood human beings to whom I am related. When I first read *As I Lay Dying* and *Light in August,* I had no idea that "Bundren" and "Bunch" would become near-sacred names in my own life; all I knew was that I identified with the "little postage stamp of native soil" (Stein interview, *Lion in the Garden* 255) that Faulkner brought to life. Now, the worlds he created in moments of genius are even more evocative for me.

There is no question that I care more deeply about my Southern roots because I have devoted my professional career to a study of the history and literature of the American South. Although I teach courses about the literature and culture of other regions, including the Frontier West, I especially love the red clay of Georgia, the islands off the coast of South Carolina, and the antebellum homes in Vicksburg and elsewhere. A scholar of the Civil War and the civil rights movement, I immerse myself in films and literature that are set in the Deep South and find the region different from anywhere else in the United States. As Conroy writes in an interview at the end of *South of Broad,* "The South is different from all other parts of America because it says it is. It proclaims it, screams it out, wears itself on its sleeve, and is a shameless promoter of its own inscrutable singularity'" (519).

In *Allegory and the Modern Southern Novel,* I describe the American South as a symbol. I argue that places—whether they are regions of the country or simply favorite ski slopes or running trails—become part of our identity and sustain us. This is hardly a novel concept; however, I also suggest that we can escape into worlds we have never experienced directly and that these worlds may become even more "real" to us than the places we know first hand.

For me, the South—from Carson McCullers' childhood home in Columbus, Georgia, to Ernest Hemingway's haunts in Key West, Florida—represents something far more evocative than dots and lines on a map. In a book about allegory and modern Southern fiction, I write about nostalgia for places and people we never actually knew:

> But the South stands, also, as a reminder of brighter days, days of porch swings, spelling bees, fireflies and honeysuckle, days of dusty roads and church socials and picnic blankets beside quiet streams. The allegories of the South explored in this study recreate a land of natural beauty and a deep commitment to religion and personal faith; they point to an American investment in the values of rural, small-town life and the human need for community. If Flannery O'Connor is correct, grace often comes through violence and despair, and the South as a region has experienced both.
>
> Our national nostalgia for the land of magnolias and roadside stands is based, perhaps, on a longing for days and times we only imagine we knew. *(Allegory and the Modern Southern Novel* 136)

In part, my nostalgia is for people I will never meet, places I cannot visit, and times gone by. Two five-inch notebooks can barely contain the pages of information about my father's side of the family, the Bunches, Bundrens, and Hursts. Collected by researchers in Claiborne and Grainger counties, the lists and short narratives are invaluable to me and to other researchers. The Claiborne County (Tennessee) Pioneer Project is representative of the organizations that make genealogical work easier and more accurate. With long-time researchers Denny and Marla Brubaker reviewing the data for the project, there is less possibility of error, although their e-mail correspondence contains the following warning: "Our information is NOT PROVEN but has been gathered from many Claiborne Co., TN reference sources, books and from researchers who have shared their information with us."

Through these records, I was able to locate my cousin Jack Bunch, and we have established what is for me a comforting and important correspondence. In a message May 23, 2010, Jack wrote, "Please send anything you want to me. I am most interested in anything you have to say. It's a one in a million shot that we ever found out about each other."

When he was a child, Jack went fishing with my father, and he remembers him with affection. Because of Jack and the way in which he has maintained connections with others in his family, I was able to talk in 2010 with Helen Cora Bunch Petre, who was, at that time, my father's only remaining half-sibling and Jack's beloved aunt. Although I knew she was ill, I did not fully appreciate how fortunate I was to have found her when I did. I corresponded with Helen and made plans to travel to her home in Corryton, Tennessee, in the summer of 2011. However, Helen went to the hospital following a fall and died of pneumonia April 22, 2010.

Born in 1938, Helen Petre was a formidable woman, who talked affectionately about her mother Cornelia Bundren Hurst Bunch and her half-brother Rutherford Hurst, whom she called "Ruford." When I asked about her relationship with my father Rutherford Hurst, she said, "I loved him better than my whole brother." Her "whole brother" was Lawrence Bunch, Jack's father, who she said didn't visit her as often as Rutherford did. My aunt described my father as a "lady's man." She said he was handsome and easy going. "Everybody liked him," she said, and he was "fully included" in her family.

Helen's father Simon Peter Bunch was so concerned about being accused of neglecting his stepson that he was "better to him" than to his biological children, she said. Helen said Rutherford had a warm and strong relationship with her father, whom she and other family members called "Sime." When Rutherford's father, Harrison Hurst, asked Rutherford to visit him because he had been diagnosed with a terminal illness, Rutherford asked his stepfather Sime to accompany him. The anecdote suggests how much my father loved the man who helped to raise him.

Because Helen Petre attended school with some of my half-sisters and half-brothers, I learned about both my father's and my mother's families by talking with her; in fact, I was able to put her back in touch with my half-sister Faustine Miracle Heiser, one of her former schoolmates, before Helen died.

I suspect I am not alone in relating immediately and warmly to Helen Petre, who was bright and funny and incapable of pretense. Her husband Robert (Tommy) Petre and one of her sisters committed suicide, but Helen maintained her optimistic spirit and her sense of humor. In our conversation, Helen said she and other children often followed my mother and father down the road, giggling when they saw them being affectionate with one another.

Losing Helen was a particularly devastating blow because she guided me into a time and place I otherwise can only imagine. I miss Helen's stories about my father, and I miss her laughter and her encouragement. There are so many places I cannot go unless she takes me with her.

As I noted earlier, in the early stages of my research, I stumbled upon a web site established by a cousin, Harry K. Till. On the site are photographs of my great-great-grandparents, great-grandparents, grandmother, and father. A photograph of David Washington Bundren, his wife Mary Barlow Bundren, and their children enchants me. Born in 1894, Cornelia Bundren Hurst Bunch, their oldest child, is in the back row. Although she cannot be more than 18 years old, she appears to be serious beyond her years. She soon would marry Harrison Hurst and give birth to my father. She later would marry Simon Peter Bunch and have several more children before she eventually died of a heart attack in Dutch Valley, Tennessee, in 1971.

Information about my parents is limited, and just as in all genealogical work, one must learn to make peace with at least a few inaccuracies. Living with the unknown or with an incorrect fact is especially difficult for a journalism professor, but I have learned to be grateful for snippets of information. Since I enjoy a demanding and exciting professional life, I have had to stop myself from making genealogical research a full-time job, although I now understand how obsessive such detective work can be for those who assemble their family histories one detail at a time.

A few public documents provide precious details. Before beginning my search, never could I have dreamed that employment forms, Social Security requests, and obituaries could mean this much to me. Each piece of paper tells me something about the two people who gave me life, and I cannot help but wonder how often biological children acknowledge the value of the documents, letters, passports, photographs, and scrapbooks that fill their homes.

Having finished high school, my mother became an inspector in a shoe factory and was later a machine operator for Camel Manufacturing, known for its production of military tents. She gave birth to 11 children, two of whom died, and I am the only child whom she relinquished. Nadine Elizabeth Nash Miracle had two daughters with Rutherford Hurst, although my parents never married. In fact, as I confirmed after a long search through legal documents, my mother never married anyone, even Foister Miracle, whose name she took. Although they reportedly were together for 17 years, Foister Miracle was married to Mary Ruth Haley Miracle and had a primary residence in Indiana. My mother gave all of her children Foister Miracle's name—except for Gerri, whose birth certificate lists her mother's maiden name.

No one notified me when my mother died Feb. 19, 1996, at the age of 76. She had been ill before she died at the Fort Sanders Parkwest Medical Center in Knoxville. The stated cause of death is liver failure, but medical records suggest that lung cancer may have spread to her liver and other organs. (Several pictures of my mother and her sisters show them smoking, and although not all lung cancer patients are smokers, of course, the risks of smoking are well documented.) My mother is buried in Bell's Campground Cemetery in Powell, Tennessee, the town where my half-sister Faustine Miracle Heiser and her husband Sam Heiser live.

In an e-mail message dated May 12, 2010, my sister Gerri wrote: "We always talk about the Miracle family. I want to hear about you and how you got where you are now." This compassionate missive prompted me to send her a long message with highlights and lowlights from my life. As I hit "send," I realized that my story would be more strange to her than would a science fiction novel. And, as it turned out, Gerri never commented on the e-mail message.

From our earliest days, we seek solace, love, and support from relationships and identify with particular cities, states, regions, and countries and call them "home." Because I grew up estranged from my adoptive parents, I depended upon friends and grew especially reliant on particular communities and geographies. When I first read about fictional Yoknapatawpha County, Mississippi, in the short stories and novels of William Faulkner, I found where I belong. Of course, to find one's home in a fictional space is infinitely problematic.

Having lived in Colorado for more than 20 years, I do not need to move to Mississippi to celebrate the folklore, the landscape, and the sensibilities of the Deep South. However, although I have spent years reveling in the grandeur of the Rocky Mountains, I experience a deep connection to Faulkner and his work, especially when I stand on the front porch of his former home, Rowan Oak. Faulkner fashioned intricate genealogies and descriptions of an extended fictional universe that are in many ways more real than my own Colorado back yard with its familiar gardens and clusters of aspens.

I cannot fully explain why I find the world of "Barn Burning" or "A Rose for Emily" or *The Sound and the Fury* so familiar. But I do know that my great-grandfather David Washington Bundren, my grandmother Cornelia Bundren Hurst Bunch, my father Rutherford Hurst, and my mother Nadine Elizabeth Nash Miracle might have stepped out of the pages of any Faulkner tale. My ancestors lived hardscrabble lives in a harsh land. Standing in front of a small cabin with a homemade quilt draped behind them, the Bundren family—their faces stern and unsmiling—posed for a photograph in 1912. They might have been characters in *As I Lay Dying* or *Go Down, Moses,* and reading these novels is one of my connections to them.

I am rooted in place. I can imagine myself waking and sleeping in any number of American cities and towns. Those of us without families are chameleons, easily taking on the dress and habits of those we meet. My ancestors—shadowy figures in my imagination—found their way into Appalachia and remained there. I love and respect those who came before me and acknowledge—always with some surprise—that I met my family in literature but was lost to them in life.

Walking down the dirt road that leads to Faulkner's home near Ole Miss, I reverently approach the square white house with its dark shutters. As the sun drops behind the trees, I imagine William Faulkner smoking his pipe and calling his dogs to his side. I think, too, of Rutherford Hurst as a young man, scowling and holding his hunting rifle—captured in a fading photograph but otherwise a stranger to me.

Born in 1897, Faulkner died in 1962, nine years before my father died. Faulkner was a genius, perhaps the greatest novelist of the 20th Century. Born in 1913, my father completed only the eighth grade and died penniless and alone. But Faulker and my father lived during the same time and in the same region of the country. Both loved to hunt and fish, and both spent hours in the woods. Because the poor whites from rural Mississippi often are linked genetically to those from Tennessee, I rely upon the art, folklore, literature, and popular culture of the post-World War II American South in order to understand times and places I would not otherwise know.

Above my desk is a watercolor painting by Darrell Warren Berry entitled "Presence at Rowan Oak." In muted colors, Berry captured the landing at the top of the stairs in Faulkner's house late one afternoon. On other walls in my office are posters from the "Faulkner and Yoknapatawpha Conference" held each summer at the University of Mississippi. I am most at home in this room, surrounded by books and images from the Deep South. Some go to Lourdes for counsel and hope. I go to Rowan Oak.

There are no memory chests in the attic.

Most of what I know about my family resulted from time-consuming online searches often punctuated by dead ends. Anyone who has conducted genealogical research can identify with this statement, although the work resembles unlocking a mystery and can be deeply rewarding. I sought information in five counties of East Tennessee, Claiborne, Grainger, Hamblen, Jefferson, and Knox, which are interconnected historically and socially.

Finding Harry K. Till's web site and tripping over an obituary dated June 8, 2008, are two of the early and determinant moments in my research. In the obituary, I read that Willie Mae Bunch Hyde died "peacefully" at 77 years of age in Washburn, Tennessee. Willie Mae, nicknamed "Bill," was my father's half-sister and the signpost that pointed me to significant information about him.

When I stumbled upon the obituary, I pulled out a 1987 file about Rutherford Hurst. The thin folder contained photographs and documents provided by Ted Hembree, a Knoxville private investigator whom my husband once hired to locate materials related to my family. As I read, I realized that Willie Mae Bunch Hyde shared the same church, funeral home, and cemetery as my father.

Even more surprising was one of the photographs in the file that I had all but ignored. In the forefront of the photograph of my father's inconspicuous grave stands a large engraved stone with the name "Johnnie Hyde" with his dates of birth and death (Jan. 13, 1922-May 28, 1971); next to Johnnie Hyde's name is "Willie Mae Hyde" with only her birth date (July 10, 1930). I had looked at that photograph occasionally for more than two decades, although neither Hembree nor I understood its significance.

Now, because of a story from the Knoxville News Sentinel, I knew that "Willie Mae Hyde" died June 10, 2008, and I knew she was my aunt. "Someone has carved the date of her death into the stone by now," I thought. I wondered if Seymour Cemetery in Grainger County was the resting place of other relatives whose identities I might never know. Some of them went to school together, some married one another, some no doubt hated one another, and all lie in the same earth at the end of the same road near the Salem Primitive Baptist Church.

My father was 57 when he died, reportedly of a heart attack, while sitting in his car. In comments to Hembree, Ruth Jones Hurst, Rutherford Hurst's third wife, said he actually died of alcoholism. I often wonder what he was thinking as he sat behind the steering wheel at the end of a road that must have been familiar to him. Was he drifting in and out of consciousness? Living in what his third wife described as no better than a cardboard box, was he thinking about being homeless, about having recently married a 20-year-old named Crettie J. Holt, about his beloved mother Cornelia and his stepfather Sime?

According to court documents, he abused Ruth Jones Hurst, stalked her after their separation, broke into her house in spite of restraining orders, and was arrested for public drunkenness. I will never know how my father might have responded to these accusations. I wish I could have talked with him about his life. If what Ruth Jones Hurst says is true, I wish I could have helped him regain his balance and self-respect. If she is incorrect, I wish I could defend him. I wonder if anyone was there for him as he gazed out of the car window on the last day of his life.

I found few records to document my father's time on earth. I was able to verify my father's employment as a machine operator for W.T. Ratcliff (1955-1963). He then worked for the Knoxville Utilities Board until 1968. When Rutherford Hurst died, he was unemployed (he had been fired from a job making $3.15 an hour). He was married to his fourth wife, although he was separated from her.

A World War II veteran, he worked for an hourly wage as a machine operator. His burial cost $800: $250 came from the Veteran's Administration, $250 came from Social Security benefits; and $300 appears to have been donated by his second wife, the late Helen Howard, whose signature appears on the death certificate.

Rutherford Hurst's grave is at the foot of a tree in Seymour Cemetery. The gravestone says he was born Aug. 31, 1913, and died April 5, 1971; the nearby military plaque states that he was born Aug. 30, 1913, and died May 5, 1971. (I believe the military records to be accurate.) His funeral was May 7, 1971, at 2 p.m. at the Salem Primitive Baptist Church, adjacent to Seymour Cemetery. Andy Vance and J.L. Wolfenbarger officiated, a detail I include because their names are so common in funeral records from this time period.

Online directions to the cemetery indicate its remoteness: "Hwy 25E north across Clinch Mountain. Turn left on to Bullen Valley Road. Go about 8 miles to Salem Primitive Baptist Church. Turn right on to Log Mountain Road. Go across Log Mountain to Dutch Valley Road. Turn left and Cemetery about 1/4 mile on right."

My father, my paternal grandmother, and my uncle Johnnie Hyde died in the summer of 1971. Both my father and grandmother died of heart attacks, he just two months before her. Born in Lone Mountain in Claiborne, Tennessee, Cornelia Bundren Hurst Bunch died in nearby Dutch Valley in Anderson County, Tennessee. I am told that my uncle Johnnie Hyde died in a car accident. Near my father's grave are the headstones of his stepfather and mother, "Simon P. Bunch (Feb. 23, 1895-April 11, 1978)" and "Cornie B. Bunch (Feb. 22, 1894-July 11, 1971)."

In 1971, I was 16 years old, alone, penniless, and afraid that I might not ever be able to afford a college education or make my way in the world. It is unfathomable to me that I did not feel anything when my father and grandmother went suddenly and permanently out of my life.

Singer Glen Campbell released an album in 2011 after being diagnosed with Alzheimer's disease. In the song "Strong," Campbell addresses the fear he sees in his eyes when he looks into a mirror and grieves the loss of his youth and his abilities as a performer and songwriter. It is the title of his last studio album that is particularly poignant. Called "Ghost on the Canvas," the album refers to his earlier life, which was full of activity and artistry. Now he faces the loss of his memory and his health. Of course, we all are ghosts on the canvas, visitors in a world we can sometimes scarcely comprehend. My father, grandparents, siblings, and aunts and uncles are lost to me, ghostly and silent.

It is cemeteries that remain. There are no memory chests in the attic, no trunks filled with carefully preserved Confederate uniforms, women's gowns, letters tied with ribbons, or photographs. I try to make peace with fragments of knowledge. Cornelia Bundren Hurst Bunch and her son Rutherford Hurst are themselves Southern fictions, and I piece them together as though they are scraps of material. Nadine Elizabeth Nash Miracle moves wordlessly through my dreams. I want more.

Chapter 3.
Memory and Knowing

The desire to understand our origins and the awareness of mortality separate us from other sentient beings. Having learned something about my birth family, I both celebrate my story and grieve what is for me a recent realization: I will never know my father, and—like other members of my family—I will die.

A friend once told me that spending time with me is "like being with a teenager." Behind the statement is an acknowledgement of the joy and energy that infuse my days. But lurking beneath her words is also an acknowledgement of something amiss, awry, not quite right with me. I'm not Peter Pan—unwilling or unable to take on the responsibilities of adulthood—but there is something missing, something left behind, or something never found.

Until I walked the dirt roads of Tennessee, I remained separated from my physical blood-and-sinew self—a "teenager"—a person whose arrested development made it impossible to fathom the ways in which others perceive the end of time, or at least their time. Some expect annihilation at the end of their days on earth; some, eternal darkness; some, a joyful afterlife. I never thought about the end of my days.

When one has no family—no personal connection to the history of a time and place, and no sense of those who gave her or him life—everything is fantastical, a dream, unreal. Am I actually here? Do my actions have consequences? What will I become? What will become of me? Can anyone see me? Will others want to know me? Who will understand me when I am a mystery to myself?

As a child, I was so disconnected from my biological family and from my own personal history that I felt invisible, surprised every time I looked in a mirror, startled whenever someone speculated about my future. I had no interest in my adoptive parents, so I had no attachment to the present moment and no sustaining context. Like Pinocchio, I thought I might one day be real. By the time I reached adolescence, I felt as though I had gotten away with something: I wasn't supposed to be born, but here I was. I began to think of every day as a gift, as a stolen treasure, but even then, I could not imagine an end of time.

In *Waterland,* Graham Swift suggests that much of life is what we reclaim for ourselves. In his richly allegorical tale about the Fens—a marshy land in East Anglia that would disappear into the ocean without an intricate system of dams, levees, and pumps—Swift compares the Fens to history, specifically, the stories we retell and preserve versus the equally valid tales that are lost to the past.

Because I have met my mother and have identified my father, I have become real. Now that I am really here—casting a shadow and hearing my own voice—I want to embrace what has been and learn as much as I can recover from the microfilm and the trunks in other people's attics. I want to identify the fictions I employed to endure an impossible childhood and the lies I told myself in order to survive. I want to develop different coping mechanisms between now and the end of my hours on earth.

Swift is among those who explores our desire to understand ourselves and to organize our existence by telling stories:

> Only nature knows neither memory nor history. But man—let me give you a definition—is the story-telling animal. Wherever he goes he wants to leave behind not a chaotic wake, not an empty space, but the comforting marker-buoys and trail-signs of stories. He has to go on telling stories, he has to keep on making them up. As long as there's a story, it's all right. Even in his last moments, it's said, in the split second of a fatal fall—or when he's about to drown—he sees passing rapidly before him, the story of his whole life. (62-63)

Writing a literary memoir requires separating what I told myself during childhood from what I believed in college from what I now know to be true. Fiction will not ultimately save me. With reality comes maturity. With reality comes responsibility. With reality comes mortality.

My mother is dead, and I will never have a relationship with her. My cousins are kind and attentive, but there are oceans we can never cross. My father lies buried in Seymour Cemetery, his life documented by two markers that are inscribed with conflicting dates of his birth and death. I have no home except the one I create for myself.

I am fortunate and deeply happy with my accidental life. Through an act of will, I have followed in the footsteps of the isolated figure in Wallace Stevens' poem "The Idea of Order at Key West." For her, as for me, there is no world "except the one she sang and, singing, made" (292). Like Arwen of J.R.R. Tolkien's allegorical tales, I left the elfin paradise and became human.

The accusatory words of my adoptive father occasionally invade a quiet moment and take me hostage: "Life is not a novel," he once said savagely, hoping, I'm sure, to make me engage with him in what he perceived to be an all-too-real present. As I stack pages of genealogical material and stare at the photos of my family—transfixed by their eyes—I understand that my adoptive father's words are sadly—and ironically—at least partially true.

And yet life is not so different from fiction, sometimes even less believable, and we are all bound by stories—those we choose, those we construct, and those we discover. Life is not a novel—except that often it is. In *The Prince of Tides,* twins Tom and Savannah Wingo engage in a conversation about real life and its embodiment in art. It is the poet Savannah—the mystic who drifts in and out of reality—who speaks for me: Tom tells Savannah, "There's a difference between life and art, Savannah." His sister replies, "You're wrong...You've always been wrong about that" (535).

"'Star Wars' must seem less strange to you."

Acadia National Park and the cobblestone streets of Portland, Maine, hold a strange allure. Did I live there in another life? Why are the windswept, craggy cliffs near Camden so familiar? In *The Prince of Tides,* Pat Conroy describes the "fierce green beauty of a Maine summer" (555), and his words transport me to Long Island, Maine, and to Street and Company, a smoky Portland seafood restaurant reminiscent of another century.

Although I discovered Maine in 1990 while conducting research about a particularly horrific child abuse case in Auburn-Lewiston, my family—Michael, Charley, and Wintry—and I tried to distance ourselves from the tragedy during the last part of our stay. We treated ourselves to Inn by the Sea in Cape Elizabeth, and if I were someone who weeps easily, I would have done so in the foyer lined with Audobon prints. Through the bright white French doors lay a perfectly groomed lawn. Beyond it were trees that partially obscured a long boardwalk to the Atlantic Ocean. Once on the beach, I watched the sails of incoming boats and looked toward weathered and immaculately kept homes on a nearby hill.

Driving in a convertible along the coast toward East Boothbay Harbor many times in subsequent years, I fell under the spell of a state as purely beautiful as Colorado and more wild, more mysterious, and more disquieting. Even in the company of those I love, I am lonely in Maine. The foghorns, the seagulls, the kerosene lamps in the cabins on Monhegan Island—Maine is a magical and seductive world.

Other sacred spaces evoke other feelings. The beaches of San Diego quiet my soul, and I breathe better and jog farther on the streets of Laguna Beach than I do in Boulder. I revel in the late afternoon light on the streets of Santa Fe and Taos. Firelight in a cabin in Steamboat Springs draws me back year after year, and I like nothing better than skiing along the tree line at Vail. I long to return to Capitola, California, and to New Orleans. I grew up belonging nowhere, and now I belong wherever I am. Like a chameleon, I take on the qualities of the people I love and settle in wherever I find myself.

Geography matters to many of us, but never more than it does to those who lack a sense of what it means to come home. Like everything else during a childhood that I erased or re-imagined, I appropriated Maycomb, Alabama, and other Southern towns and made them my own. I was born in Knoxville, Tennessee, but I spent my early life in Costa Rica, Chile, and Texas. Although I feel at home in the Texas Hill Country, kayak on Town Lake in Austin, and wander with delight along the Riverwalk in San Antonio, the beauty of West Texas and other arid spaces eludes me. I do not dismiss Wallace Stegner when he argues that we must renounce chlorophyll before we can learn to appreciate the West ("Thoughts in a Dry Land" 45-56), but "the West" is wide and varied, and I hike where it is green.

I love both the ragged Rocky Mountains and the awnings of trees on Kiawah Island, South Carolina, but I go cautiously and unenthusiastically to Nevada and other desert places. The arid landscape of El Paso, Texas, is a metaphor, signifying the years I spent in a house without laughter and without love. I do not feel safe near the desert—something that surprises and disappoints several of my friends, but aridity and childhood pain are one and the same. Even in Colorado, I hike to lakes in Rocky Mountain National Park. Water is life.

Because of its lengthy growing season, resplendent flowers, and moss-festooned trees, I am drawn to the South. Like Eudora Welty and others obsessed with place, I visit Columbus and Milledgeville, Georgia; Oxford, Mississippi; Charleston, South Carolina; Sanibel and Captiva, Florida; the Outer Banks. And now, because I know that my father died alone at the end of a road in Tennessee, I am drawn to the Appalachia and its rich mythologies as well.

Without fully understanding why, I published several scholarly articles about Appalachia and the stereotypes of its people. The titles of the essays suggest the content: "Grits and Yokels Aplenty: Depictions of Southerners in Prime-Time Television" *(Studies in Popular Culture,* 1996); "What Happened to Celie and Idgie?: The 'Apparitional Lesbians' of American Film" *(Studies in Popular Culture,* 2005); and "'American Life is Rich in Lunacy': The Unsettling Social Commentary of 'The Beverly Hillbillies'" *(The Enduring Legacy of Old Southwest Humor,* 2005). By researching Appalachia, I was not simply trying to understand the popularity of prime-time comedies such as "The Beverly Hillbillies," a television program I had rarely watched and did not appreciate during its admittedly unprecedented run and subsequent syndication. I longed to be familiar with a past that was denied me.

In 1986, when my husband Michael and I flew to Atlanta—enjoying the locales that had meant a great deal to him when he was younger—and drove toward Knoxville, I escaped into his childlike joy. Since our divorce in 1992, I often miss Michael's ability to escape the darkness of his own childhood by reveling in the day. When he took off in flights of imaginative fancy, it was a pleasure to follow. My stepchildren, Charles and Wintry, are truly blessed to know someone who can be both a guide and a playmate, and he often embodied those roles for me as well.

Crossing the state line into Tennessee, I tried to deal with the euphoria of having located my mother and the uncertainty about what the discovery might demand of me. Michael and I had our careers, the reality of his former marriage, the demands of two children, and less-than-ideal childhoods to overcome. After a restless night during which I initiated at least one argument, we drove to an apartment to meet my mother and then to a relative's house in Knoxville to celebrate Thanksgiving.

Heart hammering in my chest, I rang the doorbell and wondered again—as I had since I was six years old—what my mother looked like. To this day, I cannot remember who answered the door, whether Michael entered before I did, or who else was in the room. Nadine Elizabeth Nash Miracle walked toward me, wordlessly weeping, and I hugged her and my sister Geraldine (Gerri) Cheatham. I shook hands with Gerri's husband Kenny Cheatham. I remember nothing else except trying to breathe and form sentences.

At some point, we drove past the house in which I was born. I took pictures the way a person in an alcohol haze might try to read a book. Its paint peeling, the house suggested that the years had not been kind to those who now inhabited it. I'm sure my mother talked about living there. I'm sure Gerri was warm and encouraging, as she often is. But I remember nothing except Michael's towering and centering presence. For this and for many other things, I love him devotedly.

When we arrived at the Thanksgiving gathering, the modest red brick house was crowded with adults, teenagers, and children. In the living room were several people watching the film "Jaws." In a small room next to the kitchen were a young woman in the early stages of giving birth and at least one person attending to her. A table loaded with food testified to the importance of the holiday. In the back yard were several men drinking beer and glancing uneasily at us. Michael and I must have looked like people from another galaxy.

A strikingly handsome man who stands a shoulder above me and above the members of my biological family, Michael greeted everyone kindly and winked at me when—after he complimented a PacMan belt buckle—the man who wore it offered it to Michael as a gift. Some of those in the back yard were digging a "swim pool," someone said.

I think we ate lunch, although I cannot remember. I know I sat next to my mother on the couch as she wept and tried to make up for our years of separation by expressing her love and apologizing for leaving me. I told her I did not blame her, told her I had never been angry with her. I reassured my mother that I was happy. I asked her only who my father was. Other questions suddenly seemed less important, and I foolishly assumed I would one day ask the other questions that had always haunted me. "Your father is Rutherford Hurst," she said. Since I am a former journalist, I mentally spelled the name "Rutherford Hearst"—like the newspaper giant William Randolph Hearst. I wondered if he were alive and managed to ask. I don't remember precisely what she said, but I knew from her tears and shyness that he was dead and that I would never know him.

That evening, Gerri and Kenny Cheatham accompanied Michael and me to an intergalactic escape film. As we sat in the dark theater and I tried mightily to process the day, Michael leaned over, took my hand, and said softly, "'Star Wars' must seem less strange to you."

Later, sinking back into my Colorado life, I looked often at the photographs Michael took that precipitous day. I stared at my mother's face, searching for a resemblance, for reassurance that I had indeed come from somewhere. I thought Gerri and I looked somewhat alike, but not enough to be sisters. I wondered about Rutherford Hurst. Who was he? Had he and my mother married? If not, why not? Had my father had any other children? How did he die? Why was Nadine's last name "Miracle"? Was it a common name in Tennessee?

I wondered how Gerri could write to me and say she loved me. What should I say in response? How could I love someone I didn't know? During the months that followed, I often did not answer the phone when Gerri called. I was better at writing letters, particularly because I saw her as someone who had answers to some of the questions that my mother was too sad to answer.

I could not know then that Gerri knew almost as little as I did about our father. Five years older than I, Gerri had no memory of my birth or relinquishment. She said repeatedly that she always knew she had a little sister and wanted to have me with her. But no one, she said softly, knew where I was.

Byron Bunch and Addie Bundren are familiar to me.

On the day I met my mother, I was overly conscious of my husband's Rolex watch and our expensive rental car. Members of my biological family could not have known that Michael grew up in a poor family in the Carolinas or that his early deprivation exhibits itself in many ways.

During our marriage, Michael was the president of a software company and was able to contribute generously to people in need. A $100 tip to a valet who was working his way through school was not unusual. During one particularly memorable trip to Puerto Vallarta, I walked along the sidewalk chatting away and suddenly realized I was talking to myself. I turned to look for Michael, and found him sitting on a curb next to a woman with several children. After they talked for a few moments, he handed her money. I saw the sadness in his eyes and said nothing as we continued on our way. Such experiences were common.

My biological family could not have known Michael's life story or my own. Although I worked full time in college, I was so poor that police once confused me with a young woman whom they were investigating for writing bad checks. The house I shared with my three roommates cost us only $100 a month. With its broken front door and peeling paint, the house at 510 Wood near the Baylor campus certainly looked like a place where a criminal might reside.

When a policeman came to my door late one summer afternoon, I was so startled that neither I nor my roommates could say anything as he arrested me. He handcuffed me and led me to his car, and it took him several moments to realize that he had the wrong person. Dressed in ragged jeans and a t-shirt, I knew that I did not look like other Baylor undergraduates. Embarrassed and angry, I learned in those terrifying moments how determinant physical appearances can be.

In *Two or Three Things I Know for Sure,* Dorothy Allison describes the poverty in the South Carolina community where she grew up. With honesty and vulnerability, she explains how poverty affected her self-concept. "Peasants, that's what we are and always have been. Call us the lower orders, the great unwashed, the working class, the poor, proletariat, trash, lowlife, and scum" (1), she writes. Like Allison, I worked hard to reach the middle class, but I will never feel financially stable. Like Michael, I know what it is to be poor, and it affects the way I interact with the world. For example, I am drawn to the stories about Appalachian farmers and laborers who struggle against disease, nature, and poverty itself. I see my own fear in their faces, and I understand their responses to being called "white trash."

Transported by Sissy Spacek's voice in the Public Broadcasting System's four-part documentary "Appalachia: A History of Mountains and People," I learned about a region of the country known for its rich natural resources and the history of its people. I am tied by birth to Appalachia, a land of mountains and forests that Barbara Kingsolver says in the documentary has "as many colors of green as a dictionary has words." Having grown up in Appalachia but then spending much of her life in Arizona, Kingsolver is in some sense coming home. As I listen to her descriptions, so am I.

Funded by organizations such as the Cherokee Preservation Foundation, the National Endowment for the Humanities, the National Science Foundation, and the Southern Humanities Media Fund, the documentary series is made up of chronological sections entitled "Time and Terrain," "New Green World," "Mountain Revolutions," and "Power and Place." Footage of the Cumberland Mountains and a celebration of salamanders by authors and scientists introduce the story of English, German, and Scottish immigrants and others who share the mountains and valleys of Kentucky, Tennessee, Virginia, and other nearby states. African slaves, freed Africans, and Native Americans, especially the Cherokee, are part of the story, as are the Melungeons, mixed-race people who descended from dark-skinned Africans, Portuguese, and other nationalities; Native Americans; and Europeans.

One of the family lines from the 1600s that crosses mine is that of John Bunch, and the Bunch family is among those most likely to have Melungeon ties. Approximately 6 percent of the population of Appalachia was made up of African-American slaves. The Cherokee in southern Appalachia traded deer and beaver skins for guns and pans. The white traders slept with black and Cherokee women. As these three races intermingled, the documentary suggests that the "mysterious olive-skinned Melungeons" of Appalachia first appeared.

Given the existence of the Melungeon people, I am struck by how many of my relatives on my father's side have dark complexions. Among the Bunches and Bundrens are dark-skinned people who intermingled with white people and, later, created me. Although I have white skin, freckles, and blue eyes, my grandmother Cornelia had dark hair and skin. Helen Bunch Petre, one of my father's half-sisters—and the only one of my father's siblings with whom I have had personal contact—had brown eyes and dark skin. Helen Petre was the daughter of Cornelia Bundren Hurst Bunch and Simon Peter Bunch; my father was the son of Cornelia Bundren Hurst Bunch and Harrison Hurst. Like Helen Petre, my father, too, was dark complexioned, although he had blue eyes.

The first Europeans who sought out the new green Appalachian world were British, French, and Spanish, followed by Irish and Scottish immigrants. They encountered more than 2,000 miles of mountain ranges from what is now Alabama to Newfoundland. The mountains were inspirational and terrifying; they made the settlers feel close to God but also reminded them of a place in which witches and heretics might lurk. As time passed, the settlers would either worship and treasure the land or exploit it for profit.

Produced by the James Agee Film Project in 2009, "Appalachia: The History of Mountains and People" discusses the rich vegetation that complements the lives of those who make their home in this mysterious part of America. Chestnut oak, maple, mulberry, tulip, white oak, and other native trees inspired music and reverence in rural areas, and farmers, merchants, mountaineers, and planters tended their parcels of land in a society that would eventually be torn asunder by the Civil War. East Tennessee was the poorest of the three regions in the state and had the fewest slaves. After the war in which many (but not all) residents supported the Confederacy, companies sought lumber and built railroads through what had been lush valleys.

The history of Appalachia is characterized by both celebration and despair. In 1865, Appalachians possessed 90 percent of their forests, but by the turn of the century, the slopes were clear cut, and trains emitted sparks that set entire hillsides ablaze. The ground dried out. When rains fell, the dense forest that had been home to numerous species of plants and animals was no longer able to prevent flooding. The "slash"—branches and pieces of wood that covered the ground—burned. Erosion followed, and in 1907, massive spring floods destroyed portions of Kentucky, Ohio, and Pennsylvania.

When coal was discovered in parts of Appalachia, companies that wanted to provide fuel for cities in the Northeast turned an agrarian economy into an industrial one in 15 years and, as the documentary suggests, transformed the land from a place to live into a commodity. Immigrants were imported to work in the coal mines, and while coal barons prospered, workers spent 12-hour days in the dark. Few of these laborers lived past the age of 50; approximately three miners died each day. By 1880, nature could not reconstitute itself, and between 1880 and 1920, most of the forests were destroyed.

Connecting 11 states, the mountains provided beauty and solitude. Those who raped the land also formed opinions about the often angry and uneducated people who lived in Appalachia and, as the documentary suggests, "vilified" them as "ignorant hillbillies." Communities were "tightly knit," and they were geographically determined. Families raised corn, rice, sweet potatoes, Irish potatoes, apples, and beans. They made cornbread and biscuits. They raised and slaughtered chickens and pigs. Each "granny woman" knew and supplied herbs. Money was less important than trading with one's neighbors in what was essentially a life spent bartering. Women made quilts—some of which are prominently displayed behind my relatives in photographs—and clothes. Communities hosted barn raisings and other pragmatic social events.

Other documentaries such as "Hillbilly: The Real Story" (2008) address the origin of the Appalachian clan structure and words such as "moonshine"; the causes and impact of the Whiskey Rebellion; the hatred of "revenuers," who represented the impersonal reach of the federal government; the resistance to Prohibition; the flagrant defiance by marijuana growers of the 1970s and 1980s; and the emergence of a "rough-hewn" people who could not be subdued.

"Hillbilly" focuses upon the nature of mountain people, no less fascinating because these people are my ancestors. Appalachian settlers can trace their lineage to Ireland and Scotland, where famine and crop failure drove more than 250,000 of them to the New World between 1720 and 1775. Perceived as a "rowdy, uncouth horde," the uneducated Irish and Scottish immigrants moved from the coast of what would be the United States into the back country, where they felt more at home and where they could reestablish a familiar community and family structure. There, they battled Indians and other threats for more than 20 years.

Those who moved their families to Appalachia prized freedom above everything, even codifying at Wautauga Settlement a document that exempted them from British rule. The list of rights predates the Declaration of Independence by four years. And they were ready to fight for those rights, having had to do so in the Old Country and now in the New World. For example, on October 7, 1780, at Kings Mountain, North Carolina, Patriot militias beat British Major Patrick Ferguson's Loyalist troops soundly. More than 900 mountain men battled the British, and although sources vary, Patriots killed between 150 and 244 Loyalists and took between 600 and 800 prisoners. Fewer than 30 mountain men died.

Described as "enormously strong" by the documentary, those who settled Appalachia were passionate and tenacious. They engaged in family feuds such as the legendary Hatfields and McCoys. Often the feuds resulted from deep rifts in communities during and after the Civil War. Somewhere between the intrepid and highly moral Olivia and John Walton of the long-running "The Waltons" (1972-1981) and what "Hillbilly: The Real Story" describes as "thugs," snake handlers, and superstitious backwoodsmen lies the truth of the Appalachian people. Described by a journalist in an essay entitled "A Strange Land and Peculiar People," the "hillbillies" of East Tennessee cut trees, farmed, and toiled in coal mines, where they competed for jobs with Italian and Eastern European immigrants in segregated mining camps. Eastern venture capitalists and others maintained an unrelenting assault on the culture and social structures precious to mountain people.

Appalachia is home to millions of Baptists and Pentecostals, whose churches proliferated after the tent revivals and baptisms of the 1940s. Incongruously, perhaps, it is also the home of what the documentary calls the "redneck rebel invention" we know as stock car racing and of bootlegging. The region struggles to sustain its close-knit communities in which no one locks doors and "everyone was family to you," as Helen Vance says in "Hillbilly." This region of contradictions also gave birth to the most popular music in America—country music, a mix of gospel and bluegrass. Few but the most avid musicians and music scholars realize that gospel and bluegrass have roots in Celtic and English hill music.

When someone has no family, the history of a particular region and the stories of particular people such as "Popcorn" Sutton, a famous bootlegger, take on greater significance. No longer a compilation of stories about strangers in a college textbook, history becomes a road into one's own past. Each face in the documentaries "Appalachia: A History of Mountains and People" and "Hillbilly: The Real Story" might be that of one of my ancestors.

One such figure, who made his home in this unique area and to whom I am related, is John Bunch. The first John Bunch about whom I have information was born in 1640 in England; the second, in 1662 in England; the third, in 1690 in Virginia; the fourth, in 1715; the fifth, John Martin Bunch, in 1758 in Virginia; and the sixth, John Martin Bunch Jr., in 1785.

On Jan. 31, 1822, one of the John Bunches of East Tennessee left the following document, a will that is now part of the Grainger County Archives in Rutledge, Tennessee. Witnessed by Benjamin Craighead and Thomas McBroom, it provides details about the kind of people who populated Appalachia and reminds us that slavery was an accepted part of the landscape. I include it unedited and in its entirety:

> In The name of God. I John Bunch a Citazen of Grainger County in The State of Tennessee Being Weakly of Body but of sound mind and Memory—Do Make and Ordain The following My last Will and Testament. That is to say—My Soul I recommend to God who gave it, My boddy to The dust to be buried in a Christian like manner at The Discretion of my Executors nothing doubting but I shall Again receive The same at The General Resurrection by The Mighty power of God—and touching My worldly estate with which I have been blessed—I dispose of The Same as follows—My Estate in Lands—being The place whereon I reside about The Quantity not exactly known I give and Devise to My son Samuel to him and his heirs forever all The Land I have lying East of The Main and Easterly fork of The first Branch or hollow lying west of The Dwelling house where I reside—Changing The said Devise with The sum of Six hundred Dollars, to be by him paid as herein after provided—To my Son John all The Land I have west of The above Described Branch or hollow by his paying The sum of Six Hundred Dollars to be by him paid as hereafter provided—To My Daughter Levina Watson and her Husband David Watson I Give and bequeath—My negro girl Rachel My Negro Boys Boston and Peter

> To My Daughter Patsy Jarnagin and her hesband Jeremiah Jarnagin I Give and bequeath My Negro boy Ruben—All The rest of My property to be Equally Divided between Samuel Bunch John Bunch Polly Hickey and her husband Joshua Hickey Anna Hardaman and her husband Blackston Hardeman Patsy Jarnagin and her husband Jeremiah Jarnagin—The Twelve hundred Dollars Charged on My Real Estate To Samuel Bunch and John Bunch to be Equally Divided Between Levina Watson and her husband David Watson Polly Hickey and her husband Joshua Hickey Anna Hardeman and her husband Blackston Hardeman Patsy Jarnagin and her husband Jeremiah Jarnagin, to be Divided shear and shear alike—I by These presents Constitute Make and appoint My son Samuel Bunch and My son John Bunch My Executors to This my last will and Testament revoking all others—In testimony whereof, I have hereunto set my hand and seal This 31st day of January 1822. (http://boards.rootsweb.com/surnamesBunch/1212/mb.ashx)

A few of my relatives owned slaves (mountain people didn't own slaves as often as their neighbors who tilled the earth in the Lowland did). Because most of my relatives came to America as yeomen, I find references to slaves in the historical documents rare but troubling. And as a professor who has devoted much of her life and work to the study of diversity in literature and media, I am uncomfortable with my lineage and ashamed of the oppression perpetrated by white people in slave-owning states. Until recently, as I delved more deeply into genealogy, I did not know I was related to slave owners, although I did understand that landowners depended upon cheap labor.

Documents tucked away in an attic or basement—even wills written by strangers—become compelling narratives. As a scholar who teaches courses in media history and the literature and culture of the American South, I am drawn to the Civil War and other such landmark events. The Civil War tore congregations and families apart, with Union and Confederate soldiers worshipping in the same churches and living in close proximity to one another. Most of my relatives supported the Confederacy. Some of them excommunicated those in their churches who fought for the Union army. Others supported President Abraham Lincoln and opposed secession. Even for those immersed in the oral and written histories of Appalachia, it is impossible to imagine the chaos and paranoia that gripped the communities of this region during the Civil War.

On May 7, 2001, my cousin Nancy Cassada Nelson published "Our Hopson and Bunch Ancestors of East Tennessee." In it, she illustrates how the Hopson and Bunch families intertwined, discusses how the spelling of particular names changed, reveals the role of women in the family unit and what occurred after divorce, and documents the rifts between family members and close friends before, during, and after the Civil War. The essay follows:

> The earliest record that I have found of a Hopson in the East Tennessee area is the signature of Edward Hopson on the Watauga Petition of 1776. This was a real signature, not an "X." The connection of this Edward to our family is not known. Our first East Tennessee Hopson ancestor was Harrod, or "Old Hard," Hopson. His wife was Sarah Bunch. They are listed in the Wake

County, N.C., census of 1800 as a household containing one male age 16-26 and one female age 16-26. This couple arrived in East Tennessee soon after their marriage, along with Sarah's father Martin and some of her brothers.

In Orange County, N.C., in 1786, Richard Hopson wrote his will. He named his wife Elizabeth, his sons Richard, Daniel, Younger, and Martin, also daughters Sarah and Jane. Three sons-in-law were named, but not the first names of their wives. Sons Martin and Daniel were left 240 acres of land on Panter (Panther) Creek in Wake County, N.C. Elizabeth Hopson is head of a household in Orange County in 1790. In Wake County we find six Hobson [this is the spelling in the 1790 Wake County, North Carolina, census] families, including Daniel but not Martin. Of the six, only Daniel has sons under sixteen: three of them, and also three females (of any age) in the household. Also in 1790 in Wake County are five families named Harrod: Benjamin, James, John, Martin and William Harrod. My theory is that our Harrod Hopson was a son of Daniel, and that Daniel's wife was a daughter of one of those Harrod families. In 1800 in the census, his name is spelled Harrard Hopson, and the families are also Harrard. There is no Wake County census for 1810 or 1820. By 1830, the surviving families are Harward. I'm wondering if the name was originally Howard. The Claiborne County clerks consistently spell his name Harrod. Census takers were more creative.

In February of 1814, in Claiborne County, Harrod Hopson was already in debt and being sued by William Bunch, Sarah's brother, to sell his land and pay the debt. In 1817 Harrod bought land in the county from William Blackwood.

In 1830 Sarah Hopson was a head of household in Claiborne. In 1832 a petition was filed with the Tennessee state legislature on behalf of Sarah Hopson, requesting "femme sole" status for her. It stated that after over 20 years of marriage and 12 children, Harrod had left her bed and board and taken up with another woman. He was also running up debts and she feared that what little she was able to hoard for the support of her children would be taken to pay his debts. In 1835, Sarah was granted her femme sole status, with the proviso that she was not allowed to remarry until after his death. We assume that he had the same restriction.

In 1835, the Hopson farm was sold for debt or taxes by Sheriff John Hunt of Claiborne County. The property was bought by Anderson Jennings and deeded back to Sarah. By the time of the 1840 census, Sarah no longer appeared as a head of household, but Harrod did. There was a woman in his household, presumably the former Prudence Maples Cunningham, and an older woman who could have been her mother, Elizabeth Maples Henderson. In 1850 Prudence was listed in the household as his wife. In Elizabeth's application for a Revolutionary War widow's pension, various testimonies made in the mid-1840s call her daughter Prudence Hopson.

The second child of Sarah Bunch and Harrod Hopson was Richard, born in North Carolina in 1803 if Claiborne County census records are accurate. His wife Rhoda Yarbrough was born in North Carolina in 1805. Rhoda joined the Big Spring Primitive Church in 1834. In the 1830 census, the name of Abner Yarbrough and wife age 50-60 appears next to the name of Richard Hopson. These could be Rhoda's parents. There were no Yarbroughs in 1840 in Claiborne.

By 1845 Rhoda had died and Richard married Hannah Damewood Ritter, widow of Moses Ritter and mother of at least seven children. Over the next few generations there were many marriages between Ritter, Bunch, and Hopson children. James Bunch was a brother of Sarah and thus Richard's uncle, although he was closer in age to Richard than to Sarah. According to P.G. Fulkerson, James was over six feet tall and broad shouldered. He supposedly killed a man with one blow and it was later reported in the county that the Tennessee legislature passed a law prohibiting James Bunch from hitting a man with his fist. In 1821, James and John Bunch were fined 25 cents each for assault and battery. Their fines were paid by James Hopson.

James Bunch and Richard Hopson were partners in a fishing business on the Clinch River, and Richard's daughter Mary Jane was married to James's son Martin Van Buren Bunch. Richard's son William Younger Hopson, known as "Young," married Julia Ritter, daughter of Hannah. Unitia Hopson, daughter of Jane Bunch and an unknown Hopson, married Henry Ritter. Richard's brother Harrod Hopson Jr. married Elizabeth Mahulda Ritter.

The Bunch and Hopson families have starring roles in the saga of the Big Spring Primitive Baptist Church of Springdale in Claiborne County. The minutes of this church have been preserved on microfilm. In June of 1810, Sarah Hopson joined the church. The following September James Hopson's wife Penelope became a member. In 1816 after being "cited" to attend several meetings, Penelope was excommunicated for "the sin of dancing and refusing to face the church." Sarah and several others had been sent to labor with her.

James Bunch, brother of Sarah, and his wife Isabel Taylor, joined the church in November of 1840. James became an active member, sometimes serving as moderator at their business meetings and going to represent the church at association meetings and to other churches. In January of 1861 he admitted to being drunk with spirituous liquor and vowed not to drink any more. In March he was accused of "drunkness"—a charge that he denied, but in April he was excommunicated. Not until August of 1867 did he rejoin the church, promising not to drink anymore. Soon he was again serving as moderator. In March of 1869, he again acknowledged that he had been drinking, and the church forgave him.

When James Bunch died in 1882, a very moving and personal eulogy for him was written into the church minutes by D.H. Rosenbalm, who was at that time the church clerk and who had known James for many years.

The Civil War years were horrible ones in Claiborne County. Not only did brother literally take up arms against brother, but the county was constantly in the grip of one army or the other, or of the various unofficial armed local groups. The Big Spring meeting house was occupied by Confederate troops in April of 1862, and from that month through the end of the year the record contains the same mournful sentence "Church failed to meet." Finally in 1863 they began to hold meetings in the Tye School House, and it was not until the autumn of 1866 that the members voted to put their old meeting house in order and resume meeting there.

Richard Hopson's sons joined the Union army, and James Bunch's three sons joined the Confederate army. If this alone were not enough to end their partnership, their fishing business would have been destroyed by the war. Here is an entry from the Federal Army's Official Record regarding the Clinch River near Tazewell.

KNOXVILLE, TENNESSEE, June 12, 1862. Col. BENJAMIN ALLSTON, Commanding, Etc.: COLONEL: I am directed by the major-general

> commanding to say that Barton's command is ordered to Tazewell. He will destroy all the boats on the Clinch River, except one at Clinton, in charge of a guard. The enemy have moved to the rear of Cumberland Gap. You will occupy the valley as long as possible, retiring to the south side of Clinch River when forced, watching and defending the crossings. The general will himself move to Tazewell with such force as he can collect for the relief of Stevenson tomorrow. Major Harper with a battalion of Morrison's cavalry was ordered via Kingston to Jacksborough. I will endeavor to stop them at Kingston and bring them to this place. Continue to send your dispatches here as usual. Respectfully, your obedient servant, J.F. BELTON, Assistant Adjutant General.
>
> In July 1863, the church voted to exclude William Younger Hopson, Richard's son, from membership "for leaving his family and joining the enemy of his country to subjugate the South and the voice of the church taken he is therefore excluded." Exactly two years later, in July of 1865, they voted to reinstate him. Then in September 1865: "Big Springs Church met at Tye Branch. Charge against Richard Hopson, W.Y. Hopson, Mariah Wells, Leata [Shelton] Carpenter, Julia [Ritter] Hopson, Sarah [Ritter] Taylor, Mira Ritter for a breach of church covenant for joining other churches without calling for letters from this church and for declaring an un [sic] fellowship with all southern members for their principles for taking any part in the Rebellion. Therefore they are excluded from the [fellowship] of this church. Elder Hiram Hurst, moderator." It is sad to think that the War that divided this nation for so long was ultimately responsible for a break between the families of Richard Hopson, whose sons Brink and Young fought for the Union and James Bunch, whose sons Martin and David fought for the South and whose son James died in a Northern prison camp. These men had been as close as brothers for many years, joined by family, business, and church.

Nelson's research is representative of the work of genealogists across Appalachia. Her chronicle is significant to me because my father descended from James Martin Bunch's daughters Eliza Jane Bunch Hurst and Mourning Bunch Bundren, a fact explained later in this chapter. Elder Hiram Hurst, the church moderator mentioned in the essay, also is one of my father's ancestors. Obviously, I am descended from these members of the Big Spring Primitive Baptist Church as well. The history of the church, problems with alcoholism in the congregation, imprisonment and death during the Civil War, and the plight of women whose husbands left them for other women are for me fascinating glimpses into a world that would otherwise be lost to me.

Until I began research into Appalachia, I imagined that Faulkner's tales originated in Mississippi alone. I did not understand that Byron Bunch and Addie Bundren are based on people very much like my ancestors and those of Nancy Cassada Nelson. Much of Nelson's tale of poverty, war, and relationships takes place during Faulkner's lifetime (1897-1962) and addresses numerous themes central to the Nobel Prize winner himself.

Although I became a Faulkner scholar long before I knew about my ancestry, I now find the description of social hierarchy in his novels particularly compelling. African Americans are regarded more highly in Southern society than are the Snopes and the other poor whites. Most of my relatives—at least in my immediate family—are members of the ignominious subset of Southern society known as "poor white trash." My father was penniless when he died. My mother gave birth to 11 children and supported them on a meager factory worker's salary.

Had I not been adopted, I suspect that my life would have been similar to theirs, and, in fact, I have more in common with my parents than they know. Because I turned my back on my adoptive parents at age 15, I know what it is like to be without food and to fear being destitute. Even now, when my friends tease me about working additional jobs to pay off my house while I accrue other debt, I am loathe to tell them that I live with a secret fear of homelessness. It is not debt that terrifies me. It is shelter that is not to be taken for granted.

The stereotyping of Southerners is too broad a topic to be addressed here, but it is impossible to write a book about Kentucky or Tennessee without dealing with pejorative terms such as "hillbilly" and "poor white trash." Others have done far more than I to address the caricature of the people of Appalachia. One of the foremost scholars is Sylvia Jenkins Cook, who published *From Tobacco Road to Route 66: The Southern Poor White in Fiction* in 1976. The stereotype, she writes, "derives from the alliance of extreme material deprivation with slyness, sloth, absurd folly, and random violence" (ix).

Accurately enough, Appalachian people are often portrayed as sharecroppers and tenants who work on cotton and tobacco plantations or as mountain dwellers; unfortunately, they are often also victims of the biases of the intellectual and social elite. For example, writing in the 1720s about the North Carolina and Virginia backwoods, William Byrd created a portrait of "bizarre specimens of moral laxity and physical lassitude" (Cook 3). Farmers and factory workers became the stuff of fiction for James Agee, Erskine Caldwell, William Faulkner, and John Steinbeck as well. And in two novels set in Tennessee, T.S. Stribling "exposed the entire South as a bastion of reactionary conservatism, bigotry, and appalling self-righteousness" (Cook 30). Both *Birthright* (1922) and *Teeftallow* (1926) depict poor white Tennessee hill people and "decayed aristocrats" in a kind of "environmental determinism" (Cook 30-31).

Faulkner's portrayal of poor white Southern men, women, and children was more diverse. Although he was familiar with the stereotypes Cook exposes, he did not want to be a "polemicist or a propagandist" *(Faulkner in the University* 177). Instead, he created poor whites along a broad spectrum—including the Snopes family, who are often depicted as thieves and scoundrels; Lena Grove of *Light in August,* whose ethereal goodness and common sense make her an allegorical figure; Popeye of *Sanctuary,* a portrait of "sinister evil" (Cook 40); and the Bundren family of *As I Lay Dying,* who populate a tale of "violence, disaster, and farce" (Cook 41).

Frenchman's Bend of Faulkner's fiction was home to farmers, sharecroppers, and tradesmen. Cook argues that types play a role in Faulkner's work. There are, for example, similarities between Darl *(As I Lay Dying)* and Quentin Compson *(The Sound and the Fury),* who are both sensitive and "tending to madness"; Dewey Dell *(As I Lay Dying)* and Caddy *(The Sound and the Fury),* who are both "promiscuous" daughters; Cash *(As I Lay Dying)* and Jason *(The Sound and the Fury),* who portray the "pragmatic materialist"; and Vardaman *(As I Lay Dying)* and Benjy *(The Sound and the Fury),* who are examples of an "idiot younger child" (Cook 41).

At least in Faulkner's fictional universe, Cook suggests, "we see that people who are extremely limited materially and intellectually may nevertheless be capable of great intensities of endurance, heroism, and passion" (Cook 44) and be human enough to avoid "the pitfalls of pathos and sentimentality" (Cook 45). However, Anse, the patriarch of the poor white Southern family in *As I Lay Dying,* steals, sells Jewel's prized horse, takes Dewey's abortion money, and "betrays Darl into a lunatic asylum" (Cook 45). Clearly, he exemplifies the worst behaviors of Southern white people trapped by ignorance and poverty.

Of course, Faulkner is not the only writer who relied upon images of poor whites. In Caldwell's 1932 novel *Tobacco Road,* the Lester family members are "dispossessed tenant farmers" (Cook 67), and the novel features "mixed macabre humor and social realism" (Cook 66). Cook writes that those who populate the novel are "so intellectually debased and emotionally brutalized that we scarcely recognize them as being of our own species" and that they are "often physically warped and hideous" (Cook 66). Although one might justifiably question Caldwell's reliance upon the stereotypes that riddled the folklore of the time, his images are far more onerous and pervasive.

Other writers compensated for the negative portrayals that permeated popular culture by glorifying Southern whites who lived hardscrabble lives. James Agee, Walker Evans, and Carson McCullers, for example, betray what Cook calls their "leftist sympathies" (158) in their portrayals in *Let Us Now Praise Famous Men* and *The Heart Is a Lonely Hunter,* respectively. John Steinbeck, too, employs positive images of rural whites—many of them drawn from his nonfiction works—to create sympathetic characters in *The Grapes of Wrath* and other novels.

In a chapter entitled "Steinbeck's Retreat into Artfulness," Cook says Steinbeck's portrayal of poor whites from Arkansas, Iowa, Kansas, Missouri, Oklahoma, and Texas emphasized their "courage and generosity" and "optimism and endurance" (Cook 183). Although these elevated images are no more reliable than the negative ones, they are a welcome change, especially for those who inhabited predominantly white rural communities and who grew to despise stereotypes of a backward people in a forgotten land.

Those who immerse themselves in literature—whether they read after a demanding day at work or teach literature in the academy—know the allure of narrative. I am prepared to argue that no people are more capable storytellers than Southerners; furthermore, I believe that slavery, the Civil War, and the civil rights movement that followed made storytelling inevitable. It is through words that we are saved. It is through words that we correct historical assumptions. It is through words that we understand ourselves and make restitution to those whom we have wronged. And it is words that allow us to build community and to actualize our dreams.

My parents were poverty-stricken, uneducated people with distinctive, richly evocative Southern names. I have always been drawn to the stories of the South—an attraction that occurred long before I confirmed anything about my Tennessee roots. In *The Prince of Tides,* Conroy writes about the "fierce interior music of blood and wildness and identity" and "the beauty and fear of kinship, the ineffable ties of family" (564). Except for this fear and these ties, I know of no other way to account for the mystical connection I feel to the history of Appalachia and to the stories about my father and mother, Rutherford Hurst and Nadine Elizabeth Nash Miracle.

Adoption is a socially sanctioned lie.

My desire to write my own past began at Edgar D. Park Elementary School in El Paso, Texas, where an angry classmate, whom I accidentally injured in a rowdy game of tetherball on the playground, shouted, "Bastard!" I ran home, looked up the word in a dictionary, and thought, "Well, I guess I am."

In that moment, I understood the power of a word to define and contain. I also understood that I had a story that involved mysterious and faceless biological parents. Perhaps they loved me, I thought. Perhaps they're looking for me, I hoped.

The longing to find the people who looked like me and who were, I thought, concerned about my well-being increased as the attention afforded me in my own house decreased. In 1965 when I was 10 years old, "The Sound of Music" was released. Mesmerized by Julie Andrews, who played Maria von Trapp, I decided she was my mother. Each night, I fell asleep thinking of the Alps and of how I would find the nuns and the abbey. I was afraid of Captain Georg Ritter von Trapp, not because he blew his whistle to summon his children but because he could not readily express emotion. I believed he was not to be trusted.

In the 1980s, my husband Michael Danny Whitt and I traveled often to New York City. On one such trip, we basked in the lights and energy of Times Square and saw Julie Andrews and her longtime friend Carol Burnett. The two greeted one another and disappeared together into a limousine. Remembering my childhood fantasy, a flood of embarrassment washed over me.

Biological children, too, fantasize about their origins, especially when they are trying to break from parents and imagine their own futures. However, adopted children are from the first conscious moment participants in a lie, one they have been told and one to which some of them will learn to adapt. From the moment of birth, adopted children have two birth certificates, one real and one created by an institution. They have different birth numbers (in my case, both records list a "birth number" that begins "141-55" but is signed by two different registrars on July 19, 1955).

These legal and signed documents are the first indicators that others might tell us a socially sanctioned lie—one that is presumably told in our own best interest—and get away with it. I am grateful that I knew I was adopted. Had I believed I was the biological child of a father who was detached from me and of a mother who loathed me, I don't know how I could have maintained my own sense of self-worth. Because I was adopted, I could say to myself: "I don't belong to them." I could also say what biological children might at times wish they could say: "I don't look like them. And I am not fated to become who they are."

Obviously, adoptees have a birth family and a designated one—the first determined by chance and the second constructed by well-meaning people who match children with families as best they can. They read application forms, conduct extensive interviews, and create a situation for the child that is presumably better than the roll-of-the-dice world into which the child was born. In my case, the records were sealed immediately, and I grew up knowing I was different, knowing I was the embodiment of a secret, knowing I might never be able to confirm or deny the narratives I constructed as I matured.

Processes to place children in their new families have improved since my adoption in 1955: ideally, there are carefully choreographed home visits, interviews with extended family members, and individual and joint psychological testing for prospective parents. In 1955, there were applications and interviews. No one would have questioned the appropriateness of placing a Caucasian child with a Caucasian minister and his full-time Caucasian housekeeper wife. I had blue eyes and light brown hair. I looked as though I might belong to them. They appeared to be responsible, capable people. It must have appeared to be enough.

The original birth certificate has the following heading: "State of Tennessee Department of Health and Environment, Cordell Hull Building, Nashville, Tennessee." The certificate of live birth from the Department of Public Health and the Division of Vital Statistics identifies me as "Betty Ann Miracle." The other certificate from the "Office of Vital Records" lists the first, middle, and last name that my adoptive parents assigned me.

By the time I was in college, I could not wait to marry and take a man's name. A heterosexual woman who is a feminist and chooses to marry sometimes flounders when confronted with taking either her husband's name or keeping her father's name. I have always been unhappy with either option, but I had two choices: I could rename myself creatively as Elizabeth Joyce did in the film "Mother and Child" (see Chapter 1), or I could marry into a new family and appropriate their surname. I opted for the latter.

The decision was simple and the reality overdue. Although "Whitt" became my married name August 15, 1986, I also went to the Arapahoe County Courthouse Dec. 22, 1986, and changed my name legally to "Whitt." (Married or divorced, I was determined to leave my adoptive father's name permanently behind me.) Ironically, the middle name my adoptive parents gave me ("Janette Elizabeth")—and one I refused to use—is, in fact, my biological mother's middle name. And the name my mother gave me, "Betty," is, of course, a diminutive form of "Elizabeth."

My accurate birth certificate leaves my father's information blank but lists my mother's full name, age (36), occupation (inspector), kind of business (shoe factory), number of other children living (7), children born alive but now dead (1), and children stillborn (1). She signs her name, "Nadine Nash Miracle," and identifies my place of birth as 2212 Western Avenue, Knoxville Tennessee, which was her home. (According to Gerri, none of my mother's children was born in a hospital.) The birth numbers, registrar's signatures, and other details differ on the two documents.

After an expensive and time-consuming process, I finally received the original birth certificate stamped "March 31, 1988." I wondered why adoptees—even when they reach adulthood—can be deprived of their original birth certificates in some states. In many cases, adoptees spend a lifetime unable to give physicians accurate information about their birth families or health histories.

My complexion is similar to that of my adoptive parents, and, as a bonus, they were college-educated, seemingly moral people. Having been unable to have children, they told the adoption agency they wanted a child. I kept a paragraph from a letter written by my adoptive father, which illustrates the double life adopted children face:

> You were born in Knox County, Tennessee, the first child of a lady near 40. She had hoped to marry, so we were told, but it didn't work out. Some family member—your mother's father, or the man she hoped to marry—had (or had had) tuberculosis (not an uncommon disease in much of Tennessee); and professions of farmer, teacher and mail carrier somehow figured with the families involved. Apparently there was concern by the social worker to ascertain if we (both being college graduates) could accept a child who might not be college material. Our answer then and now is simply that we want to help our children achieve each's [sic] own potential—whether that be high school or Ph.D. (In your case, the question does now seem rather ludicrous).

What follows is a paragraph suggesting that after I turned 21, the files of the Tennessee Department of Public Welfare—"or at least some information restricted from us"—would be available.

Vague and inaccurate information that might seem unimportant to a person with genealogical data is devastating to an adopted child. For example, although my birth mother was, in fact, 36 years old when I was born, I was not her first child. When I was born, I had seven living siblings, and she had given birth to two others who died. (A brother Dwayne would be born after I was.)

"Some family member" with tuberculosis is a detail to an adoptive parent, but not to a child, and who in the family was a farmer, teacher, or mail carrier is significant. (I have not been able to confirm that anyone had tuberculosis or that anyone was a mail carrier.) Furthermore, if the child was born to people who were not college graduates, then who is the teacher in the family? Would that person not have had a formal education? My grandfather Victor Nelson Nash taught school at some point in his life, but I know little else about him. Genealogical records repeatedly identify him as a "farmer."

The next paragraph is also significant to an adopted person. Referring to the placement agency, it reads in part:

> I do not know what procedures are involved here, but this is your channel for information. Apparently you had not picked up this important detail; but again, it was not something we purposed to withhold. In fact, we not only assumed you knew the channel but that you might already have availed yourself of it.

Admittedly, not all adoptive situations suggest this level of detachment. Adoptive parents no doubt often share with their children their adoption stories; open and healthy communication may be the rule, not the exception. However, assuming that children understand institutional processes and might be able to negotiate them is unwise. In fact, it took a supportive husband, several thousand dollars, and changes in laws involving adoption records before I was able to gain accurate information. By then, I was 32 years old. Initially, only "nonidentifying information" was released to me, and it was largely inaccurate.

Assuming the pastorate of a Protestant church in a small Tennessee community, my adoptive father was 26 years old when I was born. Like all young couples, he and his wife could not anticipate fully the demands of parenting. The minister perceived himself as a servant of God and must have been aware of the respect afforded to his position. His wife had health problems that made her withdraw occasionally from public view.

Although my adoptive father could not know it at that time, his service to what was then the Southern Baptist Foreign Mission Board would be a journey that would culminate, at the age of 80, with a book about his long marriage and his devotion to God. Because of that book, I have information I would not otherwise have had. Not surprisingly, nothing about the abuse I endured appears in the book; in fact, he says he decided to leave our estrangement in God's hands and considers it mystifying. He also celebrates his long marriage, a marriage made possible—at least in part—by denial. There is no evidence my adoptive father considered what occurred when he closed the door behind him and left three children in his wife's care.

Perusing Pat Conroy's *My Reading Life,* I was startled by the dedication of his memoir. It reads: "This book is dedicated to my lost daughter, Susannah Ansley Conroy. Know this: I love you with my heart and always will. Your return to my life would be one of the happiest moments I could imagine." Although I could not help but wonder how Susannah Ansley Conroy might feel about this very public expression, I was drawn to the humility in Conroy's request for contact. Would that there were more such messages to lost daughters.

It is ironic that my adoptive father's chronicle of his development as a pastor and editor contains chapters about his childhood, teenage years, and young adulthood. Later in the book appears a chapter entitled "Extended Family Relations." There is nothing in the book that would indicate awareness that this information is a gift from his parents and others who supported him when he was a child. Like most biological children, he appears to consider the information his birthright.

Biological children can no more imagine living without information about their origins than they can imagine being born a different race or ethnicity than their own. I doubt that when he wrote the book he considered what it would be like not to have information about his parents and his sister and records and photographs from their shared life. Why would he?

My adoptive father reveals no information about why he and his wife were unable to have children, but he writes that in 1954, they applied to an adoption agency. In January 1955, a month before my birth, they had a preliminary interview with the Tennessee Department of Public Welfare. He provides no dates, but my placement occurred five months later in the summer of 1955:

> The overshadowing event of the summer was the arrival of Jan. On three days' notice we went to Knoxville to see the five-months-old baby girl which was being made available to us. After serious prayer and consideration, we decided to accept her. We named her Janette Elizabeth, after my sister and [my wife's] sister; but for practical purposes her name is Jan. The delightedly shocked church showered us with gifts of clothes, toys, and equipment for her. She was a healthy and happy baby, ideally suited for a minister's home. The happiness of our home was complete with her arrival. (30)

On Dec. 28, 1956, my adoptive parents took me from Cisco, Texas, to New Orleans in order to take a flight to San José, Costa Rica, where their missionary career would begin. The stay in Costa Rica was uneventful except for the record of a morning when they found a rat in my crib and were forced to find more appropriate housing (56).

Anecdotes that are part of any family's record appear in the book: "Jan talks constantly about grandparents and friends" (63), he writes. Having taken me to Sears, my adoptive father writes, "She always wants to try out all the tricycles and little bikes. I think she pays them more attention than the dolls!" (70). I am not surprised that I preferred bicycles to dolls, outdoor activity to domestic life. A detail that is unimportant to someone who grew up surrounded by anecdotes about himself or herself fascinates those who have no access to their own personal stories.

On Feb. 28, 1958, my adoptive parents took me to Chile for their first assignment with the Southern Baptist Foreign Mission Board. I was 3 years old. While living in Concepción, I vividly remember an earthquake that is chronicled in the book. My adoptive father carried me downstairs, where we sat by the front door, an area reinforced with strong wooden beams that offer some protection during earthquakes.

My love of stories—including those in the Bible—is obvious. When they began to tell me a biblical tale about an earthquake that involved Paul and Silas, I reminded them that I knew the story: "We were both surprised as she interrupted to say, 'Oh, yes, that's what happened when Paul was in jail and the man asked him what he had to do to be saved'" (109), my adoptive father writes. In six minutes, he adds, the third largest city in Chile endured a massive earthquake for the fifth time in the country's history.

Stories of childhood often point to who we will become. One account is especially evocative for me. In it, my adoptive mother is writing to her mother-in-law:

> She is building with her blocks now and saying "Look!" every other second, so it is a little hard to concentrate. . . She is such a sociable little somebody. Sometimes lately I have counted as many as eight children in the yard at the time, and that is not too many to suit her. She just loves people, big, little, dirty, or clean. She always notices if some of the little children are dirty but she is happy to have them just the same. (111)

As a professor at Baylor University, the University of Denver, and now the University of Colorado at Boulder, I can attest to my desire to be with people. An extrovert gains energy by being with others; although I treasure solitude, I enjoy the company of family and friends. Hearing about the lives of others is as important to me as reading books. It is no surprise then that in another letter, my adoptive father writes about my introduction to his congregation in Tennessee: "The baby just took it all in. And didn't so much as whimper! (I'm afraid she likes attention too much!) She likes people. . . and they liked her" (342).

According to my adoptive father's life story, I was adopted Wednesday, June 19, 1955. On June 20, he wrote a letter to his parents describing me. In one particularly significant excerpt, he writes, "We are mighty proud of her. To be sure, it's not quite like having your own, but it's great." On behalf of all adopted children, I often respond to those who say to new parents of an adopted child, "How lucky she is to have you!" or "It's so wonderful that he has a home." Kindly but firmly, I say, "And aren't the two of you lucky to have that beautiful child?"

While I appreciate his honesty, there is in the statement about adoption an attitude that may have contributed to the poor relationship that he and his wife had with me. "It's not quite like having your own," he writes. Does the sentence suggest that adopting a child rather than giving birth to one is better, worse, or simply different? I wish for all potential adoptive parents the counseling that will help them address this issue for themselves and their children. If they are not able to understand their own reactions to adoption, there is no question that the child will know something is amiss. There is no hiding anything from children.

No acknowledgement of the emotional and physical abuse that precipitated my inevitable break with my adoptive parents appears in the autobiography. Although my adoptive father states that I left when I was 15, he explains the separation by alluding to the Castellos. Obviously, no child opts to live with another family unless there is a catalyst. He writes:

> Many who read these lines will already know that we lost Jan—not by death, but by resignation. It might have been easier to get over her death. But precisely what died was our relationship...What neither of us fully appreciated was that Jan had, in effect, chosen a new family in Waco to which she would

> "belong." It took another 10 years for our relations to reach a final breaking point, but such a break finally came...I simply acknowledge that we lost this child. We finally worked through the loss and determined to carry on with our lives and ministries—leaving this and many other mysteries of life in the hands of our loving God. (353-54)

In excerpts such as this one, dramatic monologue reveals far more than we ever intend. I am mystified by my adoptive father's abandonment of the children for whom he was responsible and by the passivity and helplessness that characterize his response to their pain.

Parents who are able to admit fault to their children can build deep relationships with them and teach them through example that forgiveness is a habit of mind and spirit. In my case, neither of my adoptive parents accounted for the periods of explosive rage that punctuated the days, months, and years during which I lived with them. I do not disown or deny my anger toward them; in fact, it enabled me to leave and make another life for myself. But although I admit to anger—and hold it close—I also have no desire for vengeance, which, as Silvia Broome (Nicole Kidman) says in the film "The Interpreter" (2005), is just a "lazy form of grief." The cruelty and detachment I experienced while in their care are catalysts for sadness, not rage.

My adoptive father's story provides me with information I would not otherwise remember. Letters among my adoptive family members inform me that I wanted to be a writer and I enjoyed television. Given the fact that I have so joyfully spent my academic career in writing and analyzing literary, television, and film texts, I am happy to know how early those inclinations began.

Parents might tell children who become doctors about their early interest in science or tell those who become veterinarians about their childhood devotion to animals. I suspect most biological children take such information for granted. For adopted children, there also may be biological and social indicators of their career choices, but these are often lost.

My adoptive father's account suggests that I left El Paso at 15, but he does not realize I was only 6 years old when I made the decision to do so. Those who are not Baptists, which is the largest Protestant denomination in the United States, may not know that a "profession of faith" in Jesus, who is perceived to be part of the Holy Trinity, involves a public confession and baptism. Unlike Catholics, Baptists are immersed in water to symbolize their new spiritual lives, and they must be of the age of consent before they are baptized.

My baptism occurred at the First Baptist Church in El Paso, Texas, during the tenure of W. Herschel Ford, a well-known pastor and writer of sermons. Although I was very young, I wanted desperately to believe in the compassionate, fatherly embodiment of God. I wished for a nurturing creator. I loved the stories about children sitting in Jesus' lap and listened with great interest to parables about his kindness to outcasts. In real life, though, Herschel Ford was what I imagined God might be.

I wanted to be baptized as evidence of my belief in the principles Christ exemplified. But even more, I wanted Herschel Ford to baptize me. The genteel man of God stood in front of the congregation after each Sunday morning service. I often ran up to shake his hand, and he put his arm around me while he greeted church members. Having had little contact with a grandfatherly figure and having a painfully limited relationship with my adoptive father, I was devoted to Herschel Ford and relied upon his attention.

On the night when the baptism was to take place, I dressed in a white robe and walked in bare feet to the edge of the baptistry, which sat high above the congregation. Having rehearsed, I knew I was supposed to walk carefully down the steps and into the water that came all the way to my shoulders. I looked across the baptistry and to my horror saw not Herschel Ford but my adoptive father, who, as a courtesy, had been offered the opportunity to baptize me.

I thought of running away. I wondered where I would go. The organist played, and the congregation watched. My heart hammered loudly, and I tried to remember where I left my clothes moments before. In my turmoil, I wondered irrationally if my adoptive father would drown me.

Devastated and near tears, I went through the ceremony and promised myself that I would run away. I would find a way out of this family and into one I could love. I promised myself that if I couldn't find anyone, I would set out on my own. Vividly, I remember being submerged as my adoptive father spoke his high-toned words above me. I could no longer remember why I was being baptized or why it had been so significant to me only days before.

The 1961 baptism documents how early I was estranged from my adoptive parents. It may be that I never felt a connection to them. In those moments of despair, I could not know that it would be only two years until I found Martha Eugenia Angulo and only nine years until a family in Waco, Texas, would claim my heart. Nor could I know that in 26 years I would walk into the living room of an apartment in Knoxville, Tennessee, and embrace my mother, Nadine Elizabeth Nash Miracle. Although it was years until I could keep any of the promises I made to myself while standing in front of the congregation on that night, I eventually kept them all. When I left El Paso, I never returned.

Long before I knew the Castello family, I found others who cared—or they found me. One of them is Martha Eugenia Angulo. Martha would later marry Kyle Grimes, whom she met when they were both students at Hardin-Simmons University in Abilene, Texas, and I would lose touch with her. She was only 15 when I first met her, but she seemed far older and wiser than I. She was my Sunday School teacher at Primera Iglesia Bautista Mexicana in El Paso when I was 8, and each week I studied the Bible in order to gain both her praise and her affection.

Often, Martha sent me cards and short messages, which I treasured for many years. Sometimes, she gave me gifts, such as a doll dressed in the green, white, and red of the Mexican flag; a ring; and a necklace upon which were engraved the words "I Love You." I depended upon her kindness and gradually grew to love her family. Her parents, Ruben and Elizabeth, and her younger sisters Arcelia, Margarita, and Ruth shared their home with me. Occasionally, we spent time in the small house at 3416 Altura Street, making tortillas and laughing. This was the first family I intently watched—albeit from a distance—not understanding their love for one another but reveling in it.

I absorbed the beliefs that mattered to Martha. For example, terrified that I might lose her affection, I once became jealous of the other children who crowded around her. "Love is for everyone and by everyone," she said softly, kindly, and I have tried to make those words a part of the way I see the world ever since.

I reconnected with Martha in 2010. At that time, she and Kyle were working in Colombia. In her first letter after decades of separation, Martha wrote about the "awe" she felt that we would find one another again: "Of course in the perspective of eternity, it is just a breath away and only around that doorway into the next room that we were young children and that we were so much into each other's lives," she wrote. "Now here we are again, sharing thoughts and moments in time." In another missive, she talked about my letter, which I forwarded to her through her son Gabriel, a letter she describes as being "from some woman who happened to know things and times I shared with a little girl so long ago."

Devotion to Martha was my first public crime against the image that my adoptive parents promoted. I waited each week to learn if we would go to the Angulos' church or to the First Baptist Church of El Paso. I was terrified to ask, always suspecting that I would be kept from attending the congregation in which warm Latino voices filled the sanctuary for a few hours on Sunday mornings.

Now, of course, I understand that my adoptive parents knew how desperately I longed to see Martha and her family. I tried to hide my desire from them, certain that they would punish me for loving other people. They were not fooled. Little by little, I learned to hate, to hide authentic feelings, and to plan my escape from what I increasingly considered a house of horrors. I attribute the fact that Sunday was for many years my least favorite day of the week to these early experiences. It is the only possible explanation for the unremitting dread.

Although I have always preferred to be outdoors, I do not begrudge the time I spend inside a church building. I do sometimes quote Emily Dickinson's lines—"Some keep the Sabbath going to church—/ I keep it, staying at Home—/ With a Bobolink for a Chorister—/ And an Orchard, for a Dome" (153). Sundays often include a hike with my golden retrievers or a ski trip or a football party, and I am less conscious of the anxiety about Sunday—but it remains.

I don't know why characters in Pat Conroy's *South of Broad* share my feelings, but I smiled when I first read the author's description of the first day of the week: "Sunday falls upon us not as a day of rest but one of drowsy melancholy, or at best, enforced leisure. Since I was a child, God's day has felt anxiety-fraught; the Sunday afternoon willies always leave a handprint on the middle of my stomach" (253).

Ironically, in 2010 I would read about the life of W. Herschel Ford and realize that he received an honorary Ph.D. degree from Carson-Newman College in

Jefferson City, Tennessee. As a child, I would not have known about my biological family, nor would I have attached any significance to Jefferson City. However, my new-found cousin, Jack Bunch, lives in Jefferson City and has become an important touchstone. Jack communicates with me regularly, giving me a sense of belonging and sharing information about my family, many of whom live in Tennessee.

In addition to hearing from Jack and his wife Carolyn, I correspond sporadically but meaningfully with other cousins. They have sent me photos of their parents with my father and photos of my father when he was a young man. Although biological children may take such connections and documents for granted, I consider them gifts from God.

"Betty Ann Miracle" is written in her Bible.

Twenty years after my 1961 baptism at the First Baptist Church in El Paso, Texas, I received the first in a series of letters that eventually would lead me to my mother. Although the tone of the letter was kind, the information it contained was not encouraging.

On Sept. 4, 1981, Juanita Walker, a program specialist in post-adoptions at the Tennessee Department of Human Services in Nashville, Tennessee, wrote to explain why organizations such as hers are so cautious about releasing information to adoptees. Because the letter documents the struggle of adoptees to find their families, I include the letter here in its entirety:

> Please accept my apology for the delay in responding to your letter of July 3.
>
> I regret to inform you that I have no suggestions to make as to a means by which you can get any information from your sealed adoption record. The Tennessee Adoption Law is very strict about release of information without an order from the Judge of the court that granted the adoption. There are also severe penalties imposed for anyone who violates the law.
>
> Our Department is also concerned that the law does not provide for release of non-identifying birth family information to an adult adoptee. Therefore, a bill was introduced in the last session of the Tennessee General Assembly that would have authorized release of non-identifying information without a court order, but it failed to pass.
>
> I can understand your desire to obtain personal information about your birth family and your need for background medical information. You are among many who requests this kind of information.
>
> I am sure you can understand our inability, under the law, to provide even non-identifying medical information without an order from the court.
>
> If you are able, at some future date, to have an attorney petition the court, I hope you know or can obtain the name and county of the court that granted the adoption since all of the information pertaining to your adoption is in the sealed record and we would not be able to provide the name of the court.

> At this point the only thing we can do is keep your letter on file and if any member of your birth family makes an inquiry you will be contacted.
>
> We will be happy to provide court ordered information.

Included with the letter is information about the "release of information concerning biological family":

> Upon written request of an adopted person eighteen (18) years of age or older or of the adoptive parents of an adopted person under the age of eighteen (18) years, the department of human services shall provide to such adopted person or parent all nonidentifying information about the adopted person and his or her biological family as may be contained in such a person's sealed adoption record.

According to the enclosed material, the record would include the date and time of the birth and his or her weight at birth; the age of the adopted person's biological parents at the time of the birth; the nationality, ethnic background, race, and religious preference of the biological parents; the educational level of the biological parents; a general physical description of the biological parents; information about whether the biological parents had any other children prior to the birth; and available health history.

Although these details are pertinent to every adopted person, the promise to provide the information after receiving a request to do so is misleading. In 1986 when I did request whatever non-identifying information existed, much of it was missing or inaccurate. My weight at birth and a statement of general good health are included. I assume these facts are accurate. The "alleged father" is described as being approximately 5 feet 9 inches tall, weighing 160 pounds, and as having black hair and brown eyes. His complexion is described as "dark."

The list of "Other Children Born Prior to Birth of Adoptee" includes a male, 15, with auburn hair, who is said to be in the tenth grade; a female, 13, who was in the eighth grade; a female, 11, who was in the seventh grade; a male, 10, who was in the fifth grade; a female, 8, who was in the fourth grade; a male, 6, who was in the first grade, and another male, 4. A statement reads: "Health for all was said to be O.K. All were well coordinated and mentally alert. The six younger siblings had dark brunette to blonde hair."

Although the ages of the other children seem reasonably accurate, there is no mention of Gerri, who would have been four years old at the time. There was no four-year-old male in the family when I was born. Additionally, my father had blue eyes, not brown. I don't know what other information might be inaccurate.

Of course, non-identifying information is better than nothing, and eventually it led me to more answers. Once I knew my mother's name, I could conduct research about her, my siblings, my father, and my mother's long-time partner. Nadine Elizabeth Nash Miracle and Foister Douglas Miracle never married, although their relationship spanned 17 years. They had six children together, perhaps seven, and my mother gave all her children "Miracle" as their last name.

My sister Gerri is the only one in the family to have "Nash" on her birth certificate, and she didn't know her given name was "Nash" until she brought her birth certificate to a motor vehicle office in an attempt to get a driver's license. My last name, too, should be "Nash," although "Miracle" appears on my birth certificate.

In April 2011, my half-sister Faustine Miracle Heiser answered some of the questions I've had since I began to fill in my ancestry. As anyone who has conducted genealogical research knows, names on family trees cannot compare with personal narratives and oral histories. Because Faustine is 13 years older than I am, she has some memory of my birth and information about our extended family. The first child of Nadine Elizabeth Nash and Foister Miracle was Josephine, who died at three months of age from whooping cough. The second child who died was a twin named Daniel, whose neck was broken during his birth. (David, the other twin, survived, although he is now deceased.)

Because Nadine and Foister were not married, after the seventh child, there are no fathers listed on the birth certificates. I might not know my father's name at all if I had not met my mother in 1986. It is possible that I might never have contacted Faustine to ask questions; it is also possible that without my mother's consent, Faustine might not have felt comfortable discussing her family history. "I am sure your dad is Rutherford," Faustine wrote in the same letter. "The reason he and mom didn't marry was because he had a wife named Helen [Howard]. I knew her. She lived just down the road from us. We passed her house on our way to school. I have stopped [at her house] and gotten a drink."

After meeting my mother in 1986, I wrote to her periodically until her death in 1996. She corresponded with me, too, although her sorrow and guilt were palpable and prevented deeper sharing. I wish I could have spared her those feelings of guilt, especially since I did not hold her accountable for her decision to give me up for adoption. Although the decision to place me with my particular adoptive parents was ill conceived, she did not choose them.

In spite of the information I have been able to glean, I often feel invisible, a ghost. I don't know who in my biological family knew I was born. I collect documents and stories about the Bunches, Bundrens, Hursts, Miracles, and Nashes, in part, I think, because research is familiar and reassuring to me. The most significant piece of information is an off-hand comment my sister Faustine Miracle Heiser made. In one of her letters, she told me that my name appears in a treasured family heirloom: "Mom did write your name in her Bible," Faustine said. "I have the Bible."

I hope they're together in the pretty green pasture.

My life as Betty Ann Miracle is a Southern fiction, one I rarely try to imagine. I will never know who I would have been if I had lived her life. I have made peace with the past, and I am grateful to Nadine Elizabeth Nash Miracle, who gave me life.

My mother's oldest daughter, Faustine Miracle Heiser, added one especially important line to the end of a letter filled with family history: "I hope none of this upsets you but you asked and the way I know to tell you is the truth." I appreciate her kindness, but if she knew how long I have searched and how much I want to know everything about my mother's life, she would be reassured. I fear many things, but not the truth.

Those separated from their families and their roots may become strong, loving, and productive human beings. However, if they choose not to seek their biological families, they will never draw from the history that helps to define them, nor will they meet those who look like them or who flash a similar smile. If they choose not to find their roots, they either may dismiss the importance of having a biological family or ascribe too much significance to it.

My sister Geraldine (Gerri) Cheatham and I will never be close friends. We have spent too many years in parallel universes. Unable and unwilling to seek or maintain family relationships, I cannot understand what she expects of me. We have little in common. For example, as she once told me with passion and finality, she does not like to read, and my career depends upon literary study. Could we overcome such differences? Of course. But having grown up without a family, I am drawn to those who share my interests, and I have built deep connections with them. Gerri works long hours and has different ambitions and concerns. Meeting for the first time when we were in our 30s, Gerri and I are unable to create the affection, intimacy, and trust that many sisters share.

Nonetheless, I am confident that our father and mother would be proud of Gerri and of me despite our emotional and geographical distance. Gerri cares about others, giving far more than is expected of her. She works for Comfort Keepers in Knoxville, having been recognized on April 30, 2009, at the 11th Annual Caring Hearts ceremony for the compassion she shows her clients. Angela Rogers, co-owner of Comfort Keepers, nominated my sister and said of her:

> Geraldine has worked with multiple clients with Alzheimer's. She has taken the time to research this disease and how it affects the mind and body. Geraldine is always able to handle the worst situations with calm and collectedness. She strives to make sure that her current patient lives out his final days the same way he has lived his life...with well-preserved honor and dignity. These qualities make Geraldine Cheatham our Comfort Keepers Caring Heart for 2009.

Although Gerri cannot or will not provide the answers I seek, I am grateful to know her. I do not pretend we can be more than we are. Against our will and without our knowledge, Gerri and I lost a childhood together and forfeited a shared life.

I write this literary memoir fully aware that I have and will always have more questions than answers. For example, there are whispers in my ancestry about the Melungeons, a mysterious people who populated East Tennessee and who descended from Europeans, Native Americans, and dark-skinned people (I cannot say "Africans" because immigrants from Portugal, the Mediterranean, and other regions also intermingled with one another). I am part English, French, and Scottish, but when I look at photographs of Mourning Bunch, my great-great-grandmother, I see a dark-skinned woman whose surname signifies the likelihood of a Melungeon connection.

Genealogists have traced the Bunch, Bundren, and Hurst lines to England and France in the 1600s. I have far less information about my mother's family, whose name is Nash, and about the family of the man with whom she maintained a relationship for almost two decades, whose surname is Miracle. I am certain that the genealogical research upon which I rely includes errors, but after more than 50 years without any information at all, I make peace with inaccuracies and rely upon ongoing genealogical research.

Although I have a file cabinet full of documents, letters, and photographs, I will abbreviate here what I have learned about the Bunches, Bundrens, Hursts, Miracles, and Nashes. Those with a particular interest in the history of East Tennessee may find my research pertinent to their own genealogical study.

As noted earlier, the Bunches trace their ancestry to England, where John Bunch was born in 1640. The second John Bunch was born in 1662; the third, in 1690 in Virginia; the fourth, in 1715. A fisherman and a farmer, John Martin Bunch (1758-1814) married Ann Lnu (1760-1830), renounced his allegiance to King George in 1777 in Virginia, and became father to eight children.

One of those children, James Martin Bunch (1799-1882), married twice. My cousin Jack Bunch believes that one of James Martin Bunch's wives, "Isabel" or "Isabella" Taylor (1810-1853), was part Portuguese and/or Native American. Three of their children, David Washington Bunch (1839-1936), Eliza Jane Bunch Hurst (1829-unknown), and Mourning Bunch Bundren (1834-1908), are central to my genealogical discoveries.

In 1855, Mourning Bunch married Greenberry Bundren and later gave birth to David Washington Bundren (1866-1932) and seven other children, five of whom died. Mourning Bunch Bundren is my great-great-grandmother, David Washington Bundren is my great-grandfather, and David Washington Bundren's daughter Cornelia Bundren Hurst Bunch is my grandmother.

Cornelia Bundren Hurst Bunch (1894-1971) first married Harrison Hurst, and they had one child, Rutherford Hurst (1913-1971), my father. Rutherford Hurst had an affair with Nadine Elizabeth Nash Miracle (1919-1996), my mother, and fathered two daughters with her. One of them, Geraldine (Gerri) Cheatham (1950-), lives in Knoxville. I am the other daughter (1955-). The name on my sister's birth certificate is "Nash," our mother's maiden name, and inexplicably, the name on my birth certificate is "Betty Ann Miracle." My mother gave me Foister Miracle's last name, even though they were never married, he is not my father, and they were not together when I was born.

Cornelia Bundren Hurst Bunch later married Simon Peter Bunch (1895-1978), and they had John David Bunch, Nell Rose Bunch Nicely (d. 1998), Lawrence Bunch (1921-1988), Mary Elmo Bunch Vance (1925-2006), Willie

Mae (Bill) Bunch Hyde (1930-2008), and Helen Bunch Petre (1938-2011). I cannot confirm the dates of birth or death for all my aunts and uncles, specifically John David Bunch and Nell Rose Bunch Nicely. The cousins whom I mention in the acknowledgements are Jack Bunch, son of Lawrence Bunch and his wife Bonnie Jones Bunch, and Ron Vance and his sister Paula Vance Phillips, the children of Mary Elmo Bunch Vance and her husband Paul Vance.

Worth mention is the fact that Cornelia Bundren Hurst Bunch—a descendant of James Martin Bunch—married two men—Harrison Hurst and Simon Peter Bunch—who also descended from James Martin Bunch. To be clear, Eliza Jane Bunch married Henly Hurst (1819-unknown); one of their children, Henly (Hack) Hurst (1857-1922) married Louisa Simmons (1849-1932); Henly (Hack) Hurst and Louisa Simmons Hurst had Harrison Hurst (1889-1936), my paternal grandfather. Harrison Hurst and Cornelia Bundren Hurst Bunch had my father, Rutherford Hurst, in 1913.

Another of James Martin Bunch's children, David Washington Bunch, married Sarah West (1838-1901). David Washington Bunch and Sarah West Bunch had John Wesley Bunch. When John Wesley Bunch (1867-1952) and Sarah Hurst (1868-1964) married, they had Simon Peter Bunch. Simon Peter Bunch later married my grandmother, Cornelia Bundren Hurst Bunch.

The Hurst surname is as common in Tennessee as are "Bunch" and "Bundren," and the three families crisscross so often that it is impossible for even veteran genealogists to untangle the threads. The Hurst family includes constables, farmers, ministers, sawmill owners, schoolteachers, soldiers, and members of other professions. During the Civil War, many of the Hurst men served in the Confederate army. Like the Bunches and Bundrens, the Hursts joined Baptist churches, and several of them are tied closely to the historic Big Spring Primitive Baptist Church of Claiborne County, Tennessee. Known as the Big Spring Meeting House, the church was built in 1795 and completed in 1796. Minutes of the Big Spring Primitive Baptist Church are available on line, making the church a reservoir of information for historians and genealogists.

Like John Bunch, John Hurst is one of the first names one encounters when conducting research on early families of East Tennessee. John Hurst was born Jan. 9, 1700, in England and died 99 years later in Virginia. His son John "Mill Creek" Hurst (1735-1817) is the father of 17 children with two wives, Nancy Nunn Hurst and Elizabeth Breedwell Hurst. Uncovering interesting details is one of the pleasures of genealogical research; for example, when John "Mill Creek" Hurst was 83, he died when a tree fell on him.

John "Mill Creek" Hurst's son Thomas Hurst (1764-1847) was a slave owner. Thomas Hurst married Sylvia Breeding Hurst (1767-1854), and like many in the Hurst family, they attended the Big Spring Primitive Baptist Church regularly. Thomas Hurst, his son Hiram Hurst (1792-1867), and his grandson Nathan Hurst (1835-1903) all preached in the Big Spring Primitive Baptist Church. Henly (Hack) Hurst and his wife Louisa Simmons Hurst were dedicated members of the church.

The Hurst families are plentiful, but it is the descendants of the Rev. Hiram and Mary (Polly) Thompson Hurst (1795-1862) that most interest me. Hiram Hurst was pastor of several primitive Baptist churches during his career. Their descendants include their son Henly Hurst, who married Eliza Jane Bunch, the daughter of James Martin Bunch. Henly Hurst and Eliza Jane Bunch had several children, including Henly (Hack) Hurst, a farmer, who married Louisa Simmons. I located a will for Louisa Simmons Hurst, who left her son and my grandfather, Harrison Hurst, $1. The descendants of Hiram and Mary (Polly) Thompson Hurst are central in this section because of the marriage between Henly Hurst and Eliza Jane Bunch and because Harrison Hurst, my grandfather, is one of their descendants.

Because Greenberry Bundren is my great-great-grandfather, I also am the descendant of Jean Pierre Bondurant (1677-1734) and his son Jean Pierre (Peter) Bondurant (1710-1792). The first Bondurants arrived on what is now the East Coast of the United States in approximately 1700. Documents suggest that at the time that Claibourne P. Bondurant (1774-1850) and his wife Mary had children, the spelling of the surname began to give way to "Bundren."

Perhaps the name "Bundren" was more appropriate to the colonies, or perhaps family members or others whose responsibility it was to fill out documents did not or could not spell "Bondurant" correctly. Jack Bunch believes the shift occurred about 1800. Another cousin, Harry K. Till, wrote on Aug. 17, 2000, that there are those who referred to Greenberry Bundren's father as "Old Peter Bondurant" but that "Bundren" gradually replaced "Bondurant."

Genealogical study also unearths humorous and interesting names. Some of the most unusual names during the 1800s—such as "Napolean Bonaparte Bundren" and "Queen Victoria Bundren"–speak to a desire to preserve the aristocratic names of the Old Country. Often, family names reflect the time period: John Milton Bunch, Ethan Allen Hurst, America Hurst, and Daniel Boone Hurst are some of the most distinctive. Some of the most humorous are a male named Bee Summitt Funk and a female named Zippie June Bunch.

The second Jean Pierre Bondurant, better known as Peter Bundren, is thought to have fathered Greenberry (occasionally spelled "Green Berry") Bundren. As noted earlier, Greenberry Bundren and Mourning Bunch had several children, including David Washington Bundren, who married Mary Matilda Barlow (1877-1967). Mary Matilda Barlow Bundren was the illegitimate daughter of Priscilla A. Barlow and the granddaughter of Jonathan and Nancy Thomas Barlow.

David Washington Bundren and Mary Matilda Barlow Bundren, my great-grandparents, had Cornelia Bunden Hurst Bunch, William Albert Bundren (1896-1980), Laura Roxie Bundren (1898-1983), Ethel Bundren (1901-1993), Priscilla Ann Bundren (1904-1928), Lucy Jane Bundren (1908-2009), Retha Bundren (1910-1990), Woodrow Wilson Bundren (1913-1936), and Everett Bundren (1915-1916).

As I mentioned earlier, the Bunch, Bundren, and Hurst families intersect often, creating nightmares for even avid genealogists. For example, five of the seven surviving children of David Washington Bundren and Mary Matilda Barlow Bundren married Hursts. The Hurst lines also intertwine with the Barlow family. Mary Matilda Barlow Bundren is the granddaughter of Jonathan Barlow (1820-1903) and Nancy Thomas Barlow (1826-1884), who are buried in Bunchtown Cemetery.

Most shocking to me is the number of cousins marrying cousins in the Appalachian region. I have always treated the stereotype of third cousins who married one another with disdain. However, the stereotype is entirely supported by my family tree. Although I have mentioned specific names previously, I repeat several of them in the following summary in order to document the multiple intersections:

Eliza Jane Bunch Hurst, Mourning Bunch Bundren, and David Washington Bunch are siblings. Specifically, Mourning Bunch married Greenberry Bundren in 1855—two weeks after her sister Eliza Jane Bunch married Henly Hurst. My grandfather Harrison Hurst is descended from Eliza Jane Bunch Hurst; my grandmother Cornelia Bundren Hurst Bunch is descended from Mourning Bunch Bundren; and my grandmother's second husband Simon Peter Bunch is descended from David Washington Bunch. Cornelia Bundren Hurst Bunch married Harrison Hurst and Simon Peter Bunch, both of whom were related to her and to one another. All are descendants of James Martin Bunch.

Harrison Hurst and Cornelia Bundren Hurst Bunch are my paternal grandparents. As a child, my father lived with Cornelia Bundren Hurst Bunch's parents David Washington Bundren and his wife Mary Barlow Bundren, appearing as one of their dependents in the 1920 census. In the same census, Cornelia Bundren Hurst Bunch is listed as a daughter-in-law who is living with John Wesley Bunch, his wife Sarah Hurst Bunch, and their children.

One of those children, Simon Peter Bunch, married Cornelia Bundren Hurst Bunch on Dec. 19, 1919. Cornelia was 24 at this time, and my father Rutherford Hurst would have been about 6 years old. Eventually, Cornelia and Simon Peter Bunch would have six children, and they would be my father's half-brothers and half-sisters. Simon Peter Bunch and Cornelia Bundren Hurst Bunch would fully embrace Rutherford Hurst into their family circle.

Rutherford Hurst was married four times and had another child in addition to his two illegitimate children, Geraldine (Gerri) Cheatham and me. He married Georgia Hopson Jan. 8, 1931. Both my father and Georgia Hopson were from Washburn, Tennessee. Georgia was the daughter of George Caleb Hopson and Laura Alice Breeding Hopson. When my father married her, he was 18, and because Georgia Hopson was only 15, George Caleb Hopson signed the marriage certificate as her next of kin.

My father and Georgia Hopson had a child, Wanda Jo Hopson Hurst, who was born Sept. 29, 1933, in Grainger, Tennessee, and died Dec. 29, 1939, in Morristown in Hamblen County, Tennessee. Only 6 years old when she died, Wanda Jo is buried in Fairfield Cemetery next to Fairfield Baptist Church in Morristown.

On one side of Wanda Jo Hopson Hurst's grave lies her mother, Georgia Hopson Hurst Howerton. On the other are buried her maternal grandmother and grandfather. Wanda Jo Hopson Hurst is my sister, a fact unknown to me, unknown to my sister Gerri, and unknown to my cousin Jack Bunch until Nancy Cassada Nelson found her death certificate in June 2011. Signed by a physician, the document does not list her cause of death.

On June 13, 2011, I called the pastor of Fairfield Baptist Church, who was busy with Vacation Bible School, a week of biblical training familiar to those of us who grew up as Southern Baptists. The following conversations are representative of those that occur in genealogical research:

> Pastor: Yes, we have a cemetery, but we have only a few graves. Most of them are church members buried here. What do you want to know?
>
> Jan Whitt: I'm looking for a little girl who lived only six years. Her name is Wanda Jo Hopson Hurst. She was born in 1933.
>
> Pastor: Why do you want to know about her? Who is she?
>
> Jan Whitt: She's my sister.
>
> Pastor (talking to someone else in the room): Go on out there to the cemetery—would you?—and see if there's a little girl named Wanda buried there. This lady from Colorado wants to know.
>
> (A few minutes pass.)
>
> Pastor: Yes, ma'am, she's there. The plot is real small, but she's buried right there next to her momma. On the other side is a lady named Hopson.

A few minutes later, as I sat at my desk thinking about what might have happened to little Wanda Jo Hopson Hurst, the phone rang. When I answered, the following conversation occurred:

> Caller: Hello, is this Jane?
>
> Jan Whitt: It's just "Jan." I have a Southern accent.
>
> Caller: Yes, you do! I'm Bruce Morgan, and the grave is right by the driveway to our church. I just took a picture with my cell phone to send you. Do you want it?
>
> Jan Whitt: I'd love to have it, but could you sent it by e-mail?
>
> Caller: You bet I can. But if we're gonna do that, I need to get my wife. She has a high-quality camera and took classes at UT. We'll get you a good picture and send it that way. Who's this little girl again?
>
> Jan Whitt: She's my sister.
>
> Caller: And you never knew her? You've never been out here to her grave?
>
> Jan Whitt: No, sir. I was adopted, and I just found out about her. Her daddy's name is Rutherford Hurst.
>
> Caller: Well, isn't that something. We tried to block the sun and get you a good picture, but my wife will do it better. I hope this helps you some.

Jan Whitt: Yes, sir, it will. You're very kind.

Caller: We're having Sunday School right now, and we're all here. We always wondered who that little grave belonged to.

Just as my grandfather Harrison Hurst and my grandmother Cornelia Bundren Hurst Bunch are related to one another, so are Rutherford Hurst and his first wife, Georgia Hopson Hurst Howerton. Georgia Hopson Hurst Howerton is descended from James Martin Bunch's sister, Sarah Bunch. In brief, Sarah Bunch married Harrod Hopson, and two generations later, George Caleb Hopson married Laura Alice Breeding and had Georgia Hopson Hurst Howerton.

There are no records to suggest that Rutherford Hurst had any other children except Wanda Jo Hopson Hurst; Gerri; and me. After he and Georgia divorced, he married three other women, Helen Howard on June 20, 1938; Ruth Gilbert Jones on Aug. 9, 1956; and Crettie J. Holt. When he married his fourth and last wife, Crettie J. Holt, on Jan. 30, 1971, my father was 57; Crettie J. Holt, 20. I have not been able to locate Crettie J. Holt, whose last name—after "Holt" and "Hurst"—is likely to be different now. I would like to know her, since she is only four years older than I and might have information about my father during his last years.

One moment I felt as though I had no one. The next, I confronted a genealogical chart with more twists and turns than the one William Faulkner created for his characters in Yoknapatawpha County. I have more cousins, aunts, and uncles than I could possibly count. On a web site about the Barlow family (Mary Barlow Bundren is my great-grandmother), my cousin Harry K. Till writes the following about his grandmother and my great-grandmother:

> Jonathon and Nancy [Barlow] were my great-great-grandparents. They are buried in a small cemetery near a place called Bunchtown in East Tennessee. I have photos of the headstones...
>
> As you probably guessed from the name of the town, there were a bunch of Bunches in East Tennessee.
>
> My grandmother Mary Barlow Bundren was the daughter-in-law of Mourning Bunch, daughter of James Martin Bunch. Naturally, her nine children were great-grandchildren of James Martin. Six of her children married Hursts and Bunches who were also great-grandchildren of James Martin. My mother wasn't one of them. I guess I avoided being my own third cousin. However, I think my mother is also my distant cousin. In this family the family tree looks more like a bush.

I'm not certain I avoided being my own third cousin, and I appreciate the humor in the online posting. Reading it, I again acknowledged that my ancestors intermarried and that lines cross one another often and without warning. In a Dec. 20, 2010, e-mail message to Carol Margolin, a Denver friend, I attached Till's statement. "To say you have a close family is an understatement," she replied.

Because so many have investigated the Bunch, Bundren, and Hurst lines, I was able to conduct research efficiently. I have had less luck in studying the Miracle and Nash families. William Peter Nash and Sarah Catherine (Sally) Webb Nash had at least six children, including my maternal grandfather, Victor Nelson Nash (1891-1972). One of their children, Florida Elizabeth Nash Acuff (1879-1923), married J. Walter Acuff (1876-1944), and the two of them are buried in Kitts Cemetery; another, Osia [the name is also sometimes spelled "Osiah"] K. Nash (1876-1947) is buried in Avondale Cemetery. Both cemeteries are in Grainger County, Tennessee. Victor Nelson Nash married Hulda Welch (1896-1972), daughter of James Albert Welch (1869-1960) and Sarah Elizabeth Williams Welch (1866-1943). My mother was one of their five daughters.

My mother lived off and on for 17 years with Foister Douglas Miracle (1918-2004), son of Ambrose Anderson Miracle (1880-1965) and Dora Thompson Miracle (1883-1939). The Rev. Ambrose Anderson and Dora Thompson Miracle were members of a primitive Baptist church in Calvin, Kentucky, and are buried in the Buell Cemetery in Bell County, Kentucky. Ordained in 1915, the Rev. Ambrose Anderson Miracle spent his life serving several churches in the region, including churches in Kentucky and Tennessee. Foister Miracle is buried in Earlham Cemetery in Richmond, Indiana, next to Mary Ruth Haley Miracle (unknown-1987).

These facts, of course, ignore that these are real people with accomplishments, concerns, and heartbreaks. In all the years I searched for information about my family, the journalist in me pushed for answers—even when the news might be bleak or—worse—nonexistent. But genealogical research is not for the weak of heart. As it turns out, I do not want to know everything I know: My mother had 11 children and died of cancer. My father died penniless and alone. A few months before I could interview the last person who knew my father well, my aunt Helen Bunch Petre, she died from the pneumonia that followed several years of poor health and a broken hip.

Given that so many people significant to me are dead, perhaps it is illogical to say how happy I am that I began this solitary journey. However, I was 6 years old when I promised myself answers, and I am 56 at the time of the publication of this memoir. For a half century, I have reached out for my family, and the answers sustain me now.

Although I do not regret one moment spent writing e-mails and letters, making phone calls, and scanning web sites, I am sad that so many of my pilgrimages end in Tennessee graveyards. The people I would have liked to know are buried in Bell's Campground Cemetery in Powell; Bunchtown Cemetery in Tazewell, Claiborne County; Cleveland Cemetery in Grainger County; Fairview Cemetery in New Tazewell, Claiborne County; Hurst Evans Cemetery in Lone Mountain, Claiborne County; Tom Evans Cemetery in Claiborne County; and Welch Cemetery in Liberty Hill, Grainger County, Tennessee.

Seymour Cemetery in Grainger County is significant, too, because of the historic Salem Primitive Baptist Church. At one time the Rev. Ambrose Anderson Miracle was a minister there. My father Rutherford Hurst was a member of the church, and I cannot help but wonder if my father knew the pastor's son, Foister Miracle, and if my mother Nadine Elizabeth Nash Miracle attended Salem Primitive Baptist Church, too. If their time at the church coincided, then my father, my mother, and my mother's longtime partner interacted with one another. And if what I know about Baptist ministers holds true in this case, the Rev. Ambrose Anderson Miracle would have been none too happy with this particular triangle!

My grandmother Cornelia Bundren Hurst Bunch is buried in Seymour Cemetery. She and Simon Peter Bunch are buried near one of their daughters, Willie Mae (Bill) Hyde and her husband Johnnie Hyde (1922-1971). Nearby are Simon Peter Bunch's parents John Wesley Bunch and Sarah Hurst Bunch. My father's grave is also nearby.

Mourning Bunch Bundren had eight children, only three of whom survived (William R. Bundren, James H. Bundren, and David Washington Bundren). William R. Bundren (1861-1932) and his wife Harriet Jennings Bundren (1861-1916), whose gravestone reads "Hariet A.," are buried in the Seymour Cemetery, as are their children Nora Bundren Atkins (1883-1973) and George R. Bundren (1880-1914). The husband of Nora Bundren Atkins, Milton Atkins (1875-1934), is buried next to his wife.

The histories of the cemeteries in East Tennessee are themselves worth studying. Seemingly unimportant details often caught my attention as I read about them. For example, my father's ancestors Eliza Jane and Henly Hurst were buried in what is now the Hurst Evans Cemetery (Their gravestone reads "First Two Buried in this Cemetery"). The Hurst Evans Cemetery fascinates me because Eliza Jane Bunch Hurst, Henly Hurst, Henly (Hack) Hurst, Harrison Hurst, and Harrison Hurst's brother Isaac Wheeler Hurst (1884-1961) are buried there. I wonder how much my father knew about this side of his family, since it is clear that he was closer to his mother Cornelia Bundren Hurst Bunch and stepfather Simon Peter Bunch than he was to his own father. Since my grandfather Harrison Hurst died when Rutherford Hurst was only 23, I can only speculate about their relationship.

In the Welch Cemetery, there are only a few graves, and my grandparents Laura Hulda Welch Nash and Victor Nelson Nash were buried within days of one another in 1972. My grandmother's parents, James Albert Welch and Sarah Elizabeth Williams Welch, also are buried there.

One of the dubious attractions of the Bunchtown Cemetery in Tazewell, Tennessee, is the gravesite of Clarence Bunch (1911-1934), a notorious bank robber who, according to Knox County lore, planned to surrender before he was shot to death by law enforcement officers. Narratives about his life are plentiful.

The puzzle pieces don't always fit, and more than a few are missing. Ultimately, nothing replaces a human voice. For example, during a telephone interview with Helen Bunch Petre, my aunt talked about how much she loved her mother. She said she believed that she could not survive Cornelia Bundren Hurst Bunch's death in 1971. "I loved her beyond passion," she said. "When she died, I just about cracked up and even had nightmares about digging her up." One night, my aunt said, she dreamed that she, my father, and Cornelia were walking "in the prettiest green pasture." After that, she said she never had another bad dream about her mother.

With a sense of humor that sustained her until the end, Helen Bunch Petre joked on May 24, 2010, that she was "so sick she couldn't hide from the police." I find strength in her laughter and solace in her dream about my grandmother and father. As my search for answers nears a conclusion, I imagine my mother, my father, my grandmother—and now my Aunt Helen—standing together in a pretty green pasture. I wish them peace.

Chapter 4.
Children Not Our Own

A member of the ski team and a journalism major, Laura Flood stood out, even in my class of 240. She sat close to the front of the room, listened, reacted, and left after each class session with a cadre of friends.

Four months into the semester—during a routine training run at the Eldora ski area near Nederland, Colorado—Laura lost a ski and slammed into a tree. She died instantly. I read about her death on April 4, 1990, in the Colorado Daily, the university newspaper, but made no connection between the news story and the energetic young woman in my class.

During the next class session, Shauna Fisher, a friend of Laura's, handed me a note and walked quietly to her seat. I made the mistake of opening the note before I began my lecture, and it unsettled me. The note read: "I just wanted you to know that Laura Flood was in your J1001 ["Contemporary Media"] class and loved it. She mentioned how it was her favorite class and she was so excited about journalism. Every morning on the way up to Eldora in the van she would bring her newspaper so she could do well on the news quiz. She thought you were a great teacher."

During the next class session, I told the students that we had lost someone special in the campus community, and we shared a moment of silence. The students—most of whom did not know one another—cried and hugged each other after class, an acknowledgement, I think, of an awareness of our mortality, an awareness not lost even on the young.

As I look back on more than three decades of teaching, I cannot exaggerate the importance of Shauna's message about her friend. I did not know Laura personally, and except for her regular attendance and her presence in the front row, I did not know that she valued the class. However, the tragedy became a reminder of what Tennessee Williams knew so well: Humanity is a glass menagerie. We are fragile beings, bound by common experience and vulnerabilities. Our students are no less mortal than we, and this reality significantly changes the way I perceive and fulfill my teaching responsibilities. I do not take my students for granted, I do not waste our time together, and I make certain that both undergraduate and graduate students know how significant I consider our shared experience to be.

Effective classroom performance is informed by detailed, systematic, and vigorous research and enhanced by compassion and respect for students. The development and interdisciplinary nature of literary and journalistic studies profoundly influence the content of my syllabi. For example, I am convinced that 1) undergraduate as well as graduate students are capable of sophisticated textual criticism and that 2) the history of fields such as literary journalism can energize classroom discussions about contemporary ethical dilemmas in media ("What is 'objectivity?'" and "How does one go about telling the 'truth'—and whose 'truth?'" and "Which literary techniques make news more interesting without compromising its purpose?")

However, a classroom experience that engages both students and professors is not primarily cerebral. After more than 30 years of failures and successes, I know that teaching is about establishing supportive and challenging relationships. I also know that the reason I chose teaching as a career is that I care deeply about both the subject matter and the students who have—for a variety of reasons—chosen to spend a portion of their lives with me. I treasure the names and faces of many students and welcome their continued contact after graduation. Some students are especially memorable, and their stories help to illustrate the profoundly personal nature of teaching well.

Like Laura Flood, Matthew Daniel Josey did not live long enough to fulfill his marvelous potential. On May 11, 2009, Matt left a local community college, drove to Denver, and never returned. Law enforcement officials—with the help of more than 200 of Matt's friends and family—searched Denver neighborhoods, talking to residents who walked their dogs regularly, going in and out of churches to question their members, and spending time in grocery stores sharing Matt's photo with anyone who would stop and talk with them. Days after the search began, police found Matt's body May 19 in the closet of an apartment where he died after a drug overdose. Although some believed Matt had been murdered, there was little evidence prosecutors could use to pursue this claim.

The two of us met in a small and highly interactive introductory media course offered in the evenings through the Division of Continuing Education at the University of Colorado at Boulder. Matt stood out among his peers. Quiet and intense, he wrote flawless and lyrical prose. The Division of Continuing Education provides students the opportunity to take a few courses without being involved in a degree program, and Matt used the course to investigate the possibility of pursuing journalism as a career. We focused on media ethics and history, and the students wrote several papers dealing with everything from sensationalism and news production to reviews of films that address media responsibilities.

After Matt's death, I wrote a letter to the Boulder Daily Camera; attended his funeral at a Catholic church in Longmont, Colorado; and shared memories about Matt with his family at a restaurant in Niwot, Colorado, as we celebrated his writing ability and laughed about his high school exploits. Tearfully, I gave Matt's final exam to his parents, Eileen and John Josey. Matt made the only "A" on the exam and the highest grade in the class.

On the day of the funeral, the church overflowed with Matt's high school and college friends, a testament to my sense that he had lived an engaged and compassionate life. My letter of May 20, 2009, follows:

> To the Editor:
>
> Thank you for the sensitive coverage of the disappearance and death of Matthew Daniel Josey.
>
> Matt completed the contemporary media course he took with me this spring with the highest "A" in the class. He was a superb writer, was inquisitive about news events, and was dedicated to social change. I told him on April 30 that I couldn't wait to see what he would contribute to the world.
>
> Matt and other students at the University of Colorado challenge and entertain us, and as John Donne acknowledged in one of his meditations, the loss of anyone in our community "diminishes" us all. Certainly, Matt's death is a devastating loss for his family, his friends, and his professors.

My commitment to students and to the educational process is not coincidental. It is the direct result of two experiences, first, the extraordinary people who taught me formally in elementary school, junior high school, high school, and college classrooms, and, second, the caring people who taught me outside the classroom. Because I left my adoptive parents at 15, I knew nothing about balancing checkbooks, buying a car, gaining employment, or purchasing insurance. I relied upon the parents of my college roommates and upon others who reached out to me.

During my freshman year at Baylor University, I encountered one of the first strangers who would become a symbolic touchstone. To this day, I do not know her name. An employee in the bursar's office at Baylor University, she greeted me as I walked up to the counter. Desperate for money, I asked for my work-study paycheck as the bells played Christmas carols in the tower of Pat Neff Hall. The woman told me the checks would not be printed until the first of the new year. Uncharacteristically, I began to cry. The university employee, who could not have anticipated our interaction or my anxiety, gave me money out of her own wallet. Through my tears, I did not note her name. I never repaid her. Until now, I have never thanked her.

Because of incidents such as this one, Baylor University began to exemplify caring and compassion for me. To this day, I marvel at my good fortune in finding a community that embodies Christian values. I have not encountered such a place again, but it was there I learned to reach out to students who need attention, guidance, and financial help.

Rachel Moore lives at the P.O.

One of the most significant people in my personal development is Rachel Hunter Moore. I am not alone. Tributes to her are common and intensely personal.

I did not read another book with the impact of *To Kill a Mockingbird* until I took an honors literature course at Baylor University with Rachel. I have always remembered a certain class that met at 9:30 a.m. Tuesdays and Thursdays during my freshman year. What occurred on those days in Carroll Library changed my life and the lives of my classmates.

The students tramped into our English class across wooden floors, making weekend plans and grumbling about the workload. Sitting at our desks, we waited for someone to call us to order—to give us order. Accustomed to informed and passionate teaching at an institution that celebrates pedagogical excellence, I expected an honors English class to challenge me. I did not expect an experience that would transform my life and make me long to be a teacher.

From the back of the room on one sunny Waco, Texas, day came the voice of a familiar stranger with a thick Mississippi drawl. "I was getting along fine with Mama, Papa-Daddy, and Uncle Rondo, until my sister Stella-Rondo just separated from her husband and came back home again" ("Why I Live at the P.O." 57), the speaker said.

"Mr. Whittaker!" the speaker cried shrilly. "Of course I went with Mr. Whitaker first, when he first appeared here in China Grove, taking 'Pose Yourself' photos, and Stella-Rondo broke us up. Told him I was one sided. Bigger on one side than the other, which is a deliberate, calculated falsehood: I'm the same" ("Why I Live at the P.O." 57).

Surprised and a little embarrassed, the members of the class looked at each other and turned toward the voice. I smiled, knowing precisely what I would see. "Stella-Rondo is exactly twelve months to the day younger than I am and for that reason she's spoiled" ("Why I Live at the P.O." 57), the voice continued. At that moment we were able to get a good look at our guest speaker, who had moved to the front of the classroom. Adorned with a shawl, she clumped along in her heavy shoes and raised her eyes to the ceiling as she complained about her Mississippi family, who were now, according to her, all on her sister's side.

Unpredictable and charismatic, Rachel Hunter Moore had decided to teach "Why I Live at the P.O." by Eudora Welty in a way we would remember. For one and one-half hours two times a week, the classroom was transformed as we studied everything from Welty's short story to Robert Frost's longing to "unite/

My avocation and my vocation/ As my two eyes make one in sight" ("Two Tramps in Mud Time" 277) to William Butler Yeats's understanding of the "deep heart's core" ("The Lake Isle of Innisfree" 140).

Decades later, I would teach journalism and English at a research institution, the University of Colorado at Boulder. During my first few years, I would teach two classes each semester with a total of 550 students. I have been told that teaching is not supposed to be entertainment. On the university level, learning remains a serious endeavor indeed.

However, I often make room for Sister of "Why I Live at the P.O." and her rabble. Once in a while, Sister or another colorful character creeps down the crowded aisles dragging a cane or other prop and gesturing animatedly. I hear Rachel Moore's voice in my memory and see the delight and horror and confusion and embarrassment and smiles on the faces of my students. "She's just crazy," one young woman says to her friend, laughing and gesturing at me. "Yes, she is," I whisper back to them.

Students come to see me during office hours, dressed in their fashionably torn jeans, their turtlenecks, their sweaters, and their snow boots. They ask with all the intensity of 20-somethings, "How did you know what you wanted to do with your life?" I discuss their career options with them, suggest other courses, and recommend internships—wanting to help them as others have helped me. I want to encourage what Wallace Stevens describes as the "blessed rage for order" ("The Idea of Order at Key West" 292). I want them to build a productive and joyful life.

Although I have won teaching awards at Baylor, the University of Denver, and the University of Colorado, I am a pretender. I have never approximated the commitment or the talent of those who were my teachers, those who symbolized the best qualities of the professoriate. Nonetheless, the circle is unbroken.

What I hope for my students is the magic that occurred for me again and again at Baylor University—the magic of finding a teacher who loved life abundantly and who laughed readily, a teacher who communicated by being as well as by speaking, a teacher unafraid to make information entertaining as well as instructive, a teacher who celebrated the pursuit and acquisition of knowledge for its own sake.

Today, when teaching literature and media criticism, I understand, too, the words of Robert Penn Warren in *All the King's Men:* Life is, he believed, made up of events spun together like "an enormous spider web." "If you touch it, however lightly, at any point," he wrote, "the vibration ripples to the remotest perimeter" (200). I remain humble before those at Baylor who touched so many of us and who helped us to define ourselves and to celebrate our days.

Outside the classroom, Rachel Moore and her professor husband Andy J. Moore were just as significant to me as they were when they spoke to their classes from behind the podium. After my freshman year, I spent the summer working with migrants in Stockton, California, and I relied upon the cards, letters, and phone calls from the Moores and from Sherry Castello. I lived with a Latino woman who shared all she had, but she was destitute. At night, I fell asleep to the sounds of mice scurrying and chattering under the bed. They skittered through the shafts that moonlight cast on the wood floors. Out of fear that I would step on one of the rodents, I made certain I did not get up until the sun rose.

I struggled with being without others my age and, as always, stayed one step ahead of poverty. Even in 1973, a university education was expensive, and I had no financial support beyond academic scholarships and a part-time job in the alumni association. While in the Stockton area, I taught classes in Spanish and conducted Sunday School on the migrant farms. I played the piano during church services and engaged with children while their parents toiled in the relentless sun. The work was rewarding but difficult, and I was often homesick for Baylor, for the Castellos, for my friends, and for my professors.

Because of its Christian heritage, Baylor often is accused of being the "Baylor bubble." For me, that description was wholly a positive one: I needed the institutional structure, I needed reassurance about my own self-worth, and I relied upon my teachers for more than they might have realized. Separated from the Waco community I had come to rely upon, I was utterly alone and unsure of myself.

While I was in California, Rachel Moore wrote often, and my heart swelled with gratitude and pride each time I received a letter. I sent her my halting prose and confessed my fears about my financial situation and my academic future. "Speaking of favorites," Rachel wrote in one representative missive, "you know you are a special young lady to us, and we are so very proud of you...We wish you happiness and success in all you attempt, Jan—you know we love you devotedly." Another letter read: "We will be praying for you daily. Know that we admire your courage and your radiant witness in daily life. All semester you have given to me, in so many ways, the rare gift of self. Thank you for your spirit, your friendship, your sharing...We are happy to share your Baylor years."

When I published poetry in campus venues, Rachel focused on me and not on my amateurish cadence. In one particular poem, I wrote about longing for the family that had relinquished me. "Tell me the darkness is gone, that the sparkle of you is no new role, no mask," she responded. When she cleaned out her office before retiring, Rachel sent me a stack of papers I had written for her. I was horrified by the lack of sophistication and grammatical control; I can only imagine how she must have laughed when she read my early attempts at poetry and prose. But she was ever kind, ever patient, ever encouraging.

The "Moores 4," as Rachel and Andy Moore called their family, healed me from wounds I could name and ones I was decades away from understanding. Raw from early betrayals and fearful about my future, I tried to trust their belief in me. "Perhaps they are wrong," I thought. "Perhaps I have simply fooled them." But I didn't think so, and the relationship with them lights my way as I move in and out of my own classes. At the end of each semester, I make time to sit quietly in the empty, topsy-turvy classroom still smelling of potato chips, sneakers, and chalk. I thank God for Rachel and Andy Moore and for Baylor, where I first mapped my own dream.

On Christmas Day 2010, I drove to Colorado Springs to celebrate the 50th anniversary of Rachel Hunter Moore and Andy J. Moore at the Broadmoor Hotel, a historic and most appropriate place for them to enjoy their time together. The temperatures were in the 50s, and the hotel danced with holiday lights. In every hallway and gathering place, one heard the carols of the season. Having recently won the William Payden Faculty Excellence Award at the University of Colorado, I wanted to find a way to tell the Moores again how much I have relied upon their love. In spite of the champagne and the spirit of the season that enveloped us, I found it impossible to communicate how dependent I was on their encouragement during my undergraduate and graduate years.

After a lovely dinner at a restaurant near the hotel, I competed with Andy for the bill, something I rarely do, believing that those who offer to pay for meals often want to express their affection by doing so. "You must be kidding," I said. "You are not paying for Christmas dinner when you have achieved 50 years together. I'm happy when one of my relationships lasts through the weekend."

The joke defused the awkward moment, but I knew I could not say what I really wanted to say: "You must be kidding. You're not paying for Christmas dinner when—without you—I'm not certain I would ever have had this life. I rely upon the University of Colorado and upon my students. Furthermore, you are the closest thing to parents I will ever have, and I thank you from the bottom of my very full heart for this time with you."

I did not say these words. Even when—days later—Rachel sent me a photograph of the three of us in our holiday attire, I could not tell them how precious they are to me, nor would they have believed me if I had articulated decades of appreciation for who they are and how they live.

Listening to Rachel teach "Why I Live at the P.O.," I could not have known that so many years later I would embrace the Moores at the Broadmoor Hotel on their anniversary, could not have known that I would tell them about standing across the street from Eudora Welty's Tudor house, snapping pictures and smiling at the "Dukakis" bumper sticker on the back of Welty's brown Chevrolet. So few things come full circle, feel complete, provide sustenance for the days that lie ahead. But a lifetime of memories of Rachel and Andy Moore—and every magical and heartfelt moment they represent—has done just that.

Teaching is my life's work, as it most assuredly has been theirs. "If there is more important work than teaching, I hope to learn about it before I die" (65), writes Pat Conroy in *My Reading Life.* As one of his beloved teachers lies dying, Conroy sits next to his bedside:

> "Tell me a story," [the teacher] commanded, and I did.
>
> Those were the last words he ever spoke to me, and they formed an exquisite, unimprovable epitaph for a man whose life was rich in the guidance of children not his own. He taught them a language that was fragrant with beauty, treacherous with loss, comfortable with madness and despair, and a catchword for love itself. (76)

Once, after I praised Conroy as a writer who followed in the footsteps of William Faulkner, a student came up to me after class and asked if I knew that one of Conroy's children attended our university. I hoped then and now that Conroy's son or daughter found a professor whose life was "rich in the guidance of children not his own." I hope there was a professor who, like the Moores, taught him or her in "a language that was fragrant with beauty, treacherous with loss, comfortable with madness and despair, and a catchword for love itself."

When I attended college, I had no family. I was proud of my independence, but as I gazed from my dorm room window in Allen Hall during my freshman year, I could see students lining up outside of what was then a barbecue restaurant. The smells were pungent, and I was hungry. I pilfered crackers and other nonperishable items from the dormitory cafeteria during the week and on weekends relied upon invitations to the Castello home and dinners out with the parents of friends. I depended upon the kindness of near-strangers, adults who must have wondered how I could afford tuition when I couldn't afford a sandwich.

Baylor became my home, full of caring and compassionate individuals who went out of their way for me and who encouraged me, made scholarships available to me, and saw that I gained a full-time position at the Waco Tribune-Herald for the remainder of my time as an undergraduate and graduate student.

When faculty members told me I would need a Ph.D from another institution before Baylor would hire me as a faculty member, I applied to the University of Texas at Austin, the University of Denver, the University of Virginia, and Vanderbilt University. I wanted to get a doctoral degree as quickly as possible so that I could return to what had become for me a sacred place.

As was always the case, my financial situation determined my choice. The English department at the University of Denver offered me full tuition and a livable stipend for teaching undergraduate writing and literature. Although I wanted to study Southern literature and culture—and the University of Denver had no such area of specialization—I gratefully accepted the English department's offer.

I knew nothing about Colorado except that it was beautiful. Greg Hurley, one of the young men I had dated in high school, lived in Houston during my time at Baylor. One weekend, he drove four hours to Waco and took me back to Houston for a John Denver concert. While John Denver sang, his production crew played a video of eagles and hawks soaring over a craggy and terrifyingly high mountain range. I listened to "Rocky Mountain High" and vowed to spend at least part of my life in Aspen, Colorado, down the street from John Denver, a man who loved the state so much that he changed his name from "Deutschendorf" to "Denver." Of course, I had absolutely no idea how to accomplish such a thing.

I began the doctoral program in the Department of English at the University of Denver, fully intending to complete the degree and return to Waco. Suspecting that nothing could compete with Rocky Mountain National Park, Breckenridge, or Boulder, I believed the hills and lakes of Central Texas would continue to be my home. On a particularly bleak winter day in Denver, Burton Feldman, one of my English professors, walked with me to the closet in his office and gave me the textbook for his course. Perhaps he knew that I was penniless; perhaps he was simply being kind. I told him how much I wanted to go back to Texas and asked how quickly I could complete my residence work. Professor Feldman wisely and compassionately replied, "Now, Jan. We might grow on you."

It is an understatement to say that the University of Denver and the state of Colorado grew on me, and I have been richly happy here for more than 25 years. As the years whirl past, though, I wonder how much of life is determined by chance and how much by choice. Several years ago, I applied for an endowed chair position in the journalism department at Baylor, and although I was one of two finalists, the position went to a longtime Texas newsman.

Disappointed but not surprised, I remembered Burton Feldman, who warned me that Colorado might grow on me. I realized that much of my sadness about not receiving the job offer was about mortality and last chances. When I lost the opportunity to teach at Baylor and was promoted to full professor at the University of Colorado, I understood that I would not return to the banks of the Brazos River and would not teach literature in the rooms where I had come to love it. Although I was disappointed that I would not come full circle, I remain enchanted with the sunlight along the Flatirons and am intoxicated by the seasons in my home state.

Perhaps it is merely chance that guides our footsteps, perhaps we are unconscious agents of our fate, or perhaps there is some other alchemy at work. In Conroy's *South of Broad,* Leo Bloom considers the role of chance in the lives of those he loves and those who love him: "In all the rules of circuitry and the orbit of planets in their fixed, unbreakable transits, my fate begins to show itself, and I meet the main characters who will take a leading part in the dance, the great arching motion of my life" (507).

My teachers were the "main characters" who took "a leading part in the dance, the great arching motion of my life." But in this and in many other things I am not special. Many of us found our way into Rachel Moore's classroom. In "Beyond the Classroom," an article published in *The Baylor Line,* Lisa Asher writes about others who found refuge in her presence:

> Since her retirement was announced this spring, Moore has received more cards and letters from former students—now friends—than she could possibly respond to. "I've heard from dozens and dozens," she says, rattling off a list of names before stopping herself for a correction. "It's not *Libby* Broyles; it's *Courtney.* Libby is her mother," says Moore, who actually had both in class, several decades apart.
>
> She knew it was time for retirement, she says, when last fall, in one class, she had eight *current* students who were the children of *former* students. "Something just clicked," she says. "I thought, 'I don't feel old, but I am. My goodness, it got here quickly."

> But don't think Moore is going to leave Baylor without a backward glance. In fact, one of the joys of retirement, she says, will be that she'll actually have more time for those long, meaningful discussions with Baylor students that she's loved during her teaching career. "I'll have more freedom to give them more individual attention," she says, "to call and say, 'Come have a hamburger and tell me what's going on.' That's fun." (47)

While it is certainly true that Rachel Moore is a symbol of commitment to students, others at Baylor also gave and continue to give of themselves. A few of them are representative and worthy of mention here:

As I sat in a freshman journalism class taking a quiz over the *Associated Press Stylebook*, a particularly inspiring professor named David McHam leaned over my shoulder and whispered, "Would you like to work for the campus newspaper?" I could not imagine anything more wonderful, but I could only stutter, "Sure. I mean, yes, sir." The students on the Baylor Lariat staff were older than I and infinitely more skilled; while writing for them, I worked hard not to embarrass myself. Eventually, I became executive editor of the Lariat and David McHam left Baylor and taught at Southern Methodist University. On Oct. 20, 2011, in Waco, Texas, hundreds of people gathered at a dinner in his honor—a reminder that I was far from the only person whose life David changed.

J.R. LeMaster, who included my work in one of his publications about Walt Whitman, remains in touch. "Thank you for your book *Reflections in a Critical Eye,*" wrote Jim a few days before Christmas 2009. "It is a treasure of which I am very proud—of the book and of you." On June 10, 2006, Jim, who is a retired scholar in American studies, wrote in a particularly poignant message, "I am both pleased and impressed by your performance as a teacher and a scholar. I am also proud. After 47 years of teaching, one likes to think he has made a difference somewhere."

In a similar message of encouragement and affection, Thomas Hanks, award-winning teacher and Baylor English professor, wrote on Feb. 16, 2008: "Hi, Jan—I just found your name in our department newsletter, and thought back to how very much I enjoyed your company in the past. . . Godspeed, Jan—be assured that I'm still having a lot of fun in the teaching-research-writing life, and that I remember you warmly." During college, my relationship with Tom and his family extended to Lake Shore Baptist Church, where he sang in the choir and jovially greeted his friends and students in the sanctuary each Sunday.

After writing to thank Bob Baird, professor of philosophy at Baylor, for his contributions to my intellectual development, I received the following message on Jan. 12, 2008: "I started to say that you cannot imagine how meaningful and encouraging such a note from a former student is to a teacher, but as a teacher you obviously can so imagine. Thank you for taking the time to write. I assure you that your note will be saved and read again when I need an encouraging word." There might have been a time when I would have considered such a message hyperbolic, but I, too, keep particularly expressive notes from students and reread them when I need an encouraging word. Their missives are treasures.

Of course, I'm not alone in celebrating those who made the classroom experience validating and instructive. In a tribute article published in the summer 2005 issue of the *Baylor Line,* Lisa Asher writes:

> When asked to recall what made their college experience memorable, most former students will begin their list with names of instructors who influenced them, listened to them, counseled them, and taught them much more than the required curriculum. Baylor teachers—be they full professors or first-year lecturers—have historically filled a variety of roles, including mentor, surrogate parent, friend, and even spiritual guide. And students, in return, provide their professors with fresh insights, new perspectives, and, sometimes, relationships that can last a lifetime. (42, 44)

Although I have remained in close contact with Baylor professors, I lost touch with the late Herbert H. Reynolds, who was the president of Baylor during my undergraduate years. As an undergraduate reporter for both the college newspaper and the alumni magazine, I met occasionally with him. When I learned of his death, I wrote the following letter to the alumni magazine in the summer of 2007:

> It was with both sadness and celebration that I read about former Baylor President Herbert H. Reynolds—sadness that he is no longer with us, and celebration for the contributions he made, not only to teaching, research, and service but to individual lives.
>
> When I was editor of the Baylor Lariat and editorial assistant for the *Baylor Line,* Dr. Reynolds met often with me. He recorded our conversations because he insisted on accuracy, and he responded candidly to all my questions. After graduation, I asked Dr. Reynolds for a letter of recommendation, and even in the midst of his staggering responsibilities at the university and his recovery from heart surgery in 1984, he obliged.
>
> As a professor in the School of Journalism and Mass Communication at the University of Colorado at Boulder, I keep his letter as a reminder of the impact those in authority can have on those beginning their careers. In the letter he writes, "She possesses a high sense of responsibility toward her own life and toward the lives of others."
>
> I treasure these words because, although I strive to make them true of me, I know most assuredly that they were true of him. (7-8)

If I have experienced what others describe as "arrested development," it was when I was an undergraduate and graduate student at Baylor University. I prefer to think of this time as one of the happiest in my life. In spite of the fact that during my freshman year I had no funds for books, clothing, or food, I lived among people who cared about one another and who reached out to me.

During my undergraduate years, I had no money to travel and no home to return to. It was during this time that I realized I would never return to El Paso, and I made peace with my past. During Thanksgiving and Christmas when the dormitory closed, I was blessed with friends whose families took me in. On weekends during later years at Baylor, I traveled with friends and roommates to their homes in Dallas and New Mexico and happily spent a few holidays with young men I was dating.

Dot and Robert Dobbs, the parents of my roommate Saralyn, taught me to balance a checkbook and once loaned me $500. When Saralyn and I adopted a German shepherd-border collie mix named Scooter, I heard them whisper to one another, "They're not going to *keep* that dog, are they?" But Dot and Bob Dobbs became a refuge for Saralyn, Scooter, and me whenever we needed an escape from the demands of college life.

Staying with the Dobbs family and their many cats—cats who boasted literary names like "Arthur" and "Ophelia"—provided me with an example of how to reach out to others when I was an adult and had the financial means to do so. I remember with great affection how compassionate Bob Dobbs was. Having lost one of his arms (I never asked how), he sat quietly in a living room chair watching the Dallas Cowboys and petting a cat with his only hand. I loved him and envied his three daughters his presence in their lives.

During my second year at Baylor, I had no income except for student employment at the Baylor Alumni Association, and as editor of the Baylor Lariat, the school newspaper, I had little time to work outside the university. Sherry and Don Castello took me in, although it was a difficult financial period for them. Don had lost his job, and with great sacrifice, they provided for their four children, Bill, Kenneth, Laurie, and Charlie—and for me. In addition, they were parents to Gerry Sevick, now an Episcopal priest in Dallas, who became a rare and special friend. Because of the Castellos, Gerry was able to graduate from what was then East Texas Baptist College and enter the ministry.

Because of these experiences, I am especially attuned to my students who work their way through college, often taking off a semester to work full time before returning to their degree programs. Like Burton Feldman, I offer books to students who cannot afford them. Like Dot and Bob Dobbs, I help students who need to learn life skills in addition to what they can study in books.

Others at Baylor, including the Moores and Genie and Preston Dyer, invited me to babysit for them and to spend time with their families. I remember wonderful fall afternoons and evenings surrounded by the children of those who meant so much to me. Genie was my supervisor during my freshman year as a work-study student for the Baylor Alumni Association. Genie describes the magic of campus life better than I, and although she hears different chimes on a different campus, she understands how reassuring they are as they mark her days.

Genie's affection for others seems to have evolved from her own sense of belonging to a rare university community. In a column published in *The Baylor Line* in the summer of 2005, Genie Hildebrand Dyer writes:

> I love Baylor because it's always been a welcoming and accepting place for me. I transferred here as a junior, and that's a hard transition to make. But I found it relatively easy to do, because people made me feel welcome.

> I love Baylor because I have been a part of it for so long—as a student, as a staff member, at the alumni office and in continuing education, as a parent of a Baylor student, and finally as a faculty member. I love the professors I had, who presented me with new ways of viewing the world; I love the students in my classes and our exchange of ideas…I've experienced Baylor from a lot of different perspectives and found it to be a place that I can appreciate and that appreciates what I have to offer.
>
> I also love Baylor because it's where I started dating my life-mate, Preston. We knew each other before Baylor, but our dating was at Baylor and on this campus.
>
> We live on Guittard Street, which is virtually on the Baylor campus, and that keeps me young—or at least it keeps me *feeling* young. Just being around students and knowing how they are thinking and how they are living keeps you energized.
>
> Being so close and living right here on campus means I really think of Baylor as home, because it is—it's where we live. I love to be in my backyard and hear the chimes of Pat Neff ring. When we've gone on a trip and come back, I hear those chimes and think, "Oh, good, I'm home." Whenever I hear them, I have the comforting feeling that if Pat Neff's chimes are ringing, all's well with the world. (39)

In various publications about the university, tributes to faculty members such as the Moores and Dyers abound, as do the descriptions of particularly memorable classrooms and buildings. Like other alumni, I remember the way in which sunlight flooded the classrooms in the Armstrong Browning Library when Frank Leavell, who graduated from Baylor in 1950, read excerpts during his literature of the American South course. In 2005, Judy Henderson Prather, a 1973 graduate, wrote of him:

> When I reflect on those Baylor professors who most deeply influenced me, Frank Leavell makes the short list. I took him for American Lit and Literature of the South, and he was sponsor of the English honor society. How often since my Baylor years have I affectionately attempted an imitation of that mouthful-of-marbles, Tennessee-drawl, get-right-in-your-face way of speaking he had as I quoted something memorable he said or did.
>
> But it was more than twenty years after graduation before I began to realize just how often I quoted him. I had the opportunity to interview Dr. Leavell prior to his retirement in 1995. During the conversation, I was astonished to hear him say, "You know, Judy, you don't go to college to learn how to make a living. You go to learn how to make a life. You don't go to learn what you can do; you go to learn who you are."
>
> I had often said those words myself, thinking they were mine, but I realized I was just echoing Dr. Leavell. When I told him that, he replied, "That's the thrill of teaching—the widening circle. You throw a stone in the water, and the circle widens. There's a kind of immortality in that."
>
> At Dr. Leavell's funeral, Professor Ann Miller (another one from my short list) quoted Tennyson: "Our echoes roll from soul to soul. And grow for ever and for ever." Like countless others, I will gratefully continue to "echo" my teacher. There's a kind of immortality in that. (79)

Without a doubt, professors and friends at Baylor helped me "learn how to make a life." They also embodied the life I wanted for myself, one spent in the classroom as light spills onto desks and tousled heads. Not once—not ever—have I doubted my decision to spend my life in academia, where chimes in Macky Auditorium now sound the hour on the University of Colorado campus.

So much depends upon red wheelbarrows.

Choosing to teach was a deliberate act, a decision based upon accumulated experience. In our lives, so much depends upon the details, the seemingly inconsequential moments, the scenes we barely notice. So much also depends upon chance and upon our ability to reach out to others at key moments in time. In a tribute to perfect composition and to the power of art, poet William Carlos Williams writes, "So much depends/ upon/ a red wheel barrow" (318). His concept is anything but simple. To turn a day into a work of art—instead of a chaotic series of disjointed events—remains my greatest challenge.

Teaching well depends upon imagining and maintaining an active sense of community, something I gained both from Baylor University and from the church. What some experienced at a Christian educational institution was redundant, merely a reflection of the security they had already enjoyed in their families. For others, living in a small town and attending Baylor was stifling, something they needed to escape in order to embrace the future. For me, Baylor was home, a unique and stabilizing place to which I often return.

For me, teaching well also depends upon a belief system in which students are created by God and deserve my commitment and compassion. I do not privilege Christianity over other world religions, nor do I overlook the way in which people can distort its promise and dilute its power. But I am drawn to the classroom for at least one of the same reasons I am captivated by Southern literature and culture. I am inspired by the life of the historical Christ and the ways in which his teachings can be made relevant.

One of the reasons I am drawn to Southern literature is its biblical allusions and references to churches as familiar locations in the regional landscape. I am also interested in the critiques of religion prevalent in literature by William Faulkner, Flannery O'Connor, and other Southern writers. Having published *Allegory and the Modern Southern Novel* in 1985, I often lecture at conferences and in the classroom about Christian imagery in Southern literature.

Suffice it to say that finding a comfortable religious home has been as challenging for me as finding a family. Certainly, I was at home at Baylor University during my six years as an undergraduate and graduate student. I found my professors in philosophy and religion to be open and interested in diverse perspectives. None of them indoctrinated me. However, I was far more socially liberal than many of my fellow students.

Conversely, on campuses such as the University of Colorado and in towns such as Boulder, Colorado, the word "Christianity" is too often equated with dogma, fundamentalism, or social conservatism. At Colorado Christian University, adjunct professors are required to sign a doctrinal statement and undergo a lengthy interview conducted by human resources personnel. Questions about feminism, gay rights, and reproductive issues are part of the selection process. Since I am a fiscal conservative and a social liberal, I find myself ill at ease when discussing my faith and my political positions at both the University of Colorado and Colorado Christian University.

I do not celebrate the great divide between secular and religious universities, and I believe students at both the University of Colorado and Colorado Christian University deserve a diverse faculty and an opportunity to discuss controversial issues without fear. Christians who disagree with one another also have the right to teach at both institutions and to grow spiritually.

Like most progressives in the 1970s, I believed that no person was better than any other person. I believed in the role of faith—not as a stay against despair or an antidote to mortality—but as a filter that made human interaction more rewarding and life events more significant. I believed in a historical Christ who held small children in his lap and who comforted the afflicted and the disenfranchised, and I struggled to follow in his footsteps.

As a professor at a secular research institution, I have had to explain why I remain devoted to Christian principles; why I am a member of a United Methodist Church that advertises itself as an "open and affirming congregation"; and why I once taught at Rockmont College, which eventually became part of Colorado Christian University. Some are surprised to learn that my first two job interviews were in English departments at Louisiana Baptist College in Pineville and King's College, then in Briarcliff Manor, New York. I assumed I would spend my career teaching in a small church-related school that emphasizes teaching. Although those early dreams were not to be, I am fortunate indeed to be a part of the University of Colorado.

I am also devoted to the church because so many of the people who reached out to me before and after I left El Paso were Christians. Without these people, I do not know what I might have become. I relied upon their love and gradually came to believe that I was worthy of their affection and commitment to me. My self-esteem evolved because of these people and their belief in the divine.

In short, I reject the harsh and punishing faith of my adoptive parents and embrace the compassionate activism of those who reached out to me during my childhood and adolescence. Touchstones include Ruth Harrison Williams, Kay Cates, and Mary Ann Cates, formerly of Alamo, Tennessee; Martha Eugenia Angulo Grimes and her family, formerly of El Paso, Texas; Nancy and the late Earl McCuin, also formerly of El Paso; the Rev. Richard Groves, whom I knew as a youth minister in Waco and again as pastor of Wake Forest Baptist Church in Winston-Salem, North Carolina; and Sherry Boyd Castello and her family, also of Waco. Michael and I traveled to Winston-Salem in order to have Richard Groves preside over our wedding in 1986, a decision we made because of his influence on my life when he was a youth director at the First Baptist Church in Waco.

A desire to follow the teachings of Jesus was and is a part of all their lives, and they showed me that belief—like so many other human inclinations—is both a feeling and an act of will. The faith of my childhood is and is not the faith of my adult years. I continue to trust the teachings of the historical Christ, but I separate the example of his life from the repressive practices of some of his followers. I choose the faith that motivates Martha Eugenia Angulo Grimes and Sherry Boyd Castello. I see Christ's love in their transforming acts of kindness.

It is no surprise, then, that part of what drew me to the literature and culture of the American South is its reliance upon Christian imagery. Whether Southern writers are Protestant, Catholic, agnostic, or atheists with a profound understanding of Christian mythology, their writing reflects the signs and symbols familiar to those who grew up in a land infused with Christian thought. Second, Southern literature and culture emphasize storytelling and reflect a deep respect for the written word. I often have attributed this tendency to the love of Scripture that defines life in the Deep South and elsewhere.

Calling herself a fifth-generation Southerner of Scots-Irish ancestry and a "recovering Calvinist" (xv), Susan Ketchin is one of many literary critics who analyzes the "storytelling tradition common in agrarian, rural cultures" (xiii) and celebrates its contribution to regional literature. In *The Christ-Haunted Landscape: Faith and Doubt in Southern Fiction,* Ketchin cites John Shelton Reed as believing that there is "more agreement in belief and practice among southern Protestants than among non-southern Protestants or Catholics" (xi). She cites Alfred Kazin, who calls religion the "most traditional and lasting form of southern community" (xi). Ketchin writes:

> The distinguishing features of this religious tradition are its strict adherence to biblical teachings and private morality, the notion of a real and active presence of God and Satan in the world, the belief in a factual existence of heaven and hell, and an emphasis on preaching the gospel and saving souls. Strong Calvinist doctrines such as the absolute sovereignty of God and the depravity of human beings, the soul's salvation by grace alone, and the unfathomability of Divine Will constitute a significant underpinning of southern evangelicalism. (xii)

Ketchin cites Charles Reagan Wilson as believing that being born again is the "central and defining religious experience of one's life" (xii). In conclusion, the belief in baptism and a new life in Christ is most certainly at the heart of much Southern culture and literature.

Protestant hymns, a longing for abundant life, and a belief in salvation draw me back to the Christ-haunted South. Sights and smells and familiar voices lure me to Central Texas. "We will have thousands of friends, thousands and thousands and thousands of friends," says Frankie Addams exuberantly in Carson McCullers' novel *The Member of the Wedding.* "We will belong to so many clubs that we can't even keep track of all of them. We will be members of the whole world" (566). I am grateful to belong to both the Baylor and church communities, and I celebrate their contributions to many lives.

McCullers' description of adolescent angst remains one of the most acute and intense ones in all of Southern literature. Although I identify with Frankie's desire to be a part of something larger than myself, I was fortunate to embrace an academic institution early in my life and to find a rewarding profession. I celebrate my college years and the doors they opened for me. Even now, I sometimes hear the strains of "How Great Thou Art" as I awaken, and I thank God for the promise of a new day.

Although I do not use the classroom to indoctrinate students—the classroom is a safe place for them to explore their own ideas and frame their own experiences—I treat it as a sacred space. I believe in the Protestant edict that we are called to service. I might have been happy in any number of careers, but I believe that I am called to teach. While I cannot claim that registering for a literature course with Rachel Moore was anything but chance, I embraced the experience and pursued a career that has brought me great joy and has—I hope—enriched the lives of my students for more than 30 years.

Laura Flood and Matt Josey are my children, too.

Shopping in the Boulder Bookstore, I stopped short. On the cover of a book in the nonfiction section was someone who looked a great deal like Ann Miller, a master teacher during my years at Baylor. Poised and engaged, the figure was gesturing animatedly and was clearly a teacher. I purchased the book immediately and gave copies to others who might find its message inspiring.

In that book, *A Life in School: What the Teacher Learned,* Jane Tompkins advocates a "more holistic way" of defining education and argues for a method that "would never fail to take into account that students and teachers have bodies that are mortal, hearts that can be broken, spirits that need to be fed" (xiii):

> A holistic approach to education would recognize that a person must learn how to be with other people, how to love, how to take criticism, how to grieve, how to have fun, as well as how to add and subtract, multiply and divide. It would not leave out of the account that people are begotten, born, and die. It would address the need for purpose and for connectedness to ourselves and one another; it would not leave us alone to wander the world armed with plenty of knowledge but lacking the skills to handle the things that are coming up in our lives. (xvi)

Because of her own commitment to those who mentored and supported her, Tompkins longs to connect with her students, to acknowledge that knowledge is not entirely cerebral, and to address the loneliness that afflicts us all. Coming to terms with her feelings about herself and her academic life, Tompkins suggests how to assess how we really feel:

> In TV commercials, when people wake up in the morning the sun comes streaming in their windows, falling lavishly on their bedclothes, spilling onto the floor. The atmosphere is bathed in light. The air is dancing. Who wouldn't want to wake up under such conditions? When I got up, it was dark. It's usually dark inside houses in the morning, and cold, too. What matters, though, is not the dark or the cold, but the spirit of the waker. This is where the bodies are buried. You want to know what's going on in someone's life? Ask them how they feel first thing in the morning. (9)

Like many of those who spend their lives in the academy, Tompkins immersed herself in books while she was growing up. Provocatively, she writes about the function of literature and thereby reveals a great deal about herself and her desire for security. She finds both escape and safety between the covers of books. "Then there was reading in bed," Tompkins writes. "A great pleasure and comfort, for a book made you feel doubly safe. Safe from the world and safe even from your own thoughts, though I wouldn't have put it that way then" (43).

Tompkins' life parallels mine in that she fell in love with literature and enjoyed her classroom experiences when she was young. Like me and so many others, she decided to go to graduate school in order to prolong the joy and sense of belonging that the classroom offers. She writes about herself and her classmates in graduate school, celebrating the mind and heart:

> It was love that had brought us there, students and professors alike, but to listen to us talk you would never have known it. The love didn't have a conjugation or a declension; it couldn't be articulated as a theory or contained in a body of information. It wasn't intellectual—that was the shameful thing—though it had an intellectual dimension. Being amorphous, tremulous, pulsing, it was completely vulnerable. So we all hid it as best we could, and quite successfully most of the time. (79).

In this excerpt and others, Tompkins challenges the separation of the heart from the mind and reminds fellow academics that passion lies at the heart of the intellectual enterprise: "It's commonly supposed that the suppression of passion makes for intellectual development," she writes. "When the horses of passion are under control, the thinking goes, reason holds sway and progress can be made. In my experience just the reverse is true" (81).

A Life in School challenges not only preconceptions about the role of the intellect in higher education but the importance of teaching. Tompkins asks tough questions about why we teach and how we are trained. She suggests that most professors know very little about their role in the classroom and about how to relay information effectively. She writes:

> When I look back on it now, I'm amazed that my fellow Ph.D.'s and I were let loose in the classroom with virtually no preparation for what we would encounter in a human sense. If nothing else, I wish I had been warned about what an ego-battering enterprise teaching can be. Teaching, by its very nature, exposes

the self to myriad forms of criticism and rejection, as well as to emulation and flattery and love. Day after day, teachers are up there, on display; no matter how good they are, it's impossible not to get shot down. (90)

As though she is describing the best teachers whom I remember and emulate at Baylor University, Tompkins challenges college professors to consider their audiences and to make the classroom experience safe and encouraging for students. She writes:

> Yet I believe that school should be a safe place, the way home is supposed to be. A place where you belong, where you can grow and express yourself freely, where you know and care for the other people and are known and cared for by them, a place where people come before information and ideas. School needs to comprehend the relationship between the subject matter and the lives of students, between teaching and the lives of teachers, between school and home. (127)

Focusing upon the real lives of the students who populate the campus, Tompkins acknowledges the human element in making education work and juxtaposes the life of the classroom with real life. She confesses that she was unprepared for the world outside of the academy, and when she confronts it, she wants to return to the familiar:

> Though there was always fear associated with sitting in rows—am I too different? will I pass the test? does anybody like me?—the desks and chairs and tasks provided an escape from fear by giving me something definite to do. Add the column of figures. Learn the causes of the war.
>
> Now, wandering the world outside of school, having transcended "rows," nothing to do, no place to go, I am terrified. In the huge, dark, unfurnished world without rows, I cower and tremble. Give me back Mrs. Colgan. Let me be in 1B again. Let me learn to add, to subtract, to carry and to borrow numbers. Give me a problem to do.
>
> I see the light-filled classrooms, rows on rows, desks, chairs, waiting to be filled: let the lesson begin. "Our first assignment will be to learn the periodic table." Let me back in. Please. Let me sit down again, open my notebook to the first blank page, start writing. When is the exam? (155)

As though she is quoting Frank Leavell, Tompkins suggests that education is not as much about learning particular skills as it is about helping students interact successfully with others, to learn self-discipline, to learn to laugh and to enjoy the day, and to pay tribute to the role of passion in our lives. "Although parents might object—what, all that tuition and no ticket to financial security and social success?—it would be more helpful to students if, as a starting point, universities conceived education less as training for a career than as the introduction to a life" (223), Tompkins says.

I revel in the time I spend in the classroom, but my commitment to students extends to helping them learn to write and speak effectively and with greater confidence. Critiquing verbal and written expression requires that I be both sensitive and demanding, encouraging and honest. It is not an easy line to walk.

I try to confess my own blunders and help the students to learn from theirs. Professors often keep examples of particularly amusing student prose, and although I do not belittle students—having made many of the same mistakes myself—a few excerpts from course evaluations and correspondence suggest why my colleagues and I emphasize effective writing.

For example, a student in a 1998 media history class wrote on an evaluation form: "Every day is a different day, something new. She tries to connect the history with our *lifes* and make it *relivent.*" Apparently, the student did not enjoy everything about the class, however, since a complaint follows: "She grades writing assignments *to* hard, pays attention to *gramatical* stuff more *then* content" (the italics are mine). A student in a critical thinking and writing course in 2005 writes that she hated the "quizes" and recommends that I "not grade so difficultly," saying that I am "very strickt on grammer."

Some of the messages that bring a smile to my face come by e-mail. Although I do not find it humorous that the student who wrote the following message in 2005 is worried about his friend, I do find his explanation for his absences quite interesting:

> Miss Whit this is Colby, i have been trying to email u for the last week about my project I hope you got at least one of my emails, there seems to be a problem with me reaching you. I told you that there had been an emergency and that is why I wasn't able to be in class. I found out a few weeks ago that my friend was getting worse. He has an illness which slowly eats away at his ablities. He came out this week to visit my friend and I. I am just trying to spend as much time with him as I can that is why I haven't been in class. This has been hard to everyone involved in this situation. I hope you cam understand why I haven't been in class and why I haven't been there for my project, I really want to figure something so i will call once my friend has left.

Below are two other messages, the first in 2006 from a student named Nick and the second in 2004 from Lauren. The first is amusing because of the last line; the second, because the student thanks me for helping her to become a better "writter":

> dear jan,
>
> i know you gave us a fairly detailed guide for the test, but im still confused. do we need to know anything on the early development of television? i think it might save me time to skip the review of chapter 8, but im unsure. please help, im lost in pages of confusion and i think my mind is going to explode.

Here is Lauren's assessment of our class at the end of the semester:

> hey its Lauren. i was just rememinding you to send me my grade. i had a great time in your class this semester, you were an awesome teacher and even though

> i cant beat those comma splices, i feel like you have definately helped me become a better writter. thanks again and sorry to dissappoint you on the rewrites.

One of my favorite messages is from Phil, who wrote on March 12, 2008, and apologized for missing an appointment: "I want to apologize for not coming to see you yesterday," he said. "I misread your message. I thought it said sue me instead of see me. I will come by tomorrow after class."

I do not keep only the humorous correspondence. Sometimes the messages students send make it clear that they are feeling vulnerable. One young man named Fred, who signed his otherwise anonymous course questionnaire, wrote: "Before your class I'd been at a school for six years since my father passed away. I tried getting back in before, but you are the first teacher since high school that I've just loved. Thank you."

It is not possible to enjoy the students more than I do. However, like Nick, I often feel "lost in pages of confusion" and "think my mind is going to explode." Because of the opportunity to interact with motivated young people and to repay those who reached out to me so long ago, I often can't wait for the next semester or a new school year to begin.

There are other voices, other rooms.

Long before I knew of my origins and my Tennessee homeland, I fell in love with the sometimes stark and sometimes lyrical prose of the South. It was a classroom on the ground floor of the Armstrong Browning Library at Baylor University that proved my undoing. On one particularly memorable day, Frank Leavell lowered his tall frame briefly into a chair at the front of the room before leaping back onto his feet and beginning a lecture about the history and literature of the American South.

Professor Leavell's class became one of many transformative experiences during the 1970s, and, as Tompkins suggests, students responded to the subject matter because a passionate professor confided in us his fears and discontents. He let us know him, let us in. The real world meshed with the stories that lay between the covers of our books, and we were our teacher's trusted companions on a well-traveled road.

One either might celebrate the college classroom or find its archaic and often immutable practices stultifying. For my part, I loved its four walls and its sense of order and higher purpose. I loved the smell and the feel of books. Although I reveled in journalism, music, photography, psychology, religious studies, and other classes, I came to revere especially the printed word. Specifically, I became a devotee of literature and culture, especially the writers of the 20th-century American South.

In *The Literature of Memory: Modern Writers of the American South,* Richard Gray writes about the following "brave madmen": James Agee, Truman Capote, James Dickey, Randall Jarrell, Carson McCullers, Flannery O'Connor,

William Styron, Peter Taylor, Robert Penn Warren, Tennessee Williams, and Thomas Wolfe (220). As I worked my way through college as a reporter at the Waco Tribune-Herald, the words of these unreconstructed Southerners became my escape into a world of red clay, dense forests, and whippoorwills.

In real life, I wrote farm copy, covered crime, and edited obituaries from 2 to 11 p.m.; then, late into the night, I studied literature and other texts for classes in the morning. Paying tuition and living expenses was exhausting, but I didn't complain: With each morning came new friends and new books and a new confidence in myself.

I learned to analyze character and to dissect plot and theme. I gravitated to the New Critics, also known as the Agrarians, who called Vanderbilt University their home and who championed rural values and physical labor. In 1915, a group of students that included Donald Davidson, Allen Tate, and Robert Penn Warren met weekly with John Crowe Ransom, their professor, to discuss philosophy and literature. From 1922 to 1925, they published *The Fugitive,* a regional poetry magazine. In 1930, 12 writers, including poets, a journalist, and a historian, published *I'll Take My Stand,* a manifesto that deals with civility, courtesy, families, farming, the land, manners, and the past.

For an entire generation of literary scholars, the New Critics' belief that the text is preeminent became central. I learned to read and analyze literature by employing formalism and relying upon the tenets established in Ransom's 1941 *The New Criticism.* The literature into which I had escaped as a child became even more wondrous. The New Critics did not ignore class, gender, geography, race, regionalism, or religion; they simply believed that an author such as Flannery O'Connor could be significant to readers even if they did not know (or care) that she was a Catholic. Formalism gave literary critics special authority, and I began to enjoy scholarship as much as I loved teaching.

In Professor Leavell's classroom, I began to consider the importance of my birthplace, Knoxville, Tennessee. The cities and rural areas of East Tennessee lay at the heart of Agrarian philosophy, and Vanderbilt and the New Critics held a strong allure. Tennesseans of literary note include James Agee, Cleanth Brooks, Donald Davidson, Shelby Foote, Andrew Lytle, John Crowe Ransom, Allen Tate, and Peter Taylor.

The documentary "Appalachia: A History of Mountains and People" describes an Appalachian renaissance in country music, folklore, and literature during the 1920s. Writers featured in the documentary are Tennesseans Ron Eller, a historian; Tom Gish, an editor; and Thomas Wolfe, a novelist. Others included in the documentary are Wendell Berry, Annie Dillard, Charles Frazier, Nikki Giovanni, Barbara Kingsolver, Bobbie Ann Mason, and Lee Smith. Together, these women and men helped to tell the story of Appalachia and to combat the prevailing stereotypes of ignorant, lazy, and violent hillbillies.

Ray Willbanks highlights the literature and culture of Tennessee, where my ancestors settled and where most of them remain. He writes in the *Literature of Tennessee* that the hills of East Tennessee are an area "rich in individuality and folklore" (vii). Most students of American history and literature have read about the Dayton, Tennessee, Scopes trial of 1925, which culminated in the play *Inherit the Wind* (1955) by Jerome Lawrence and Robert Edwin Lee. In addition to individual works of literature, the "flatlands" (vii) of Western Tennessee, Willbanks writes, contributed black and Native American culture, while the Cumberland Plateau of Central Tennessee is known for frontier humor and local color (vii-viii).

Well-known Tennessee writers include James Agee, who was born in Knoxville and wrote *The Morning Watch* and *A Death in the Family;* Cleanth Brooks; Donald Davidson, who grew up in rural Middle Tennessee; Shelby Foote, who was born in Mississippi but claimed Tennessee as his home; Nikki Giovanni, who was born in Knoxville; Andrew Lytle; John Crowe Ransom, who grew up in Middle Tennessee; Peter Taylor, who was the grandson of a three-term Tennessee governor and who was born in Trenton in West Tennessee; Allen Tate; and Robert Penn Warren, who was born in Kentucky but attended high school in Tennessee.

The literature and culture of the American South both seduce and alienate readers. Stereotypes of ignorant hillbillies, racists, trailer park trash, and other such negative images abound. In the film "Sweet Home, Alabama" (2002), for example, a perturbed Melanie Smooter (Reese Witherspoon) says: "People need a passport to come down here." Although the line elicits laughter, the statement is also an acknowledgement that the Old South haunts the New South and that one road trip to Atlanta does not a Southern aficionado make.

"The truth is, it goes by quickly, doesn't it?"

In college, I devoted myself to earning a living at the local newspaper, to reading with a new eye and a new purpose, and to making the most of every moment of a blessed and happy life. More than three decades later, I am in my office late at night, reading e-mail messages from my passionate, frustrating, determined, and often charming students.

Since 1978, I have been at home in the classroom. I read excerpts from Franz Kafka's *The Stranger* and William Faulkner's *Light in August* and Michael Cunningham's *The Hours.* I communicate my enchantment with the poetry of Emily Dickinson and T.S. Eliot and Gerard Manley Hopkins. I screen film excerpts and debate the meaning of phenomenology with students.

Visiting me on summer evenings in my suburban home, students gather outside on the patio and talk about the parents they love and the homes that define and shelter them. They share their fears about growing up and articulate their dreams. I listen far more than I speak. I marvel at their maturity and their desire to contribute to a world that must be both inviting and mystifying.

The students I greet each day know that they will probably change careers an average of seven times. (Their parents are terrified; the students, on the other hand, often are giddy with anticipation.) They know that William Randolph

Hearst built a castle in San Simeon and that I want them to visit it. They know that gender issues in advertising matter and that they can continue the work begun by Jean Kilbourne and Warren Farrell by creating new images of women and men in popular culture. They have read *Fried Green Tomatoes at the Whistle Stop Café, Bastard Out of Carolina, The Heart Is a Lonely Hunter, Invisible Man,* and other Southern novels that challenge normative beliefs about race, ethnicity, and sexual orientation.

As I run to a media studies class one warm fall night, I cross the street and am greeted by Tori Peglar, a former student who is riding home on her bicycle, her pajama-clad infant daughter wearing a helmet and strapped into a seat on the back of her mother's bicycle. "Tori!" I shout. "I'm so happy to meet your beautiful baby at last. Does she know she'll be expected to ride bicycles, hike, rock climb? She must be exhausted thinking about it. Well, it's wonderful to see you." We embrace, and she rides away, lost in the Colorado night. And I have promises to keep and a room full of freshmen waiting across campus for class to begin.

On May 7, 2009, Tori wrote to invite me to an event connected to her role as director of alumni association communications. "Your energy, enthusiasm and intelligence never cease to amaze me," she said. "I owe where I am today to you for mentoring me through the Critical Thinking and Writing classes, then helping me get work in the writing program. Both jobs have helped me tremendously in my job as editor. Thank you!"

On Aug. 1, 2011, I received a message from a former student named Kim. I wish students could know how much they elevate our spirits when they take time to reconnect. Kim writes:

> Dear Professor Whitt,
>
> You won't remember me but in 1992 I applied for admission to CU. I'd previously attended another school in upstate New York and for a number of reasons had a very poor GPA. CU duly rejected my application, but you made a case for me and I was therefore accepted. Just thought you should know that your efforts were not in vain. After graduating in 1997 with a double major in English and Asian Art History (minor in Physical Anthropology) I went off to teach English in China and then Korea. Subsequently, I worked for *Town and Country* magazine. In 2003 I moved to London where I continued my education. I have just completed my Ph.D. at University College London, Institute of Archeology.
>
> None of these adventures would have been possible if you had not supported my application to CU. So, thank you very much. You took a chance and I very much appreciated it at the time and even more so now.
>
> I wish you the very best luck…and hope that you personally are happy and well.

I do not remember this particular student, but I like to think of her as representative of all those who find their way. I appreciate her gratitude, but, in fact, students such as these will succeed with or without my help. I do recognize in her message the same kind of appreciation I feel toward so many of those who cared about me. I simply pay it forward.

As students stream in and out of my office and years go by, I realize that it's past time to say "thank you" to their parents. I want to thank them for their children, for the generations of students that make me smile every morning when I wake. I decided early in my life not to have children, but I will continue to know, and choose, and love the children that belong to others.

Dressed in hiking boots and loaded down with backpacks and textbooks, these young people visit me during office hours and greet me as we collide serendipitously in the middle of campus. These young people share their fears, tell me about their most recent loves and losses, and ask my advice about careers. I know the best of these children—these children who are not my own.

In one university annual review, the faculty appraisal committee addressed a statement I made in my report to them. Members of the committee wrote: "Consider the implication of saying, 'Teaching is my primary emphasis' in a research institution." I smiled, knowing that the suggestion was a not so thinly veiled criticism of my priorities. Truthfully, I have considered the implication, and I am joyfully, hopefully, overwhelmingly grateful for the opportunity to teach, to engage with, and to grow with these extraordinary students.

Daily, I am surprised by how fast the days go by, how much more I want to do with them. In the film "Something's Gotta Give" (2003), Erica Barry (Diane Keaton) and Harry Sanborn (Jack Nicholson) walk on the beach and share their surprise at how quickly life spins past them. "But the truth is, it goes by fast, doesn't it?" Barry asks. "Like the blink of an eye," Sanborn replies.

In many ways, I am still the freshman who sat wide-eyed in my first college literature class. I identify with so many of my students, especially those who question, who argue, who push against boundaries, who send me e-mails at midnight. These young people have made my life in the academy a joy, a challenge, and a privilege.

Conclusion. Reconstructed (But Unregenerate)

On Oct. 29, 1986, I picked up my mail as I walked to class at the University of Denver. I sighed as I recognized the Tennessee Department of Human Services return address on the thin envelope. The news from the agency was never good, and this envelope appeared to contain only one sheet of paper.

For more than 10 years, I had been writing to the human services department. New laws made it possible for an adopted child to leave a letter on file asking for contact with his or her birth mother. I had written such a letter. Then I had settled in for what I was certain would be a long—probably fruitless—wait.

I walked to the front of the classroom, dropped my books on the desk, greeted the students, and wrote the day's agenda on the blackboard behind me. As the students took a quiz, I unfolded the letter. It read:

> At your request and in accordance with the Tennessee Adoption Law a search was initiated for your birth mother.
>
> Your birth mother has been located and she has given the Department permission to release to you her identity. She is Mrs. Nadine Miracle, 6331 Pleasant Ridge Road, Apartment 1103, Knoxville, Tennessee 37921.
>
> We would appreciate your letting us know when you contact your birth mother.

I stood in front of my class, unable to move or to think clearly. Somehow, I completed a lecture about the history of newspapers and then fled to my office to call my husband and to think about what to do next.

I decided that writing to my mother would be better than calling, that she could ignore a letter if she chose to do so, that she might have changed her mind about wanting to know me. Even though she had responded immediately, I was convinced there had been an error. Perhaps I was someone else's child. Perhaps the information at the Tennessee Department of Human Services was inaccurate. "Miracle," I said aloud to myself. "What an unusual name."

On Nov. 4, 1986, I wrote to my mother. I remember thinking that there should be a template for such a letter. I remember wondering how many times a lost child had sought, identified, and contacted a parent. In part, my letter reads:

> Thank you so much for being willing to let me contact you. I was so afraid that you would be worried about hearing from me, and I want very much for you to know that I have only positive feelings about you and have wanted to know about your life and your other children for many years. More than anything else, I want to thank you for giving birth to me. I understand that you had seven children when I was born, and I know what a struggle we all must have been for you…
>
> I wanted to call you this week because knowing where you are has been the answer to many prayers. However, I was afraid I would cry, and my husband suggested that a letter would be kinder to you. Therefore, I want you to have this picture of me and to think about whether or not you want to meet me. Mike and I would love to come to Knoxville soon...I can't tell you how many questions I have, or how fond I am of you—even without knowing you.
>
> Please write to me if you feel comfortable doing so. I am enclosing my home address and phone number below. I hope that you will not always be a stranger to me.

What followed is a blur. After visiting my mother at Thanksgiving, I received a letter from her. Dated Dec. 2, 1986, the correspondence reveals her insecurity and pain. I wish I could have reassured her. I also wish that she and I could have had more time together before she died in 1996. I treasure her correspondence:

> I'm sorry I didn't get to talk to you more. After you saw and talked to your sisters and brothers, I had planned to bring you to my house so I could be alone with you which didn't work which my plans never do. It seems the Lord gave me one more chance to be with you which I failed. I hope your visit wasn't too disappointing…I never stopped missing you, no matter how much I loved my other children…I love you so much if I do make so many mistakes in my life. I have to quit writing now. I can't keep from crying. With all my love, your mother.

I cannot explain what it is like after more than 30 years of searching to find one's mother. The chance that the Tennessee Department of Human Services—

in a time before the Internet—could have located her is miniscule. The chance that she was willing to communicate with me is even more miniscule. But miraculously, my mother lived where human services staff members could locate her.

Nadine Elizabeth Nash Miracle is my mother. She was willing to meet me. And out of all my days on this earth, I was able to spend a special one with her.

Reading great books saved my life.

Written by Tennessean John Crowe Ransom, "Reconstructed But Unregenerate" is an essay about the culture and literature of the American South and about protecting our integrity and maintaining our character. An explanation of formalism and a description of what is best about the South, the essay also is personal.

I pilfered the title of Ransom's famous essay because Ransom is a Tennessean, because he is a proud Southerner, and because being reconstructed and unregenerate is his description of himself and of his homeland. I, too, am reconstructed—changed by what I have experienced, by the people I have known, and by the books I have read. I am also unregenerate—willing to learn from my mistakes, determined to embrace the world around me, adept at survival.

A proud son of the South, Ransom is changed but defiant. The first paragraph of the essay establishes Ransom's regional sensibilities:

> It is out of fashion in these days to look backward rather than forward. About the only American given to it is some unreconstructed Southerner, who persists in his regard for a certain terrain, a certain history, and a certain inherited way of living. He is punished as his crime deserves. He feels himself in the American scene as an anachronism, and knows he is felt by his neighbors as a reproach. (1).

Sometimes we reconstruct ourselves; sometimes, the changes occur against our will. Either way, we are a patchwork quilt of experiences and relationships. I am fortunate to know the people who look like me, fortunate to know my name, fortunate to live life abundantly. At long last, I know more fully who I am.

While conducting research for a chapter about the television series "Men of a Certain Age," I discovered an essay by an anonymous black man who also sought and found his mother. Calling himself Thaddeus Goodavage, he attributes his inability to form long-lasting and sustaining relationships to his adoption and to growing up in a dysfunctional adoptive home. "I began to see how my history limits me from reaching my potential in the world, particularly as an intimate partner (because the most intimate historical space for me—my relationship with my mother and father—was so unusual" *(Faith of Our Fathers* 225-26), he writes.

Having sought his biological family for many years, Goodavage learned that his father was dead and his mother had tried—twice—to abort him, once with a coat hanger and once with pills. She was 14 years old when she became pregnant. She was white; the author's father, black. The author was determined to locate his mother—no matter what the emotional cost –and the meeting was transformative. "She knew me," he writes, and with those words, he speaks for me as well. Nadine Elizabeth Nash Miracle and I were intimate strangers, as were he and his mother. He writes:

> Trains, planes, and a rental car finally brought me face to face with the woman whom I had grown inside of. When I saw her nose, her hair, her chin, her ears, her face, her shape, her walk, her laugh, I felt a different kind of link to the earth. I felt a different kind of link to myself. We communicated with the movements and gestures and feelings and hopes and sadnesses that only we knew. She knew me. This was quite a significant experience for me, and I felt as if my loneliness was fading. *(Faith of Our Fathers* 222)

As I addressed in Chapter 1, the flip of the coin, the luck of the draw, the roll of the dice determine much of who we are; in other cases, we are the result of decisions that we make. At the end of our lives, the sum of our actions, beliefs, and relationships constitute a story. Those who write memoirs have the opportunity to construct their stories with impunity, but we all tell the stories of our lives—often in excerpts over cups of coffee with friends, during a road trip, or over long romantic dinners. We want to tell our own stories. We believe we know them best.

Rain on a Strange Roof is primarily a "literary memoir," a manuscript about the power of literature to comfort, instruct, and transform. It is at its heart a narrative about those who spend their lives immersed in books and how such an existence both comforts and unsettles them. In *My Reading Life,* Pat Conroy pays tribute to the authors and the narratives that changed him: "I've always wanted to write a letter to the boy I once was, lost and dismayed in the plainsong of a childhood he found all but unbearable," Conroy writes. "I believe that the reading of great books saved his life" (322). Like Conroy, I am quite certain that reading saved my life and that it sustains me now.

Those who love literature understand the purpose of Conroy's literary memoir and my own: Books provide fictional and non-fictional maps. *Rain on a Strange Roof* is a thinly disguised celebration of the humanities and their essential role in human life and in the academy. It is through literature that some of us understand ourselves and learn to contribute to the world. It is through literature that some of us are saved.

"And so they are ever returning to us, the dead."

My Appalachian mother and father are buried in Tennessee. Victims of poverty, they were not accomplished people. Rutherford Hurst finished the eighth grade; Nadine Elizabeth Nash Miracle graduated from high school. Out of 11 children, I am the only one whom my mother relinquished for adoption.

Determined to escape a difficult childhood, I learned to love school and to rely upon my teachers for affection and encouragement. I spent 12 years gaining a bachelor's degree in journalism and English, a master's degree in English, and a doctorate in English. By some standards, I am accomplished. I am a college professor, I am financially independent, and I am a successful scholar and teacher. However, a vague, directionless longing sometimes descends upon me like fog, a ghostly whisper, a haunting.

I know Addie Bundren and Byron Bunch now, and I will never read *As I Lay Dying* or *Light in August* in the same way again. My great-grandparents David Washington Bundren and Mary Barlow Bundren gaze solemnly at me from a 1912 photograph. Hard work awaited them after the shutter snapped. In another photograph, my father holds a rifle and stares back at me without expression. I try to read his eyes. But I was not yet born when the photograph was taken—an unsettling thought—and in 2012 I will be 57, the same age Rutherford Hurst was when he died alone in his car at the end of a road in Claiborne County, Tennessee.

I want to know their stories, want to hear their voices, want to make peace with the people who left me to find my own way. Literature replaced the emptiness with magic, with evanescent whispers. I don't know why—as a freshman at a university in Texas—I was drawn to the literature of the Deep South, particularly works by William Faulkner, but I no longer speculate. Like "Hurst," "Nash," and "Miracle," "Bundren" and "Bunch" are names that connect me to my sister, my half-sister, my cousins, and the fictional residents of Yoknapatawpha County.

"Bundren" devolved from "Bondurant," changed by my forbears who left France and made a home in the New World. "Miracle," like "Merckel," "Merkel," and "Markel," originated in Germany. "Hurst" is English and Scottish. I am part French, part English, and part Scottish, and the blood of the Melungeon people also runs through my veins. I am a child of Appalachia.

When Michael Danny Whitt and I returned from our 1986 pilgrimage to Knoxville, I was more quiet than usual, concentrating on the memory of my mother's face and on how I might locate information about my father. Never one for too much introspection, Michael asked if I planned to change my name to "Miracle." I said the academic community already knew me as "Jan Whitt." Without changing expression, Michael suggested I hyphenate my name—"Miracle-Whitt"—and consider having a son whom we could name "Kraft."

I remain deeply grateful to Michael, who once said I was the other side of his coin. Without his encouragement and without his having hired an attorney and a private investigator, I would not have located my two birth certificates or my family history. I would most certainly never have met my mother before she died. He cannot understand his contribution—any more than anyone who possesses extensive information about his family can understand—but he was willing to accompany me to Tennessee and all it represents.

I am rich with family, part of a tradition all my own. I have written a story of the past—one detail at a time. I live in the present with a deepening sense of what has been. For all adopted children, some of what came before is real; some, forever elusive. In *Requiem for a Nun,* Faulkner writes, "The past is never dead. It's not even past" (535). Shadowy figures invade my sleep and my waking hours, demanding attention. Some of those who appear in my subconscious moments originate in my everyday life—students, colleagues, friends. Others who invade my thoughts are strangers—my father, my grandmothers and grandfathers, all but two of my siblings, all but a few of my cousins. I long to be part of their lives, but they are lost to me.

Winfried Georg Sebald, former professor of German and author of *The Emigrants,* writes hauntingly: "And so they are ever returning to us, the dead" (23). For Sebald, history is a mosaic, not a linear progression. Images we thought we had forgotten resurface. Thoughtlessly or cruelly spoken, certain words and phrases echo in memory. I am drawn to Sebald's tales of the dead, to the tribute he pays to remembrance. Able to name my mother and my father at last, I am aware of my mortality. *Memento mori.* My sense of self, once spectral, has become a hymn of praise, a liturgical celebration of identity.

I was not there when Nadine Elizabeth Nash Miracle died Feb. 19, 1996. I did not know she died. Years later, I read her obituary with its formulaic style and neutral tone. Her funeral was at 8 p.m. Feb. 21, 1996, at Gentry-Griffey Chapel in Knoxville, Tennessee. The Rev. Richard Mellon officiated.

My mother died four days before my birthday. I wonder what I was doing the day she left me a second time. I wonder if I took my golden retrievers on a walk that day. I wonder if I finished reading a novel in preparation for class. I wonder if I was watching television, or listening to Vivalde, or enjoying dinner with friends when she left this world. I try to imagine standing at the gravesite during the interment service at Bell's Campground Cemetery.

My mother's funeral program includes a well-known excerpt from the Bible, which begins, "I will lift up mine eyes unto the hills, from whence cometh my help" (King James Version, Psalm 121.1). I wonder if she looked up into the hills. I wonder if she found help there. I was not at my mother's side when she died. But Nadine Elizabeth Nash Miracle is my mother, and if anyone were to ask, I would say that I loved her.

In *South of Broad,* Pat Conroy introduces Starla and her brother Niles, orphans whose mother and grandmother abandoned them. Their memories of their family resonate for those of us without family. Niles and Starla discuss their sadness with their friends and try to explain the hope that kept them alive and their reluctance to let that hope go:

> "We never saw our mama again. We never saw Meemaw either.That night we began our lifelong tour of orphanages. Starla and I always thought they were going to find us. We heard they both went to prison. We knew that when they got out, they wouldn't quit until they found us. That dream kept us going for all these years. That dream and nothing else," Niles said.
>
> "I've still got that dream," Starla said. "I need them to hold me again."
>
> "I'll show you their graves tomorrow," Niles said. "They're in the family plot up the hill a ways." (396)

Starla dreams about connection. Niles understands the futility of her dream. Throughout Conroy's novel, protagonist Leo Bloom identifies with and reaches out to Starla and Niles, trying to understand the depth of their loss. "I think about Niles in the orphanage on the day I met him, and guess he had wanted someone, anyone, to hold his hand during the long, dreadful forced march of his childhood" *(South of Broad* 461), he says. I understand the longings Starla and Niles express in their own awkward and dissimilar ways. I grieve for their inability to come home.

I acknowledge that not all adoptions are ill fated. I celebrate those who find caring and embracing parents. But as soon as I was old enough, I fled the abuse and despair before it crippled me. The long and terrible silence that characterized my relationship with my adoptive parents reminds me of Dr. Benedict Copeland's daughter Portia, who says, "It don't take words to make a quarrel" *(The Heart Is a Lonely Hunter* 65). As novelist Carson McCullers understood, sometimes a relentless grief obliterates whatever love might have been possible.

I do not forgive my adoptive parents because to forgive them is to forget what I learned and to dilute my passionate advocacy for others. "I could grant no amnesty to the man who did not touch me as a child except when he was backhanding me to the floor" (486), Tom Wingo says of his father Henry in *The Prince of Tides.* Anger made it possible for me to escape, and it protects me still.

I grew up in a house held together by what author Pat Conroy calls "laws of concealment and secrecy": "I learned that silence could be the most eloquent form of lying" (420), he writes in *The Prince of Tides.* In the novel, Tom Wingo loves his parents in spite of the horrors he and his siblings Luke and Savannah endure, but he regrets his complicity in keeping the family's dark secrets:

> It was a private and binding covenant entered into by a country family remarkable for its stupidity and the protocols of denial it brought to disaster. In silence we would honor our private shame and make it unspeakable.
>
> Only Savannah broke the agreement, but she did it with a wordless and terrible majesty. Three days later, she cut her wrists for the first time.
>
> My mother had raised a daughter who could be silent but could not lie. (420)

After they confront their childhood pain and begin to heal, Tom and Savannah Wingo are able to discuss truth and its power over their lives. "The old Mom technique," Savannah says at one point. "Truth is only what you choose to remember" *(The Prince of Tides* 533).

To some extent, the secrets my adoptive parents kept can be explained by their desire to maintain their piety in the eyes of others like them. In religious fundamentalism, there is little place for confession and forgiveness; instead, followers too often exist in the grip of failure, original sin, and self-doubt, expecting and fearing punishment.

Two 2011 news documentaries, "Shattered Faith" and "Ungodly Discipline," address the abuse perpetrated in the name of God. Both reveal the techniques Christian fundamentalists employ to humiliate and control children and to break their spirits. Jocelyn Zichterman, director of Freedom from Abuse, shared her story on "Ungodly Discipline," which aired Sept. 2, 2011, on CNN. She and others dealt with what the documentary described as "biblical chastisement" and the desire of fundamentalist Christians to break the will of a child in order to control her or him.

According to "Ungodly Discipline," spiritual training often devolves into sadistic beatings and terrifying threats—both in single-family homes and in child care facilities funded and maintained by fundamentalist Christians. The latter are often free from secular oversight and escape investigation and prosecution. Abused when she was young, Zichterman devotes herself to protecting others from misguided Christians who engage in and promote corporeal abuse. I am, of course, encouraged by her courage and her single-minded purpose, and I look forward to the day when Christian ministers are held accountable for their treatment of their families and when they can seek help for dysfunction.

For me, the bleak and harrowing days are long, long past. I have spent half a century pursuing who I am and learning how better to contribute to my profession, my friends, my family, and my students. My mother lost two children and suffered a nervous breakdown before I was born. I am grateful to be alive, and I think of each day as stolen time. In Cormac McCarthy's *No Country for Old Men,* Ed Tom Bell says, "I didnt know you could steal your own life...I think I done the best with it I knew how but it still wasnt mine. It never has been" (278).

I, too, have stolen my own life. I carry it gently, tentatively. In a message dated May 14, 2010, my cousin Jack Bunch wrote, "You must have inner strength to have turned out so well." I don't know about inner strength. I don't know if I have turned out so well. I do know that I have been well loved.

With the Miata top down, I drive along Marshall Road on my way to the university, reveling in the blue and seemingly limitless Colorado sky. I lift up mine eyes unto the hills. I sing in gratitude to Rutherford Hurst and Nadine Elizabeth Nash Miracle who—although they must remain fictional characters in an incomplete story—make possible the promise of each new day.

Appendix

Author's Note: These obituaries are included to help those who might have a particular interest in the Bundren, Bunch, Hurst, Miracle, and/or Nash families of East Tennessee. Several of the death notices are not otherwise available; others are compilations of published material.

Names are listed alphabetically. I cannot attest to the accuracy of each entry, although I have corrected obvious errors and misspellings. I am unable to provide additional dates because they are sometimes omitted in the original documents.

SIMON PETER BUNCH

Simon Peter Bunch, 83, on Route 1, Washburn, died at Doctor's Hospital, Morristown, 4 a.m. Tuesday. He was a veteran of World War I.

Survivors: son, Lawrence Bunch of Jefferson City; four daughters, Mrs. Paul (Mary) Vance of Talbott, Mrs. Johnnie (Bill) Hyde, Mrs. Robert (Helen) Petre of Washburn, and Mrs. Edmond (Nell) Nicely of Heiskell; two sisters, Mrs. Sally Branson and Mrs. Minnie Arnwine of Knoxville; 13 grandchildren; five great-grandchildren.

Funeral 2:30 p.m. Thursday at the Salem Primitive Baptist Church where he was a member, Rev. Andy Vance, Elder Johnny Robbins officiating. The body will be taken to the church at 2 p.m. to lie in state. Grandsons will be pallbearers.

Burial in Seymour Cemetery. The family will receive friends 7-9 p.m. Wednesday at the Smith Funeral Home in Rutledge.

GEORGIA HOPSON HURST HOWERTON

Georgia Hopson Hurst Howerton, 83, of Jefferson City Health and Rehabilitation Center went home to be with Jesus, Saturday, March 27, 1999.

She was a member of Praise World Outreach Center and the widow of James J. Howerton.

Survivors include a son, Bobby (B.J.) and Kaye Howerton; daughter, Dorothy (Elmer) Howerton; grandchildren, Kim and Tim Howerton of Morristown and Rick and Debbie Davis of Haines City, Florida; great-grandchildren, Jonathan and Megan of Jacksonville, Arkansas, Matthew and Sara Davis of Knoxville, Tennessee, and Tyler and Casey Davis of Rogersville, Tennessee; beloved sister-in-law, Mary Ruth Hopson; step-daughter-in-law, Wilma Howerton; step-daughter, Ethel James; stepson, George Howerton; eight step-grandchildren; 13 step-great-grandchildren; several nieces, nephews, and cousins and a host of friends because she loved everyone she met.

Funeral services will be at 8 p.m. Monday, March 29, 1999, at Mayes Mortuary with Rev. Ron Sills officiating. Graveside services will be at 10 a.m. Tuesday at Fairfield Cemetery.

The family will receive friends from 6 to 8 p.m. Monday evening prior to the services at the mortuary. Mayes Mortuary is in charge of arrangements.

HARRISON HURST

Harrison Hurst, 42, died Tuesday, April 22, 1936, at 7:30 a.m. at his home at Midway after a lingering illness.

He is survived by his wife; one son, Rutherford Hurst, of Jefferson City; one step-daughter, Virginia Hord [the name is spelled "Horde" on the tombstone] of Richmond, Kentucky; two sisters, Mrs. Emma Evans, Tazewell, and Mrs. Mary Rosenbalm, Pleasant Hill, Missouri; one brother Wheeler Hurst, Tazewell.

Funeral services will be held Thursday by Rev. Arch Buchanan in Hurst Cemetery.

RUTHERFORD HURST

Rutherford Hurst, 57, of Washburn died suddenly Tuesday night.

Survivors include his wife, Crettie Holt Hurst; stepfather and mother, Mr. and Mrs. Simon P. Bunch; half-brother, Lawrence Bunch, Jefferson City; Mrs. Johnnie Hyde, Washburn; Mrs. Edmond Nicely, Heiskell; Mrs. Robert Petre, Washburn; and several nieces and nephews.

HELEN CORA BUNCH PETRE

Helen Cora Bunch Petre, 73, of Corryton, Tennessee, passed away peacefully April 22, 2011, at her home surrounded by her loving family. She was a member of Emory Valley Baptist Church.

She was preceded in death by her parents, Simon Peter and Cornelia Bunch; husband, Robert (Tom) Petre; infant son, Timothy Dean Petre; brothers, Lawrence Bunch and Rutherford Hurst; sisters, Mary (Elmo) Vance, Willie Mae (Bill) Hyde and Nell Nicely.

Survivors include her son, Keith Petre of Corryton; daughters, Sheila Roberts of Knoxville, Kim and Stan Coffey of White Pine, Karen and David Collins of Washburn; grandchildren, Hollie Collins and Jacob Winstead; loving family pet, Buckwheat. Special thanks to Dr. Bruce Avery, Dr. Michael Brunson and to her cousin and family friend, Dr. Fred Hurst.

The funeral service will be held at 8 p.m. Monday in the chapel of Bridges Funeral Home with Rev. Richard Nicely and Rev. Dean Brantley officiating. Family and friends will meet at 10 a.m. Tuesday at Bridges Funeral Home and proceed to Cleveland Cemetery in Washburn for the interment at 11 a.m.

Pallbearers: Jacob Winstead; Pete, Ryan, and Simon Hyde; Luke Singleton; and Keith Roberts. The family will receive friends from 6-8 p.m. Monday at Bridges Funeral Home, 5430 Rutledge Pike, 523-4999.

NADINE ELIZABETH NASH MIRACLE

Nadine Elizabeth Nash Miracle, 76, of Knoxville, passed away Monday afternoon at Fort Sanders Parkwest Medical Center.

She was preceded in death by her daughter, Linda Louise Miller.

She is survived by her daughters, Faustine Heiser of Powell; Joyce Miracle of Halls; Geraldine Cheatham of Seymour; Jan Whitt of Englewood, Colorado; sons, David Miracle of Knoxville, Sammy Miracle of Powell, James Miracle of Knoxville, and Dwayne Miracle of Seymour; 16 grandchildren; 10 great-grandchildren; sisters, Mildred Monday of Sevierville, Lonette Welch of Knoxville, Julia Ann Lucas of Atlanta; and several nieces and nephews.

Funeral arrangements are incomplete and will be announced later by Gentry-Griffey Chapel.

SEWELL NELSON (SAM) MIRACLE

Sewell Nelson (Sam) Miracle, 64, of Powell passed away Monday, March 23, 2009, at St. Mary's Medical Center in Knoxville.

He was a member of Trinity Baptist Church. Sam was employed at C & D Tire Company in Knoxville and was a U.S. Vietnam veteran and a diehard race fan.

He was preceded in death by his mother, Nadine Nash Miracle; father, Foister Miracle; brother, David Miracle; sisters, Linda Miller and Joyce Miracle.

Survivors include his wife of 34 years, Anna Lou Miracle of Powell, Tennessee; sons, Sam and Lucy Green of Knoxville, Will and Angela Green of Morristown, Jerry and Tionna Green of Maryville, Eddie Landon and David Landon, both of Virginia; daughters, Terry and Ben Morrison of Knoxville, Missy and Darrell Chapman of Powell; beloved sister, Faustine and Sam Heiser of Powell; sister, Geraldine Cheatham of Knoxville; brothers, Gerald and Larry Miracle, both of Indiana, James and Dwayne Miracle, both of Knoxville; eight grandchildren, one great-grandchild; several nieces and nephews.

The family will receive friends on Wednesday, March 25, 2009, from 6-8 p.m. at the Holly-Gamble Funeral Home. Funeral services will follow at 8 p.m. in the chapel with Rev. Louis Branch officiating.

Family and friends will meet at 1 p.m. on Thursday, March 26, at Marietta Baptist Church Cemetery for graveside services. Holley-Gamble Funeral Home in Clinton is in charge of the arrangements.

VICTOR NELSON NASH

Victor Nelson Nash, 80, died at his home, Route 1, Washburn, 7 a.m. Monday [the tombstone reads "Jan. 3, 1972"]. He was a member of Puncheon Camp Baptist Church.

Survivors include his wife Hulda; daughters, Mrs. Mildred Monday; Mrs. Nadine Miracle, Knoxville; Mrs. Valerie Hickam, Sevierville; Mrs. Lonette Welch, Corryton; Mrs. Julia Ann Lucas, Marietta, Ga.; son, James William Nash, Sandusky, Ohio; 26 grandchildren; 16 great-grandchildren.

Closed casket funeral 2 p.m. Wednesday, Rev. Andy Vance officiating. Burial in family cemetery, Liberty Hill.

Family will receive friends 7-9 p.m. Tuesday. Smith Funeral Home, Rutledge, in charge.

MARY (ELMO) VANCE

Mary Elmo Vance, 82, of Talbott, passed away Thursday, May 11, 2006, at Jefferson Memorial Hospital. She was of the Baptist faith.

She was preceded in death by her husband, Paul L. Vance; her parents, Cornelia and Simon Peter Bunch; one sister; and two brothers. She is survived by her daughter, Paula Phillips and Daren of Knoxville; her son, Ron Vance, and granddaughter, Elysia Vance, both of Dandridge; her sisters, Willie Mae (Bill)

Hyde of Washburn and Helen Petre of Maynardville; and several nieces and nephews.

In lieu of flowers the family request that memorials be made to the family. A celebration of life will be held Monday May 15, 2006, at Fielden Funeral Chapel at 8 p.m. with Rev. Jerry Epperson officiating.

The family will receive friends Monday 6-8 p.m. at Fielden Funeral Home, New Market, 475-3468.

Works Cited

Allison, Dorothy. *Bastard Out of Carolina: A Novel.* New York: Dutton, 1992.

———. *Two or Three Things I Know for Sure.* New York: Plume, 1996.

"Appalachia: A History of Mountains and People." Dir. Ross Spears. Agee Films, 2009.

Asher, Lisa. "Beyond the Classroom." *The Baylor Line* (Summer 2005): 42–47.

Coleridge, Samuel Taylor. *Biographia Literaria. The Norton Anthology of English Literature.* 5th ed. Vol. 2. Ed. M.H. Abrams. New York: Norton and Co., 1986. 14:397–402.

Conroy, Pat. *The Prince of Tides: A Novel.* Boston: Houghton Mifflin, 1986.

———. *My Reading Life.* New York: Doubleday, 2010.

———. *South of Broad.* 2009. New York: Dial, 2010.

Cook, Sylvia Jenkins. *From Tobacco Road to Route 66: The Southern Poor White in Fiction.* Chapel Hill: University of North Carolina Press, 1976.

Dickinson, Emily. "Some keep the Sabbath going to church." *The Complete Poems of Emily Dickinson.* Ed. Thomas H. Johnson. Boston: Little, Brown, 1960. 153–54.

———. "There's a certain Slant of light." *The Complete Poems of Emily Dickinson.* Ed. Thomas H. Johnson. Boston: Little, Brown, 1960. 118.

Dyer, Genie Hildebrand. Letter. *The Baylor Line* (Summer 2005): 39.

Eliot, T.S. "The Love Song of J. Alfred Prufrock." *The Norton Anthology of Modern Poetry.* 2nd ed. Ed. Richard Ellman and Robert O'Clair. New York: W.W. Norton, 1973. 482–85.

Faulkner, William. *As I Lay Dying.* 1930. New York: Modern Library, 2000.

———. *Light in August.* 1932. New York: Vintage, 1990.

———. *Requiem for a Nun. William Faulkner: Novels (1942-1954).* New York: Library of America, 1994. 471–664.

Flagg, Fannie. "A Conversation with Fannie Flagg." *Fried Green Tomatoes at the Whistle Stop Café: A Novel.* New York: Fawcett Columbine, 1987. n.p.

———. *Fried Green Tomatoes at the Whistle Stop Café: A Novel.* New York: Fawcett Columbine, 1987.

Frost, Robert. "Design." *The Poetry of Robert Frost.* New York: Holt, Rinehart, and Winston, 1969. 302.

———. "The Death of the Hired Man." *The Poetry of Robert Frost.* New York: Holt, Rinehart, and Winston, 1969. 34–40.

———. "Two Tramps in Mud Time." *The Poetry of Robert Frost.* New York: Holt, Rinehart, and Winston, 1969. 275–77.

Goodavage, Thaddeus. "Are You My Father?" *Faith of Our Fathers: African-American Men Reflect on Fatherhood.* Ed. Andre C. Willis. New York: Dutton, 1996. 207–27.

Gray, Richard. *The Literature of Memory: Modern Writers of the American South.* Baltimore, Md.: The Johns Hopkins University Press, 1977.

Gwynn, Frederick L., and Joseph L. Blotner, ed. *Faulkner in the University.* Charlottesville: University of Virginia, 1995.

"Hillbilly: The Real Story." Dir. David Huntley. A & E Home Video, 2008.

Ketchin, Susan. *The Christ-Haunted Landscape: Faith and Doubt in Southern Fiction.* Jackson: University Press of Mississippi, 1994.

King, Florence. *Confessions of a Failed Southern Lady.* New York: St. Martin's Press, 1985.

Lee, Harper. *To Kill a Mockingbird.* 1960. New York: Warner Books, 1982.

Luscombe, Belinda. "Finding Mom on Facebook." *Time* (16 Aug. 2010): 45–46.

McCarthy, Cormac. *No Country for Old Men.* New York: Alfred A. Knopf, 2008.

McCullers, Carson. *The Heart Is a Lonely Hunter.* 1940. *McCullers: Complete Novels.* New York: Library of America, 2001. 1–306.

———. *The Member of the Wedding.* 1946. *McCullers: Complete Novels.* New York: Library of America, 2001. 459–605.

Meriwether, James B., and Michael Millgate. *Lion in the Garden: Interviews with William Faulkner (1926-1962).* Lincoln: University of Nebraska Press, 1980.

"Mother and Child." Dir. Rodrigo Garcia. Sony Pictures, 2010.

Nelson, Nancy Cassada. "Our Hopson and Bunch Ancestors of Tennessee." 7 May 2001. http://www.whitsettwawall.com/Hopson/Hopson_History.htm. 16 June 2011.

O'Connor, Flannery. "The Displaced Person." *A Good Man Is Hard to Find and Other Stories.* 1948. New York: Harvest, 1955. 196–252.

———. "A Good Man Is Hard to Find." *A Good Man Is Hard to Find and Other Stories.* New York: Harvest, 1955. 1–22.

———. *Wise Blood (*1949). *The Violent Bear It Away* (1955). *The Complete Stories* (1946). New York: Quality Paperback Book Co., 1992. 8–232.

Poe, Joe T. *Life at 80 as I Have Lived It.* El Paso, Texas: Casa Bautista de Publicaciones, 2009.

Pols, Mary. "Good Grief." *Time* (28 Feb. 2011): 7.

Porter, Katherine Anne. *Letters of Katherine Anne Porter.* Ed. Isabel Bayley. New York: Atlantic Monthly Press, 1990.

———. "Old Mortality." *The Old Order: Stories of the South.* 1930. New York: Harcourt Brace Jovanovich, 1969. 105–82.

Prather, Judy Henderson. "Frank Leavell." *The Baylor Line* (Summer 2005): 79.

Ransom, John Crowe. "Reconstructed But Unregenerate." *I'll Take My Stand: The South and the Agrarian Tradition.* Baton Rouge: Louisiana State University Press, 1991. 1–27.

Rosenblatt, Roger. *Making Toast: A Family Story.* New York: HarperCollins, 2010.

———. "Once Upon a Time." 24 Dec. 1999. Online NewsHour with Jim Lehrer. http://www.pbs.org/newshour/essays/2000. 31 Jan. 2006.

Sebald, W.G. *The Emigrants.* 1992. New York: New Directions, 1997.

Snodgrass, W.D. "The Campus on the Hill." *Heart's Needle.* New York: Alfred A. Knopf, 1975. 34–35.

"Something's Gotta Give." Dir. Nancy Meyers. Columbia Pictures, 2003.

Stegner, Wallace. "Thoughts in a Dry Land." *Where the Bluebird Sings to the Lemonade Springs.* New York: Random House, 1992. 45–56.

Stein, Jean. "Interview with Jean Stein Vanden Heuvel." *Lion in the Garden: Interviews with William Faulkner (1926-1962).* Ed. James B. Meriwether and Michael Millgate. Lincoln: University of Nebraska Press, 1968.

Stevens, Wallace. "The Idea of Order at Key West." *The Norton Anthology of Modern Poetry.* 2nd ed. Ed. Richard Ellman and Robert O'Clair. New York: W.W. Norton, 1973. 291–92.

"Sweet Home, Alabama." Dir. Andy Tennant. Touchstone, 2002.

Swift, Graham. *Waterland.* 1983. New York: Vintage, 1992.

Tompkins, Jane. *A Life in School: What the Teacher Learned.* Reading, Mass.: Perseus Books, 1996.

Warren, Robert Penn. *All the King's Men.* 1946. Norwalk, Conn.: Easton Press, 2000.

Welty, Eudora. "Why I Live at the P.O." *Welty: Stories, Essays, and Memoir.* New York: Library of America, 1998. 57–69.

White, Aaronette M. "Ain't I a Feminist?" *African American Men Speak Out on Fatherhood, Friendship, Forgiveness, and Freedom.* Albany, N.Y.: State University of New York Press, 2008. 156–74.

Whitt, Jan. *Allegory and the Modern Southern Novel.* Macon, Ga.: Mercer University Press, 1994.

———. "'American Life is Rich in Lunacy': The Unsettling Social Commentary of 'The Beverly Hillbillies.'" *The Enduring Legacy of Old Southwest Humor.* Ed. Ed Piacentino. Baton Rouge: Louisiana State University Press, 2005. 229–47.

———. *Burning Crosses and Activist Journalism: Hazel Brannon Smith and the Mississippi Civil Rights Movement.* Lanham, Md.: University Press of America, 2010.

———. "Grits and Yokels Aplenty: Depictions of Southerners in Prime-Time Television." *Studies in Popular Culture* 19 (October 1996): 141–52.

———, ed. *Reflections in a Critical Eye: Essays on Carson McCullers.* Lanham, Md.: University Press of America, 2008.

———. "Remembering Dr. Reynolds." *The Baylor Line* (Summer 2007): 7–8.

———. *Settling the Borderland: Other Voices in Literary Journalism.* Lanham, Md.: University Press of America, 2008.

———. "What Happened to Celie and Idgie?: The 'Apparitional Lesbians' of American Film." *Studies in Popular Culture* 27.3 (April 2005): 43–57.

Willbanks, Ray, ed. *Literature of Tennessee.* Macon, Ga.: Mercer University Press, 1984.

Williams, William Carlos. "The Red Wheelbarrow." *The Norton Anthology of Modern Poetry.* 2nd ed. Ed. Richard Ellman and Robert O'Clair. New York: W.W. Norton, 1973. 318–19.

Yeats, William Butler. "The Lake Isle of Innisfree." *The Norton Anthology of Modern Poetry.* 2nd ed. Ed. Richard Ellman and Robert O'Clair. New York: W.W. Norton, 1988. 140.

———. "The Second Coming." *The Norton Anthology of Modern Poetry.* 2nd ed. Ed. Richard Ellman and Robert O'Clair. New York: W.W. Norton, 1988. 158.

Index

About the Author

Jan Whitt is a professor of journalism, literature, and media studies at the University of Colorado at Boulder. *Rain on a Strange Roof: A Southern Literary Memoir* is the story of her 50-year search for her parents, Rutherford Hurst and Nadine Elizabeth Nash Miracle.

Having begun her career as a reporter and editor in Texas, Whitt published *Burning Crosses and Activist Journalism: Hazel Brannon Smith and the Mississippi Civil Rights Movement* (2010), *Settling the Borderland: Other Voices in Literary Journalism* (2008), *Women in Journalism: A New History* (2008), and *Allegory and the Modern Southern Novel* (1994). She also is editor of *Reflections in a Critical Eye: Essays on Carson McCullers* (2007).

Reflections in a Critical Eye garnered first place in the culture category of the 2008 Eric Hoffer Book Awards and second place in the women's issues category of the 2007 *ForeWord Magazine* Book Awards and was one of three finalists in the anthology/collections category of the 2008 Colorado Book Awards. *Allegory and the Modern Novel* won the Kayden Book Award from the University of Colorado in 1991.

Current projects include a book about Utah author and environmental activist Terry Tempest Williams for Mercer University Press and a collection of essays about film and literature for Peter Lang International Publishing Group. Whitt has completed a proposal for a book entitled "*Voices in the Wind-Bent Wheat": Truman Capote's Failed Masterpiece,* a study of the stories that Capote omitted from *In Cold Blood* and a critique of the Southern literary giant's motives and misrepresentations of fact.

Whitt teaches undergraduate and graduate courses in American and British literature, literary journalism, media studies, popular culture, women's studies, and writing. She has received teaching and advising awards at Baylor University, the University of Denver, and the University of Colorado at Boulder.

Whitt received her B.A. degree in English and journalism from Baylor University in 1977 and her M.A. in English from Baylor in 1980. She received a doctorate in English from the University of Denver in 1985.

A volunteer with Golden Retriever Rescue of the Rockies and Wyoming Herding Dog Rescue, Whitt enjoys gardening; hiking; reading; running; skiing; and traveling.

www.ingramcontent.com/pod-product-compliance
Lightning Source LLC
Chambersburg PA
CBHW020944310726
48980CB00001B/43
9780761858294